PHOTOGRAPHING CHILDREN
PHOTO WORKSHOP

SECOND EDITION

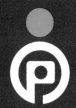

PHOTOGRAPHING CHILDREN
PHOTO WORKSHOP

SECOND EDITION

Ginny Felch

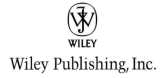

Wiley Publishing, Inc.

Photographing Children Photo Workshop, 2nd Edition

Published by
Wiley Publishing, Inc.
10475 Crosspoint Boulevard
Indianapolis, IN 46256
www.wiley.com

Copyright © 2011 by Wiley Publishing, Inc., Indianapolis, Indiana

Published simultaneously in Canada

ISBN: 978-1-118-02453-9

Manufactured in the United States of America

10 9 8 7 6 5 4 3 2 1

For general information on our other products and services or to obtain technical support, please contact our Customer Care Department within the U.S. at (877) 762-2974, outside the U.S. at (317) 572-3993 or fax (317) 572-4002.

Wiley also publishes its books in a variety of electronic formats and by print-on-demand. Some content that appears in standard print versions of this book may not be available in other formats. For more information about Wiley products, visit us at www.wiley.com.

Library of Congress Control Number: 2011930292

About the Author

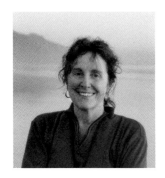

Ginny Felch, as a child of the '50s, was given a Brownie camera by her father. She was encouraged by his kind compliments about her sensitivity and composition. The beauty and nostalgia of New England as well as Ginny's mother's eclectic eye for beauty and her appreciation of art and design were gifts that contributed to her developing eye. Ginny was trained as a wedding photographer after years of studying black-and-white photography. Later, her love for children, spurred by devotion to her son, Zachary, led to an inspired career creating children's portraits.

Under the name of Virginia Clayton, she exhibited and lectured her way to becoming a Master of Photography through

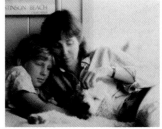

Professional Photographers of America and has been coached by some great photographers, including Marie Cosindas, Morley Baer, Ruther Bernhard, Robert Farber, Sara Moon, and Josef Karsh. Ginny has had speaking engagements across the country and in Europe. In 1990, she visited the Soviet Union while documenting the Heart to Heart Children's Medical Alliance as part of a group of volunteer doctors and nurses from Oakland Children's Hospital.

Shortly after returning home from working with parents facing the possibility of losing their children, Ginny endured the tragedy of losing her own 15-year-old son in an automobile accident. Soon thereafter, her home and all belongings were destroyed in the Oakland Firestorm of 1991. This was the beginning of a challenging and courageous journey of healing and discovery. Her survival and reclaimed zest for life were due in no small part to her relationship with her husband, Will, and his family.

When Ginny finally did return to her life as a children's photographer, she found it all the more poignant and meaningful to be a part of the joy and appreciation of children and life. Ginny is motivated deeply by the moody and sculptural effect of natural light on a myriad of subjects, creating a sense of place and feeling of timelessness. Her children's portraits are known for those qualities as well as her warmth and ability to connect with and relate to children.

Her philosophy about photography is that the equipment and technology take a back seat to vision, creativity, and passion. Above all, Ginny seeks beauty.

"Beauty has a dignity and poise that takes us beyond our smallness and negativity; beauty brings us in to remembrance. Beauty is the bridge between the real and the ideal. Not everything is beautiful; yet when we develop a graceful and gracious eye, we can find beauty in the most unexpected places." — John O'Donohue

Credits

Acquisitions Editor
Aaron Black

Project Editor
Chris Wolfgang

Technical Editor
Haje Jan Kamps

Copy Editor
Lauren Kennedy

Editorial Director
Robyn Siesky

Business Manager
Amy Knies

Senior Marketing Manager
Sandy Smith

Vice President and Executive Group Publisher
Richard Swadley

Vice President and Executive Publisher
Barry Pruett

Project Coordinator
Sheree Montgomery

Graphics and Production Specialists
Samantha K. Cherolis
Jennifer Henry
Andrea Hornberger
Jennifer Mayberry
Heather Pope

Quality Control Technician
Jessica Kramer

Proofreading and Indexing
Toni Settle
Sharon Shock

Acknowledgments

What really touches me and inspires me to no end is the generosity of photographers who have enthusiastically and steadfastly contributed to the energy and content of this book. The feedback they gave me from the first edition provided the wind beneath my wings for the revision. I never stopped thinking about them and my inspiring audience in the process of the revision. My Facebook Group, Photographing Children, has given me years of fun and feedback, and I feel I have many wonderful friends there.

Mary Schannen of Melange Photo (www.melangephoto.com) has been instrumental in supporting this project with her enthusiasm, her boundless energy, and inspiring images. She was one of the original members of the Facebook Page, Photographing Children, with feedback about how the first edition of the book inspired and helped her. Her vast networking with vendors and on Flickr greatly inspired the last chapter on creative post-production. Her passion for photography inspires me.

She brought in Melinda Meredith, who reviewed and suggested updates for much of the technical input in the book. She has one of those amazingly balanced brains that can produce lovely imagery and understand every bell and whistle of her camera.

Kylie Banks contributed helpful assessment of post-production software. Thank you all so much!

When the original publication of *Photographing Children Photo Workshop* was released in 2008, the vibrant networking fever had just barely begun. Since that time, hundreds of thousands of camera-toting moms across the world have jumped on the bandwagons of Facebook and Flickr to share and improve their photography. I have been very fortunate to have met many of them online and established wonderful relationships with them, watching their children grow before my eyes. Our Facebook contests, where Adobe has generously contributed coveted prizes (Lightroom, Photoshop Elements, and Photoshop), have created the heartbeat of the forum. Watching the elevation of the quality of photography has really been inspiring.

It is daunting to me to see how much these moms can do in one day. Annie Manning nursed her baby to sleep while she emailed me her workflow in Chapter 11 for the deadline! Mary Schannen dealt with snow days, playdates, and dinner parties while helping me come up with some new ideas. Liz Sanford's photography has improved by leaps and bounds since we met on the Facebook Group, and she never stops moving!

In the meantime, they and many others, are running their own businesses and creating impressive images. My heart and thanks go out to them.

When I first started attending PPA meetings in the '80s, I was often the only female photographer in the audience. I remember pledging to myself that I would grow to become an influence on other women who had the vision and heart for the work but were not enthusiastic about jumping into the science (like myself!) This has been the gift of writing my books and being part of the whirlwind of mamarazzi photographers. Now I am a proud grandmarazzi and you will see evidence throughout the new edition!

For Will, Kristin, Jason, Anahi, and Nico.

Thank you for the love, support, great food, wine, and family vacations! You make my life very rich and sweet.

Contents

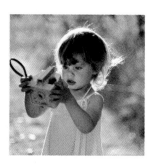

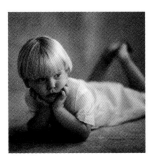

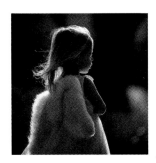

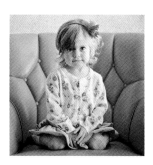

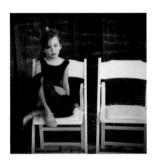

CHAPTER 6   What's Your Style?   **113**

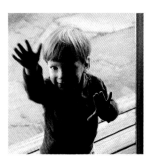

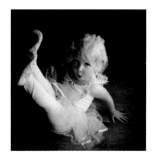

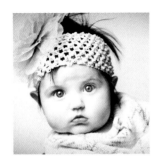

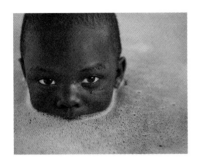

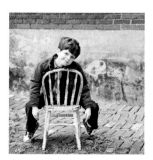

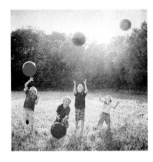

Introduction

The sheer miracle of childhood is something few can deny. The intrinsic innocence, honesty, spontaneity, and whimsy of children have been the subjects of prose, poetry, and paintings throughout the history of man. Since the introduction of the art and craft of photography, the depiction of children has been a popular and passionate quest.

What a thrill it is to have such a long and fun-filled career as a photographer of children. It has always been my desire to share the passion and the craft with those who feel the same stirrings of attraction to this field. I know that some are put off or discouraged by the threat of the supposed technical challenge of photography and equipment.

It truly makes me sad to think of the unexpressed vision of those who hold back due to that fear or intimidation. I believe this challenge is manufactured; the flames of fear continue to be fanned by some manufacturers of camera equipment, authors of books, and teachers of photography.

Don't get me wrong; there is a place for understanding how to better execute fine photographs technically, but your vision, passion, and personal tastes have a deeply profound effect on what you produce. It excites me to think that I can be any part of encouraging you to follow your bliss, your heart, and your passion for photographing children. That has always been my point of view whether teaching, mentoring, or producing children's photographs.

Even when working in the darkroom, I was interested in keeping the process more of a mystery and a magical experience. To see an image rise up out of the paper submerged in water is still a miracle to me! I continue to feel that magic when I peer through a lens and even when I work on an image in Photoshop. I want to know less about why things happen and more about making my images sing.

Those who are primarily looking for scientific definitions and formulae for sharp and perfect images might look elsewhere. Books abound with such information. I hope that in this book you find inspiration and encouragement to follow any urges you have had to make photographs that capture the spirit of a child.

WHO SHOULD PHOTOGRAPH CHILDREN

Everyone who enjoys and appreciates children and who wants to learn to capture their energy should photograph children. I would guess that a large majority of cameras are purchased when parents see their firstborn child.

With the advances of digital technology, anyone can take an acceptable image of a child — in that the exposure is good. That is almost guaranteed. The issue here is how to take an exceptional photograph of a child, one that holds your attention for years.

I believe that parents have the potential to be excellent photographers of their children. The motivation is great, in creating a history of the life of a child, as well as to surround yourself with images that bring you back to that day. The opportunity is there, as parents usually spend an inordinate amount of time watching, playing with, and tending to their children in all manner of activities. Most importantly, parents have the heart connection built right in! That is the key that opens the door to the potential for creating beautiful images of children.

Certainly, other people cherish children and love to observe and photograph them. The ingredients needed are passion and an interest in learning to see! Right there, you have most of what you need, even with a simple point-and-shoot camera.

Wonderful photographs of children have so many uses. You can create brilliant scrapbooks, slideshows, and even customized books, as well as post to galleries, blogs, Facebook, and Flickr. Wouldn't you just love to improve your photography by leaps and bounds just by learning to see and understanding a few photography basics? I think your time has come!

WHAT I'VE LEARNED FROM COACHING PHOTOGRAPHY

Most people contact me for two reasons: Either they have been photographing children for years and want to learn to go beyond their existing work, or they are just starting out and are put off or intimidated by some of the technical elements of the camera and computer. The second group is my favorite.

Dispelling fear is a beautiful thing. When you are fearful, your mind tends to shut down, and things make less sense. You get discouraged, and you give up. Fear is the enemy of creativity, and creativity is what you need to nurture the most if you want to improve your photographs. On the other hand, entering into the zone of creativity can allay bigger fears and can open you up to new experiences and joys.

Heritage Illustrated Dictionary's definition of creativity, "to cause to exist, bring into being, originate," makes me think of giving birth. No two babies are alike (identical twins, the exception), and each one is uniquely created from two unlike parents. A new being comes forth, with new possibilities, much like the creation of an idea, or an image.

Shouldn't that give us all hope? The potential for new ideas is within ourselves, and we are all potential creators or artists. You can look outside of yourself for inspiration, but your point of view, your sense of timing, and your personal interpretations are all the resources you need to spring forth with more extraordinary imagery.

WHAT IS AHEAD

I really hope that this process of learning about improving your photographs of children will be fun, inspiring, and relaxing and that you will learn to trust yourself above all. And don't just trust yourself, but *value* and *honor* your true nature and your unique vision. You have something unique to contribute to the volumes of photographs that have been created over the years. I really believe that.

Through exercises about seeing and appreciating light and composition, you will expose yourself to a beauty you might never have appreciated. Learning to see the light has enhanced my life immeasurably, let alone my photographs of children. What used to be mundane, ordinary moments will be brightened by more acute observation of your surroundings. A simple walk on the beach, in the park, and down the street will become a more enchanting engagement with life. That is what I truly hope for you.

Choosing children as your subjects can bring you so much insight into your own life. Children really are our teachers. They have all the wisdom that we come into the world with, and we can learn a great deal from them. They are honest, spontaneous, and often carefree little beings, to say nothing of their graceful gestures and penchant for playfulness.

In your interaction with children, in your deep observation of them in order to create lasting images, and in your exploration of their nature, you will be entertained and inspired. Hopefully that inspiration will come through in your photographs.

You are embarking upon, or continuing on, a very fruitful and rewarding path. Let's celebrate and begin!

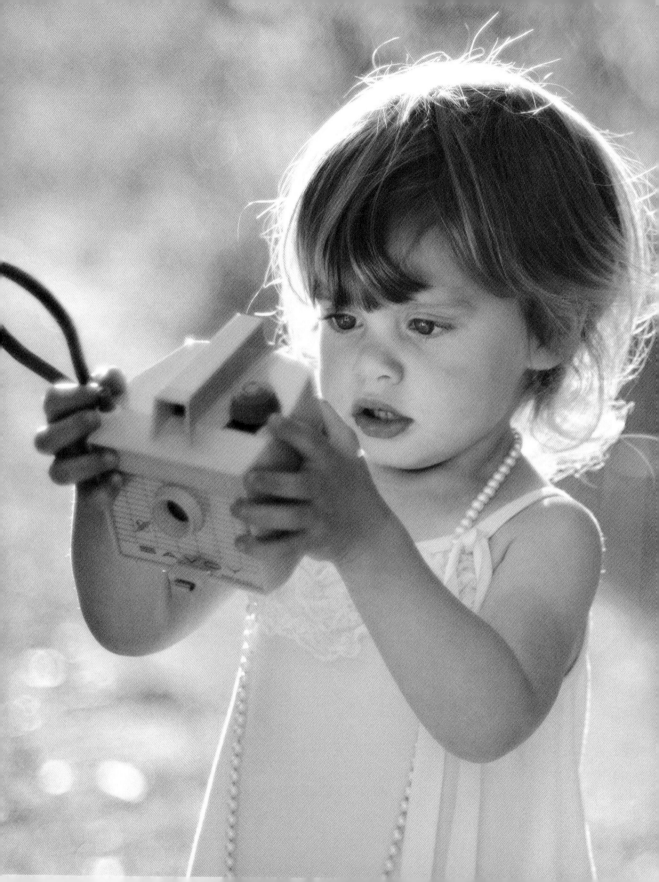

THE ART OF PHOTOGRAPHING CHILDREN

© Valeria Spring / www.theredballoonphotography.com

Photographing children is not for the faint of heart. Just ask any child photographer and you will hear enough stories about fussy newborns and stubborn toddlers that it might make you think twice about this genre of photography. Certainly, a bowl of fruit is much more cooperative than an 18-month-old. You can find great light, and spend all afternoon working the angles for the perfect shot of fruit. Not so with children.

Subject to every whim of the children they photograph, the children's photographer must be part Pied Piper, part parent, part psychologist, and, oh yes, part photographer. Making images of children can tax you in every possible way. Chasing them is a physical workout, while trying to coax a 2-year-old (or a 14-year-old, for that matter) to see things your way takes every psychological skill in your arsenal. Add to all this the technical challenges of learning photography in general and your camera in particular, and you might feel like giving up before you even start.

While photographing children may not be the easiest hobby or way to make a living, it might turn out to be one of the most rewarding adventures you ever pursue. Children simply are the most fascinating subjects. Young children in particular haven't learned to be guarded and self-conscious. Every thought and mood is transparent on their faces, which allows for images with great expression. Sometimes, you lift your camera at just the right moment, the planets align, and you capture a photograph of something so precious that you forget all the challenges and you are reminded of your love for photographing children.

Whether you are a parent or professional, being successful at children's portraiture requires you to get in touch with your inner child, and to reach inward to find out what really inspires you both visually and emotionally. This chapter explores what you should know when you begin your journey photographing children and offers a starting point for inspiration.

ADVICE FOR THE ASPIRING PROFESSIONAL

Judging by the popularity of digital cameras, it's apparent that photography has become an international pastime, if not a downright obsession. Prices and availability have made cameras more affordable than ever, and technology continually presents point-and-shoot capabilities that result in amazingly good exposures. Now even the cell phone cameras have entered the competition.

What is it, then, that pushes you over the edge to want to become a professional photographer, to make images that are better than the rest, good enough to be called, dare I say it ... art? Has being a photographer been a lifetime dream? Or have your ever-improving photographs of your own children caused friends and neighbors to ask if you'll photograph their kids? Do you have a true love for and patience with children? Are you willing to put up with a shy child who doesn't want to leave her mother's side, as in 1-1, or do you have the patience to wait for a newborn to fall asleep in her father's arms?

 *note*

Perhaps you only have a point-and-shoot camera — this is fine; this is enough. Don't be intimidated by all the latest advances and technology. The advent of digital photography will allow you to be more successful, more quickly than ever before. You will know when you need to advance, but to start all you need is a camera and a child.

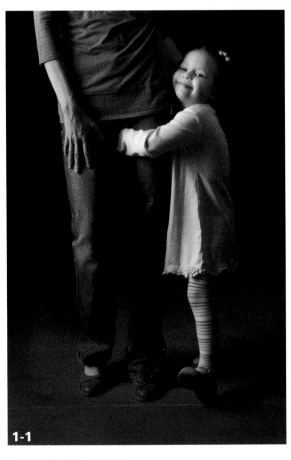

1-1

ABOUT THIS PHOTO *Children can be among the most challenging and rewarding of photographic subjects. Taken at ISO 100, f/3.5, and 1/250 second. ©Allison Tyler Jones / www.atjphoto.com*

Before you dive headfirst into the art and business of photography, think about what draws you in and what your aspirations are as a photographer. Taking time to evaluate your goals and motivations will inform every decision, whether it's the type of equipment you need or the kind of business you might want to have.

"A photographer's work is given shape and style by his personal vision. It is not simply technique, but the way he looks at life and the world around him." ~Pete Turner

Ask yourself questions such as

- Are you happy simply recording your immediate and extended family history and your friends' lives?

- Do you love to find the beauty and complexity in things around you?

- What type of photographer are you and where are you now?

- Do you have enough technical skill to feel confident charging for your services or do you have a passion to photograph children as more of a hobby at this point?

If you are considering photographing children as your career and don't feel a draw or some sense of enchantment toward little ones, you would be much better off finding another subject or specialty.

BE INSPIRED

Whether photographing children for fun or profit, paying attention to your creative journey, past and present, helps you develop your own individual style or signature. That signature enables you to create more captivating, inspiring, and authentic photographs.

A NOTE TO PARENTS A large percentage of photographers who decide to photograph children, either as a hobby or a vocation, do so when they become parents. Suddenly nothing is more profound than nurturing and observing your perfect and beautiful creation. Watching his or her every move and expression, the softness of the cheeks, and the miraculous achievements made each day is awe-inspiring. Using the downtime with a baby or young child and taking advantage of these precious moments enable you to begin to really see this child. Morning light through the window, sleepy eyes, and grateful smiles suddenly become your favorite subjects. Maybe you are a new parent now reading this book for ideas on ways to better capture your own child. Relax and enjoy the pleasure of making simple and spontaneous images of your child.

Who has a better potential to photograph your child than you? If you've ever taken your child to a mass-merchant photo studio to have his or her picture taken, you know that those photographers aren't exactly tuned in to the individual child. As a parent, you have the inside track on your child's expressions, moods, and quirks. You have access to your child 24 hours a day, allowing you to document the full range of activities, interests, and expressions.

But don't forget, your child also has the inside track on you. Somehow, kids just know how to push their parents' buttons, and a friendly photo shoot can go from, "Come on over here, sweetie, and let's take your picture" to "Stop touching your brother! Do you want a time-out?" Before you know it, you're ready to send them all to their rooms all because you wanted a nice photo for you to remember how much you love your kids.

And so, a caution to all parents out there: Remember why you're taking these photographs in the first place. Be patient with those little ones (even when they aren't so little anymore). When you're first learning about photography, you can be so worried about "getting the shot" that you forget to *be in the moment* with your child. Maybe one time you could photograph the neighbor's children and alternatively, she could photograph yours. You know you'll be nicer to her kids than you are to your own; they'll be on their best behavior too — for a while anyway!

If you were to ask ten people to photograph the same child in the same environment, you would see ten different approaches and styles, because the eyes of the photographer are inevitably filtered by past experiences and personal vision (whether the photographer knows it or not). So why not hone in on this tendency and begin to develop your own vision and style?

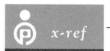 **x-ref**

As you discover different styles of portraiture, you might wonder how different effects are achieved. Chapter 6 explores the most common types of children's portraiture, from classic studio work to the emerging popularity of environmental portraits. Chapter 11 gives you some creative post-production tips to enhance your photographs and help create your style.

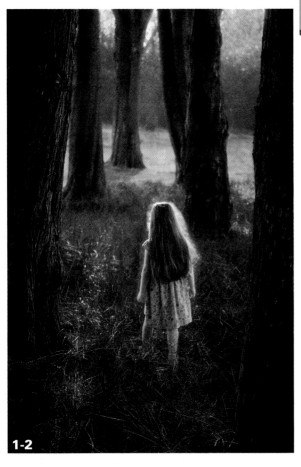

1-2

ABOUT THIS PHOTO *I was inspired by lovely late afternoon light and a cooperative and romantic child to add my own style to this image. Taken at ISO 640, f/5, and 1/200 second. ©Ginny Felch / www.photographingchildren.com*

A good place to start is by studying the masters of the art of photography and painting. Absorbing the work of other photographers and artists can help you see what you do and don't like, which is the very beginning of identifying your own style.

Nothing is wrong with learning the way of the masters as you amble along your path. But as you do this, honor yourself, as you have embedded in your soul your own style and vision, which is fervently waiting to be noticed and tapped in to.

> "Art is not so much a matter of methods and processes as it is an affair of temperament, of taste, and of sentiment...in the hands of the artist, the photograph becomes a work of art... in a word, photography is what the photographer makes it — an art or a trade." ~William Howe Downs

Along the way, go ahead and learn the skills and approaches of others, but eventually your very own style will begin to surface and resound. Yes, traces of this mentor or that mentor might show up in your images, but your own vision will shine through, as in 1-2. In fact, you couldn't hide it if you wanted to.

The photo in 1-3 is a new take on an old subject, the family portrait. Taking the best of classic portraiture combined with new elements of more photojournalistic style, this photo of a young family says something fresh and interesting about their lives together. This *lifestyle* photography has become a very popular style.

Do you ever take the time to think about what inspires you deeply? Do you love the mountains, the beach, or midtown Manhattan? Are you a dreamer or an athlete? Are you an avid reader or art aficionado? Do you love movies, bicycle rides, or traveling to Indonesia? All of your tastes, your passions, and your fascinations are what make you unique and who you are. Never take this for granted; in fact, refining, developing, and acknowledging your tastes and passions all contribute greatly to your creativity.

Looking around your home might give you some clues as to what inspires you and what you love. Do you have a style? Is there a consistency to what is around you; for example, a theme such as nature or the arts? Are you surrounded by colors and textures that you enjoy? Maybe you haven't seen the details in your home as a choice, and pieces have been dictated by what was free,

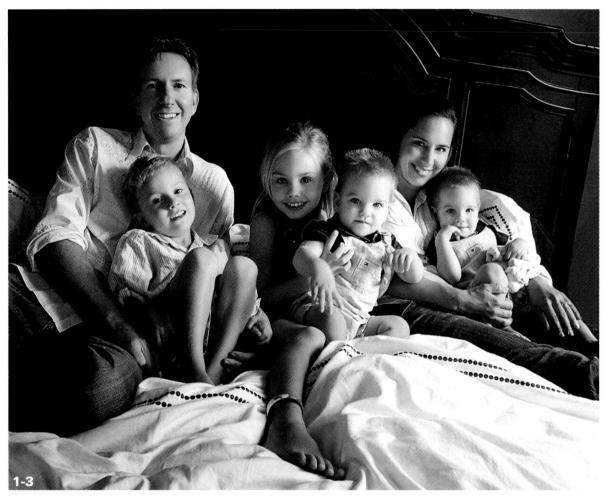

ABOUT THIS PHOTO *A new take on the family portrait. Combining a more candid casual feel, this photographer has put her own spin on a timeless photographic tradition. Taken at ISO 2000, f/6.3, and 1/60 second. ©Mary Schannen / www.melangephoto.com*

inherited, or chosen by others. Do you realize how much you are influenced by your surroundings? They feed into you, either negatively or positively, on a daily basis. Would you choose to photograph your surroundings, or do you have to go to another location or country to be inspired? Would you photograph a child in your home? Whose home would you prefer, and why?

Many people believe that they don't have the choice to influence their physical environment for a myriad of reasons. However, your surroundings

are a very important part of your creativity, so take steps every day to pay attention to what you create around you. This pays off when you design your photographs.

Another source for the roots of your creativity might be to remember what inspired you as a child. What did you have around you, in your bedroom, for example? Did you have collections? Can you see a theme running through any of your knickknacks? Did you have a favorite toy or a

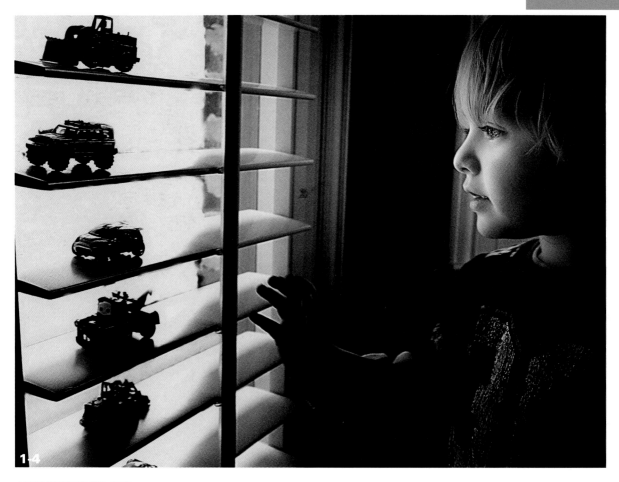

ABOUT THIS PHOTO. *Beautiful, contouring light from a bedroom window highlighted the photographer's son's face and his treasured model collection. Taken at ISO 400, f/4, and 1/50 second. ©Mary Schannen / www.melangephoto.com*

favorite place? In a whimsical portrait of a little boy in 1-4, the photographer brings back memories of her own childhood collections.

RESOURCES FOR INSPIRATION

Living an enriched life, living as fully as possible, and drawing from your intuition for guidance significantly affect what reflects back in your photographic images. As a photographer of children, these things can affect your attitude, your taste, and your inspiration for creating more artistic and meaningful portraits. Here are some ideas that you might consider for further exploration.

■ **Attending workshops.** Nothing is more inspiring than spending days or a week with a group of fellow photographers, as in 1-5. The environment of sharing and cooperation in moving your photography forward is very motivating. Away from the demands of family and work, you are in a very special and protected place. From personal experience and reputation, I recommend Maine Photographic

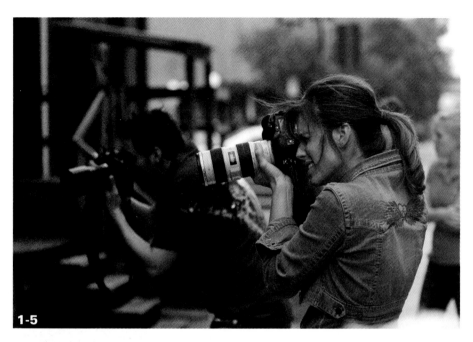

1-5

ABOUT THIS PHOTO *Photography workshops are a great place to get some hands-on practice. Taken at ISO 200, f/2.8, and 1/125 second. ©Allison Tyler Jones / www.atjphoto.com*

Workshops and Santa Fe Workshops for hobbyists and professionals alike. Professional trade organizations such as Professional Photographers of America (www.ppa.com) and its local affiliates hold lectures and workshops throughout the year, many of which focus on the business of photography.

- **Working with mentors.** Many accomplished photographers are willing to mentor photographers who are newer to the craft. Mentoring is more hands-on and longer term than just taking a workshop. Because it is one-on-one, you can really cut to the chase and learn exactly what you wish.

- **Reading books.** Literature can call you into a sense of place with words alone, tickling your imagination. Books by other photographers can be provocative for aspiring photographers.

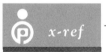 *x-ref*

You can find many wonderful opportunities for studying with photographers you admire online. See Chapter 11 for a resource list.

Books on great artists and their lives speak to you from a valuable point of view and move you with the artist's creations. Take the time to peruse art and photography books at your local library.

- **Reading magazines.** Magazines can motivate you by keeping you current on styles of clothing and imagery. Whether it's a GapKids ad or an editorial about child rearing, every page can give you new ideas on photographing children. These resources can give you insight into contemporary styles that might influence your work. Clip your favorite photos and start

ABOUT THIS PHOTO *Keep current on all the latest trends in children's photography by joining an online forum of photographers. Taken at ISO 640, f/2.8, and 1/60 second. © Mary Schannen / www.melangephoto.com*

1-6

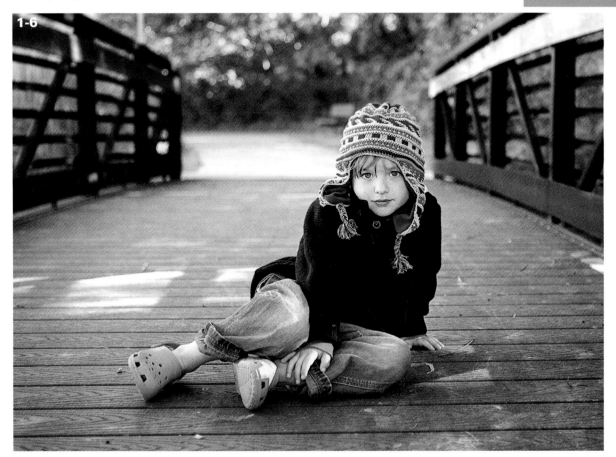

tip

When you are watching a movie, view the bonus features on the DVD you are watching. Study lighting setups in the movie scenes to get great ideas on how to light your own work. Or just pay close attention to the lighting and composition in the next movie you attend. Notice how each frame is composed just so. Movies directed by Martin Scorsese and Akira Kurosawa, among others, are known for their masterful lighting. You will begin to see how important light and composition are to create a mood and tell a story.

an idea file to inspire you when your motivation is running low. Notice how your collection changes as you move through the months.

■ **Visiting museums and galleries.** Author and artist Julia Cameron encourages all artists to have "artist's dates" frequently. It is one thing to visit a museum and quite another to go with the intention of keeping your eyes wide open for inspiration. Taking another artist friend along can make it a fun adventure and influence your work in new ways, such as inspiring you to use new colors, compositions, and forms of light.

■ **Exploring culture.** Theatre, ballet, and opera can open your eyes and lead you to new ways of thinking and seeing. With a photographer's eye, watch the delicate and sophisticated lighting used to dramatize dance and theatre.

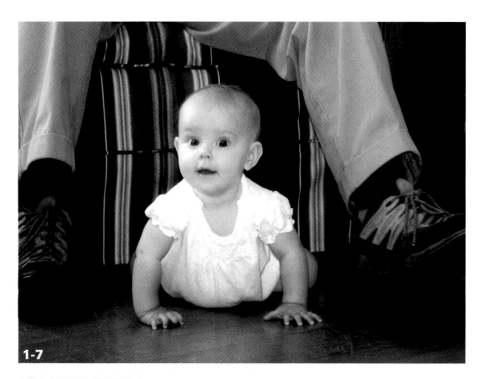

1-7

ABOUT THIS PHOTO *I couldn't resist this opportunity at a family reunion when I saw my little great neice so tiny next to Gumpaw's feet! Photographing from ground level offers whimsical backgrounds and can surprise and delight the subject. Taken at ISO 400, f5.6, and 1/60 second. ©Ginny Felch / www.photographingchildren.com*

Notice the gestures, movement, costumes, and fabrics. These observations might move you to experiment. The performing arts may influence you to seek out more dramatic lighting situations and backgrounds for your portraits of children.

■ **Traveling.** An olive tree in your front yard doesn't hold a candle to one in Tuscany — it just doesn't! Moving outside of your everyday environment makes you not only appreciate the styles and light of other cultures, but also your own environment. New colors, new faces, styles, architecture, food, and foliage expand your vision at every turn. Observe children of other cultures, their clothing and their activities. When you arrive back home,

idea

Try this creative exercise: Make 20 photographs that include a child and contain one of the following elements: Texture, harsh light, color, junk as art, a window, a face, shadow, reflection, round, smooth, and partnership.

you are forever changed, and you won't be able to help seeing your environment differently. These are experiences that imprint your cells and change you forever, feeding your spirit and your vision.

■ **Checking out the Internet.** Bookmarking your favorite photographer's websites or blogs is the way to keep a virtual idea file. Join an online forum to share your work in a cooperative spirit with other photographers from

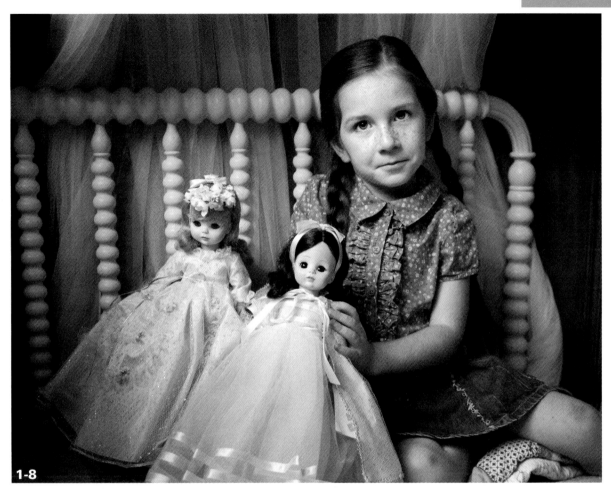

1-8

ABOUT THIS PHOTO *I was deeply enamored with dolls as a child, and was invited to share the passion with Daisy. Taken at ISO 1600, f/5.6, and 1/100 second.* © Ginny Felch / www.photographingchildren.com

> **quote** "Pretending is a great way to exercise our imagination. Pretending takes us back to our kidhood...it unleashes our creativity." ~Kevin Eikenberry

around the world. The critique and encouragement from these forums can help you improve very quickly. The Internet is so of-the-moment, giving you access to the latest trends in child photography, such as the contemporary-style portrait in 1-6. You could spend days on Flickr perusing photographs of children and finding great inspiration!

■ **Doing creativity exercises.** You don't have to take a class to do creative exercises. Make up your own using all the inspiration you've gathered from the previous suggestions. Choose your own subjects, but narrow it down, be specific, and work within a timeframe. Join in with friends to work on creative exercises and

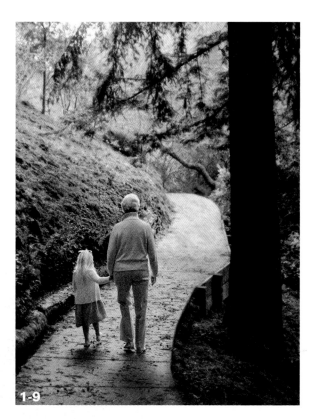

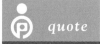

ABOUT THIS PHOTO *Grandmother came along on the shoot to help with the children. Even though the children were the intended subjects, I couldn't resist capturing this pictorial scene, focusing on the close and trusting relationship. Taken at 1600, f/5.6, and 1/200 second.* ©Ginny Felch / www.photographingchildren.com

share the results on a blog or Facebook. Work your way through the assignments at the end of each chapter in this book and you might be surprised at how you start examining and appreciating what you see every day and how that influences your work.

THE IMPORTANCE OF PLAY

Can you remember how important playing pretend was when you were a child? It was a natural part of playing, whether it was about cowboys, Star Wars, or dolls. Almost everyone eventually learned that pretending was for children and sacrificed this behavior for the sake of growing up. Time to turn back the clock!

Your ability to play is an essential skill when photographing children. When you get down low, at the child's level, as in 1-7, viewing life from this perspective and entering into the child's world, how can your photography not be influenced?

Children, as a whole, are very good judges of character and can detect a phony a mile away. If you really aren't interested in them or are intimidated by them, they know it. Take the time to sit with them and let them get used to you. Ask the child to show you her room, as in 1-8, or her favorite toys. Children are no different from adults in this aspect; they like people who are genuinely interested in them. Ask them about school and their teachers, friends, and interests. Let them look over your camera and show them a few shots throughout the shoot so they feel a part of what is going on. If you are working with a particularly timid child, allow this child to first get comfortable by letting her stay with Mom or Dad, Grandma, or a babysitter, for a bit, as in 1-9, before she is expected to perform for you. In this case, a whole new story was told.

Taking time to play a little and see the world from the perspective of the child you are photographing can only help you expand your vision in capturing real and touching images. Spending a little time on the floor can change your viewpoint not only by putting yourself at the child's level but also by allowing you to explore new angles and approaches to your subject. Take the chance! You might like it down there!

Assignment

Show Us Your Style!

You should understand that who you are and what has inspired you shine through in the portraits you create. After reading this chapter, you have probably given some thought as to what influences you, what your tastes are, and what your passions are. Now that you are more aware, create a children's portrait that reflects some of who you are and your style. You can show this through your choice of colors and tones, clothing, background environment, or general attitude. Use your imagination and try to come up with something really unique, something that separates you from the crowd.

Living by the beach opens up great possibilities for photographing children and families. In this photograph of an extended family of young people, the atmosphere was relaxed and comfortable, inspired by my lifestyle. I am definitely influenced by summering on Cape Cod as a child, and I am now known for beach portraits. Casual and relaxed, this portrait of first cousins was thought out ahead of time to achieve color harmony. I spoke with the family about wearing clothing that would create a sense of unity in their style. Taken at ISO 400, f/9, and 1/800 second.

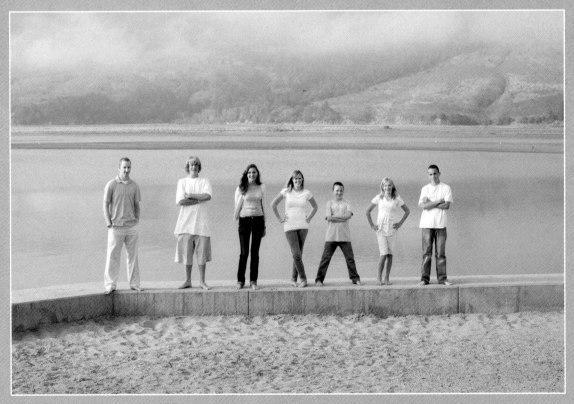

©Ginny Felch / www.photographingchildren.com

 Remember to visit www.pwsbooks.com after you complete this assignment and share your favorite photo! It's a community of enthusiastic photographers and a great place to view what other readers have created. You can also post comments, read encouraging suggestions, and get feedback.

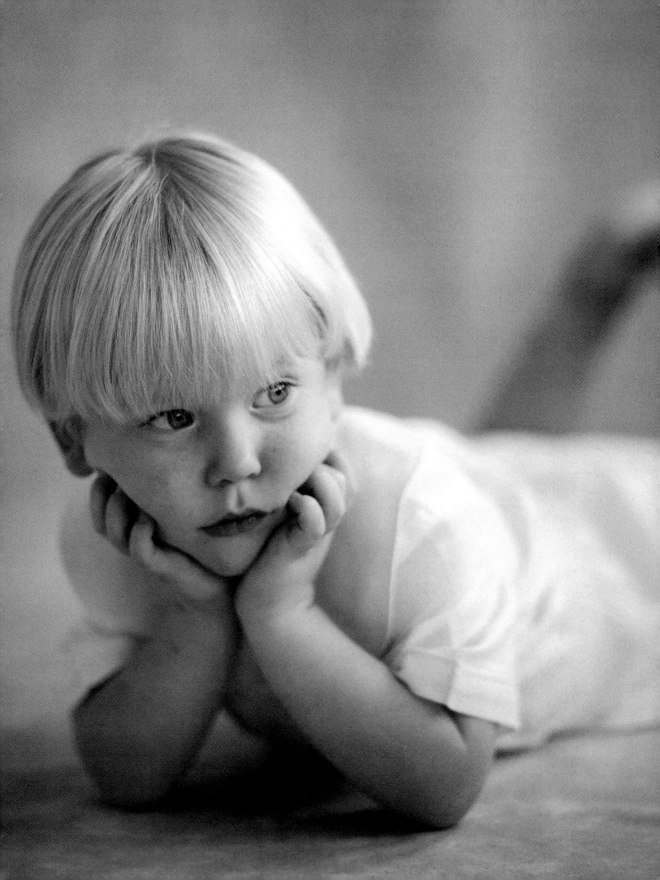

©Scarlett Hendricks / www.photographybyscarlett.com

While intimidating at first, learning the more technical aspects of photography and how to use your camera will, in the end, give you more tools at your fingertips. These tools enable you to repeat those lucky shots you get from time to time and, later on, to realize your creative vision for photographing children.

If you are a beginner, try working through the assignments at the end of each chapter using your camera's automatic mode and autofocus. Then, when you feel ready for the next challenge, you can gain more control by placing your camera into specific program modes or priority modes. If you have a point-and-shoot camera that limits your choices, you can still apply much of the information in this book. As you read through the book, notice that under each photograph there is a description of the image as well as technical information provided that gives you information as to how the photographer got that shot, as in 2-1. This chapter helps you understand what those numbers mean and how they can affect the look of every photograph you take.

YOU DON'T NEED TO KNOW EVERYTHING

You don't have to know everything about the mechanics of your camera to make great improvements in your photography. If you do nothing else, both learning to see and recognize beautiful light and working on your compositional skills will greatly improve your work. However, if you plan to pursue photography as a more serious hobby or are considering making photography of children a sideline or full-time career, learning the more in-depth workings of your camera will help you to achieve the photographs you envision.

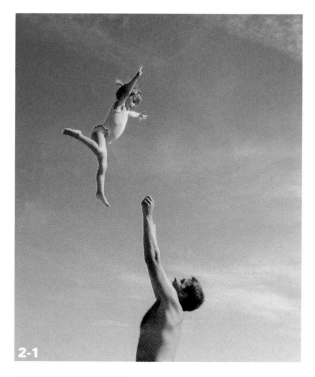

2-1

ABOUT THIS PHOTO *In her greatest ballerina form, this girl was caught midair, as her dad waits carefully in anticipation. The camera was in Program mode. Taken at ISO 400, f/7.1, and 1/1600 second. ©Sarah Felch*

quote "Only a fraction of the camera's possibilities interests me — the marvelous mixture of emotion and geometry, together in a single instant." ~Henri Cartier-Bresson, *Aperture 129*, Fall 1992

Beginning photographers are consistently befuddled about the issues of exposure, depth of field, and settings on their cameras. While new technology makes it easier than ever to make a proper exposure, the bells and whistles that come on today's cameras can further compound the problem.

Knowing that this part is confusing to just about everyone should help you feel a little better. However, there is no substitute for practice, and the more you practice with your camera settings, the quicker you learn to use your camera. If you have already advanced to other modes (besides Auto) on your camera, the following information should help you to better understand what you are doing and why.

GOING BEYOND AUTOMATIC: EXPOSURE BASICS

If you are using Auto mode, you may have discovered that it often results in a photograph with everything in focus — foreground and background. When Auto isn't giving you the results you're looking for, you may need to change the settings on your camera to capture your subject differently.

Cameras come from their manufacturers with set defaults that allow them to create a good image in most situations. However, there are times when you need to do something more specific to the settings to accommodate the situation in which you are shooting. For example, maybe you want to capture your child dancing in a rain puddle and freeze every single drop of water in the splashes she's making. Maybe you want to get a shot of your boys running through a meadow of grass with the golden light in their hair but still capture light in their faces. Both of these situations would present some problems for the typical camera in Auto mode.

If you are using Auto mode, you may have also discovered that it often results in a photograph with everything in focus — foreground and background — which is the default choice made by the computer elements in your camera. What if you want to make an image more like some in this book, where the subject is in focus and the background is blurred? You can achieve the image you want in all sorts of situations by learning more about exposure.

Exposure is what happens when the shutter on your lens opens and lets light into your camera, exposing the film or digital sensor to create an image.

There are three key elements to exposure:

■ Shutter speed

■ Aperture

■ ISO

Each of these elements (when set correctly) creates a properly exposed image. Understanding these elements so you can use them in creative ways can dramatically change the look of a photograph.

SHUTTER SPEED AND FREEZING MOTION

Shutter speed is relatively easy to understand. It is, essentially, time. Specifically, it is the amount of time that your shutter is open to light in order to record an image on your camera's digital sensor. Shutter speeds for photographing children are usually in the range of 1/60–1/500 second.

How long the shutter is open determines whether the image will be tack sharp or soft and blurry with regard to the movement of your subject. A fast shutter speed, such as 1/1000 second, freezes movement, whereas a slow shutter speed, such as 1/15 second, blurs movement. The longer the shutter is open, the more likely it is that movement will be recorded. The faster the shutter speed, the more likely it is that any movement will be frozen.

In most situations, you want your subject to be sharp and in focus so your shutter speed needs to be fast enough to accomplish this. For example, if you want to freeze the movement of your son at the peak of his jump off the diving board, a fast shutter speed is called for. If, instead, you'd like to capture the blur of the movement of a child kicking sand (see 2-5), you might want to try a slower shutter speed. A fast shutter speed of 1/320 second was used to capture the girls in 2-2 playing ring-around-the rosy.

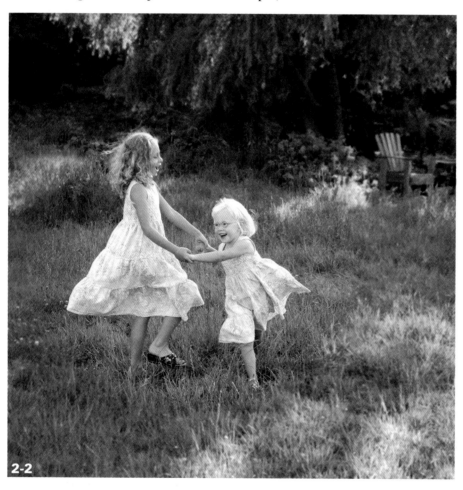

2-2

ABOUT THIS PHOTO *I chose the shutter speed of 1/320 second to freeze these sisters playing ring-a-round-the rosy. Taken at ISO 400, f/4.5, and 1/320 second. ©Ginny Felch / www.photographingchildren.com*

MOVEMENT

Choosing your shutter speed then, is based on movement. Is your subject a wiggly preschooler or a more mature adolescent? The too-slow shutter speed and (as in 2-3), can cause unwanted blurring. Remember, your subject isn't the only person who's moving. If you are holding the camera in your hands (also known as shooting handheld)

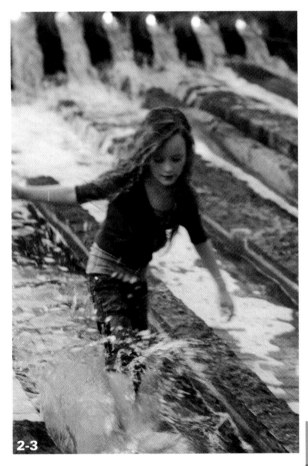

2-3

ABOUT THIS PHOTO *The shutter speed of 1/60 second was too slow to freeze the droplet of water that the little girl was kicking up and camera shake caused the rest of the photo to be out of focus. Taken at ISO 100, f/2.8, and 1/60 second. ©Allison Tyler Jones / atjphoto.com*

you have to take your own movement into consideration. Many shots have been ruined due to camera shake, which is when the photographer moves, causing the camera to shake resulting in a blurry photo.

If you examine the blurry photo carefully, it's usually easy to tell when there is camera movement versus a moving subject. Camera shake blurs the whole photo; in a photograph with a moving subject; only the part of the subject that is moving is blurred.

Inexperienced photographers usually cannot hold a camera steadily with a shutter speed of less than 1/60 second and might be better off using 1/100 second or faster. In other words, if your camera (in an Auto mode) chooses 1/60 second or faster, you should be able to hold your camera steadily without a tripod, which is explained in more detail in the next section. If your camera selects a shutter speed below 1/60 second and you don't have a tripod, try the following tricks to steady your camera:

- Take a deep breath, let it go, and as you exhale, press the shutter release button.

- Rest or lean the camera against a conveniently located still surface such as a fence post or wall.

- Hold your arms very tightly against your body and widen your stance, making your body into a kind of tripod.

tip

Some camera lenses offer "image stabilization," a device in the lens that compensates for camera movement and the resulting blur. This device is very handy for photographing in low-light conditions and prevents accidental blurring.

SHUTTER SPEED TIPS Here are some shutter speed tips for when you are handholding your camera, assuming you are using lenses commonly used for portraits, i.e. 50mm, 85mm and 100mm:

- Too slow for handholding (that is, you need a tripod unless you are experienced or have a very steady hand): 1/4, 1/8, 1/15, 1/30 second

- 1/60 second is borderline if you don't have steady hands

- Fast enough for hand-holding: 1/125, 1/250, 1/500, 1/1000, 1/1500 second

- To freeze movement: 1/250, 1/500, 1/1000, 1/1500 second

Because this is a book about photographing children, it is assumed that, for the most part, you will be handholding your camera. Working with tripods and chasing toddlers don't often mix.

SHUTTER SPEED SELECTION

A good rule of thumb for choosing a shutter speed that ensures your subject is in focus is to select a shutter speed that is at least the reciprocal of the lens' focal length. On the front of your lens you will find numbers such as 18-70mm or 50mm. For example, if you are shooting with a 50mm lens and you want your subject in focus, you don't want to shoot with a shutter speed any

slower than 1/60 second. You can always set a faster shutter speed; you just don't want to go slower because there is a greater chance of blurring the image. If you have an 18-70mm zoom lens, you should be shooting with a shutter speed of no less than 1/100 or 1/125 second; either of these is fine. Determine the focal length of your lens, such as 50mm, and set your shutter speed accordingly. If you aren't sure what the focal length is, you can find it printed on the barrel of your lens.

Table 2-1 offers some shutter speed settings that are a good starting point to achieve non-blurry photos in a variety of child photography situations.

Table 2-1

Common Shutter Speed Settings

Situation/Subject	Shutter Speed
Sleeping baby	1/60 to 1/125
Roaming toddler	1/125 to 1/250
Kids running	1/250 to 1/500
Child on swing	1/500 to 1/1000

FREEZING MOVEMENT

If you are photographing fast-moving subjects such as children swinging, running, riding, and so on, you might need an even faster shutter speed to freeze the movement. Shutter speeds of 1/250, 1/500, 1/1000 second, and faster stop almost any action. The movement in the photo shown in 2-1 of a little girl being tossed into the air by her dad was frozen by a fast shutter speed. In 2-4, the ebullient little girl's jumping movement was also stopped by a fast shutter speed.

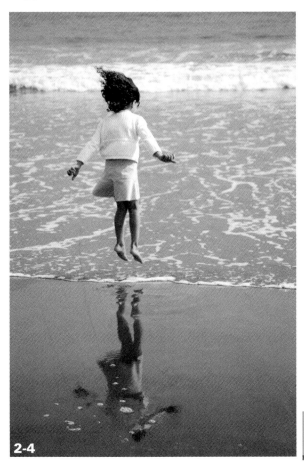

2-4

ABOUT THIS PHOTO *I used a shutter speed that was fast enough to freeze the motion of this exuberant little girl as she jumped in the surf. Taken at ISO 100, f/5.0, and 1/1000 second. ©Ginny Felch / www.photographingchildren.com*

> **tip**
> An easy way to remember which way f-stops go is to think of f-stop numbers as fractions — where f/2.8 becomes 1/2.8 and f/11 becomes 1/11 — then it makes more sense that the smaller numbers are larger openings.

BLURRING MOVEMENT

If you're feeling a bit more adventurous, you might want to try blurring the movement of your subject on purpose for a creative effect. Kids on a playground or a little girl kicking sand at the beach, as in 2-5, are all good subjects for trying your hand at blurring movement in your photos. Choose a slower shutter speed but not too slow; you want the moving subject to blur but everything else to be in focus.

APERTURE

In photography, aperture refers to the opening in the lens of your camera. When the shutter is released, the aperture determines how much light is allowed to come through the lens into your camera. Aperture is measured in f-stops, such as f/2.8, f/5.6, f/8, f/11, f/16, and so on. The smaller the number, the larger the opening in the lens — f/2.8 is a much larger opening than f/16 (see 2-6 and 2-7).

Thinking about shutter speed and aperture together is easier when you think of your eyes. Your eyelid is the shutter of your eye, and it is either open or closed. Your pupil is the aperture of your eye. When it's bright outside, your pupil contracts (or closes down) to let less light into

> **quote**
> "Photographs are not made by cameras, which are only tools. We make images with our hearts and minds. What must be brought to photography is an ever-open and seeking mind." ~Arnold Newman

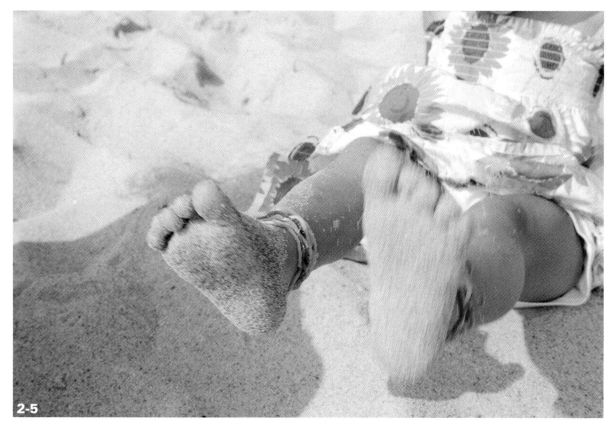

2-5

ABOUT THIS PHOTO *Photographing children always provides the opportunity to capture action; here the slow shutter speed blurred the kicking, sandy feet to liven up the photograph. Taken at ISO 400, f/4.5, and 1/30 second. ©Zofia Waig / www.zofiaphoto.com*

your eye. When light is low, your pupil dilates (opens up), letting in the maximum possible light so you can see. What do most people do when they can't see something very well? They squint. They are closing down the aperture of their eye to allow more of what they are looking at to be in focus. This is an easy way to remember how aperture works when the numbers get confusing.

Now that you know what aperture is technically, how do you think it can affect your photograph? It is really quite simple. Your choice of aperture determines just how much of your photograph is actually in focus. That brings us to depth of field.

The aperture or f-stop you choose determines the depth of field in your photograph. *Depth of field* is the field or area in the photograph that is in focus. Choosing a small aperture, such as f/16 or f/22,

Depth of Field - A Simple Visualization

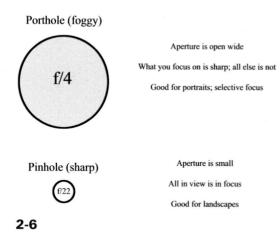

Porthole (foggy)

f/4

Aperture is open wide

What you focus on is sharp; all else is not

Good for portraits; selective focus

Pinhole (sharp)

f/22

Aperture is small

All in view is in focus

Good for landscapes

2-6

ABOUT THIS FIGURE *This very simple diagram reveals the relative sizes of the aperture openings of the lens, or f/stops. Notice that the larger the opening, the smaller the number – because the number is actually a fraction.*

creates a photograph with everything in focus from front to back, as in 2-8. This is called a wide or deep depth of field.

A photograph where just the family is in focus but everything else in the foreground and background is out of focus would have a narrow or shallow depth of field, as in 2-9. Have you noticed that many of the portraits that grab your eye are not in focus throughout? In these cases, the subjects are in focus, but the foreground and background are out of focus. This is how your eyes perceive things as well. If you are looking at someone, the foreground and the background are not sharp. Aperture choice gives the photographer the ability to show the viewer what is important using focus and lack thereof.

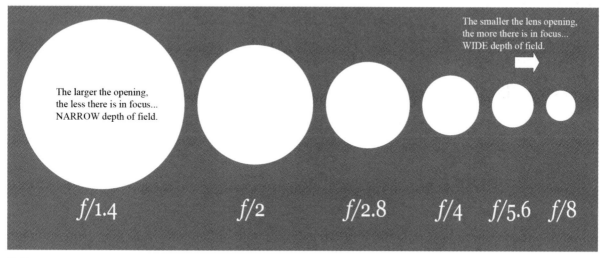

The larger the opening, the less there is in focus... NARROW depth of field.

The smaller the lens opening, the more there is in focus... WIDE depth of field.

$f/1.4$ $f/2$ $f/2.8$ $f/4$ $f/5.6$ $f/8$

2-7

ABOUT THIS FIGURE *If you can picture in your mind the lens opening at larger apertures versus the lens opening at smaller apertures as in this figure, it will be easier for you to understand how to set your camera.*

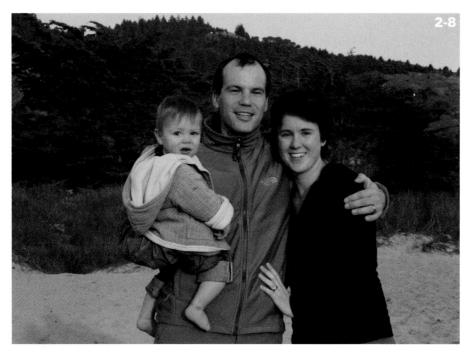

2-8

ABOUT THESE PHOTOS
In 2-8 you can see a photo of a young family I photographed at the beach using an aperture of f/22 at 1/50 second, giving focus throughout. In 2-9, I photographed the same family using an aperture f/2.8 at 1/320 second, causing the subjects to be in focus and all else blurred. Taken at ISO 400, f/4.5, and 1/320 second. ©Ginny Felch / www.photographingchildren. com

Here are few more important items to know regarding depth of field:

■ **Wide depth of field.** Apertures of f/8 and smaller (f/11, f/16, f/22) all produce a photo with a reasonably wide depth of field. These settings are perfect for shots where you want to include the environment as part of the image, such as when photographing a child in his room and including the detail of all the toys.

A wider depth of field is also good when shooting groups of people, such as a family, so that everyone in the photograph is in focus from the front row to the back. When you see images of children at a distance or portraits in which all things in the image are in focus, the photographer is often using smaller apertures of f/11 to f/16 or smaller, which results in a wide depth of field. This technique is often referred to as shooting stopped down, meaning the aperture of the lens is smaller and more closed down.

■ **Narrow depth of field.** Apertures of f/2.8, f/2.0, and even f/1.4 or f/1.2 are not uncommon in narrow depth of field photos. These settings work well for isolating your subject from the background, as in 2-10. The f-stops used on most of the photographs in this book were anywhere from f/1.4 to f/5.6. That isn't much of a range considering that there are so many other possibilities (f/8, f/11, f/16, f/22, f/32, and some stops in between).

Throughout the book, you see many portraits of children where you can clearly see their faces, yet the background is blurred. In these instances, the photographer was using larger apertures, such as f/3.5 to f/2.8, or larger. The larger apertures create a narrow depth of field. This technique is often called shooting wide open, meaning the aperture is as wide open as it can be. The photo in 2-10 was shot wide

2-9

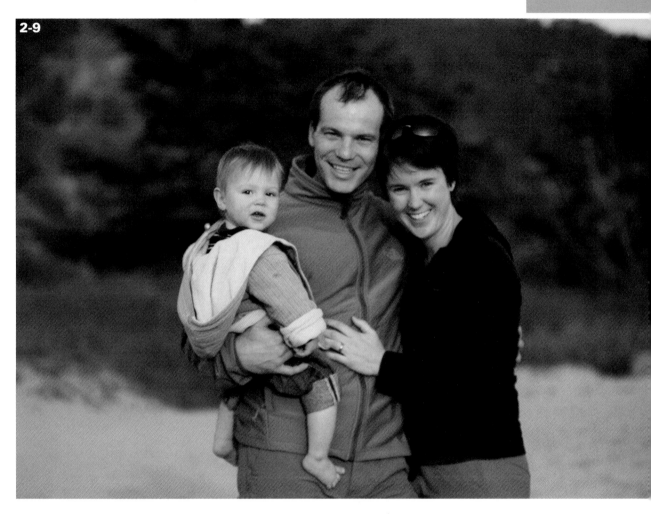

---

tip Choose which aperture/f-stop you want to use. You can see that the larger f-stops (smaller numbers) — that is, f/4 and f/5.6 — give you a pleasing depth of field for portraits. Your best way of deciding which one to use is through experimentation.

tip Manipulate your depth of field by playing with your aperture settings. Shoot the same subject in the same setting and only change your aperture for each shot. This gives you an instant library of how the aperture of your lens affects your images.

open with an aperture of f/3.5. The newborn is in focus and her proud big sister watches with amusement in the background. Similarly, in 2-11, the photographer used f/2 to blur background and sharpen the very handsome little cycler.

ISO

On most digital cameras there is a button or menu setting that enables you to choose the ISO setting. ISO, which stands for International Organization for Standardization, refers to the

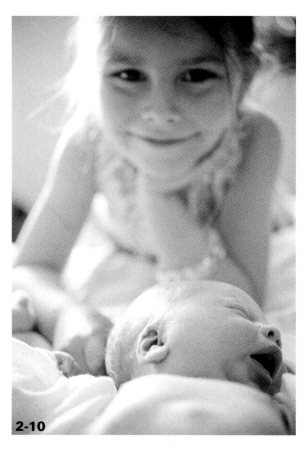

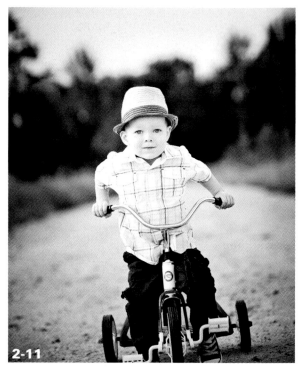

ABOUT THIS PHOTO *The blurred or out-of-focus background created by a wide aperture separates the uptown tricyclist from the woods in the background. Taken at ISO 100, f/2, and 1/640 second. ©Cama Cathrae / www.camacathraephotography.com*

2-10

ABOUT THIS PHOTO *A large aperture was chosen by the photographer to isolate the newborn, yet reveal the delighted sister in the background. Taken at ISO 800, f/1.8, and 1/60 second. ©Zofia Waig / www.zofiafoto.com*

light sensitivity of your camera. ISO ratings originally applied to film speeds, such as 200, 400, and so on. Just like film, the higher the number rating, the more sensitive the sensor on your digital camera is to light. For example, if you need your camera to be very sensitive to light, such as when you are shooting in low light, then you'd want to choose an ISO of 800 or higher. The ISO setting is often the easiest variable to manipulate when you need a specific aperture and shutter speed combination.

Generally speaking, in order to keep your photographs crisp and free of noise, you should use the lowest ISO you can while still keeping your preferred shutter speed and aperture. On most cameras, ISO 100 is the lowest setting. When you use higher ISO settings — generally 800 and higher — you begin to see noise in your images, which gives a grainy appearance.

Refer to Table 2-2 as a starting point for choosing ISO settings in different situations. Most cameras can deliver excellent, noise-free results when you use ISO settings of 100, 200, and 400. The settings in the table are only a starting point for various situations that you may find yourself in and are designed to allow for high enough shutter speeds to enable you to hand-hold your camera.

Table 2-2

Common ISO Settings

Situation	ISO Setting
Sunny day	100
Porch light	200
Overcast day	200 to 400
Window light	400
Indoor w/o flash	800 and up
Stage performances w/o flash	1600
Indoor sporting events w/o flash	1600

USING PROGRAM MODES

The previous discussions of shutter speed, aperture, and ISO are to give you an idea of how your camera works so you can manipulate it as you desire. Many cameras have program modes that move beyond the general Auto mode and give you more control over your final image. These program modes allow you to choose the type of subject matter you want to photograph; you can match your camera's program mode to the subject you are photographing. Table 2-3 is a list of some common program modes your camera might offer.

Table 2-3

Common Camera Program Modes

Mode	Indicated by	Results
Auto mode	A	Your camera makes all the decisions.
Program mode	P	Camera chooses shutter and aperture; you choose metering mode, ISO setting, focusing mode, and so on.
Portrait mode	Icon	Camera favors a narrow depth of field to blur background.
Sports mode	Icon	Camera favors a fast shutter speed to freeze action.
Landscape mode	Icon	Camera favors a wide depth of field (everything in focus).
Macro mode	Icon	Camera favors a narrow depth of field and macro lens settings for very close-up shots.
Shutter Priority mode	S or Tv	You choose the shutter speed; the camera sets the aperture.
Aperture Priority mode	A or Av	You choose the aperture; the camera sets the shutter speed.
Manual mode	M	Total control. You set everything: shutter speed, aperture, and ISO.

Your camera is a precision instrument that has been designed to successfully capture your image. Let the camera do some of the work for you when you are learning. The program modes go beyond the more generic Auto mode and can increase your chance of success in specific shooting situations.

PORTRAIT MODE

Choosing Portrait mode tells your camera that you want your subject in focus but everything else can be out of focus. Portrait mode favors a narrow depth of field where possible. If you make the same image twice, using Auto and then using Portrait mode, you should see a difference in what is in focus. Portrait mode is a precursor to using Aperture Priority, which gives you more control, allowing you to choose the exact aperture you require and letting the camera set the shutter speed.

SPORTS MODE

Sports mode defaults to a fast shutter speed, allowing you to capture fast-moving children or the action in sporting events. This program mode is a precursor to using Shutter Priority, which allows you to set the exact shutter speed required and lets the camera take care of the aperture.

LANDSCAPE MODE

Landscape mode favors a wide depth of field setting to allow everything — foreground and background — to be in focus. This mode is not used a great deal in child photography but might come in handy when photographing children in an outdoor setting where you want to include the detail in the background. You might also use Landscape mode to photograph a large group to ensure that everyone is in focus.

CLOSE-UP OR MACRO MODE

Macro mode is great for isolating the bee that just landed on a flower but more applicable to the children's photographer is using this setting to get in close on baby toes, eyelashes, ears, and fingers.

APERTURE PRIORITY MODE

Many digital cameras have a mode called Aperture Priority, often abbreviated as A or Av. This mode enables the photographer to choose the aperture or f-stop, and the camera correspondingly selects the correct shutter speed to give you a proper exposure. Aperture Priority is a better choice than Portrait mode once you understand the concept of depth of field, because it gives you more control over your image. You are able to set the exact aperture you need and let the camera do the rest. Aperture Priority is the mode favored by many professional portrait and wedding photographers.

This mode is a great choice for general use but particularly for children's portraits. It simplifies the process, allowing you to be spontaneous while ensuring an accurate exposure. You already have enough on your mind when working with children without having to concentrate on camera function. All you need to decide is what should be in focus (narrow versus wide depth of field).

Many photographers are now stylizing their portraits using an even larger f-stop, such as f/1.5 or even f/1.2. This creates a more selective focus and really throws all else out of focus except for what

ABOUT THIS PHOTO *I chose a large aperture to hone in on the brand new little feet of a newborn. Taken at ISO 100, f/1.5, and 1/250 second. ©Ginny Felch / www.photographingchildren.com*

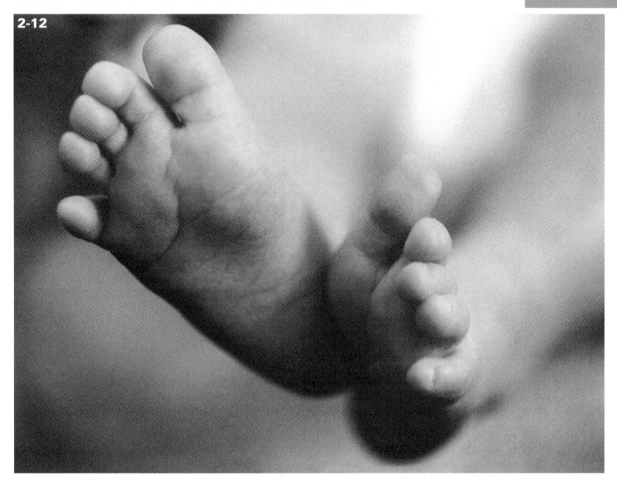

2-12

you choose as your main subject. It can be the face; it can be the foot. Ah, creative liberty! Just remember that when you are shooting this wide open, as in 2-12, your margin for error is very slim. It's easy to get everything out of focus, so practice, practice, practice.

SHUTTER PRIORITY MODE

Shutter Priority mode allows you to determine the best shutter speed for your subject, and the camera does the rest. So, if you are shooting your daughter's softball game and you want to

tip When you are using Aperture Priority mode, and the aperture you choose causes the camera to select a shutter speed that is too slow to handhold your camera (1/60 second and slower), you can increase your ISO until an appropriate shutter speed is selected.

freeze the big run for home, as in 2-13, set your camera on Shutter Priority mode, dial in a fast shutter speed, and let the camera take care of the rest.

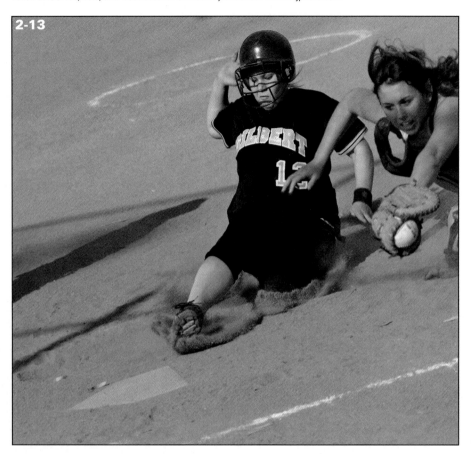

2-13

MANUAL MODE

Manual mode gives you free reign, allowing you to choose both the shutter speed and the aperture. Some photographers swear by it, but it takes experience and understanding of the built-in metering capabilities of the camera.

WHAT DO YOU WANT?

If you've made it this far in the chapter, give yourself a pat on the back. That is a lot of technical information to wade through, but your patience will pay off if you learn to practice even one or two of the techniques discussed. The important thing to remember is that every one of these topics is just a tool in your image-making arsenal. Before you take your next photograph, ask yourself this question, "What do I want?" Do you want a gorgeous close-up of your toddler with the background blurred so you can concentrate on her face? Perhaps you'd like to freeze the motion of your 12-year-old skateboarding off the neighborhood ramp. Rather than just letting your camera do its thing, why not take control and start making some informed decisions about the images you are making? Set your aperture with your subject in mind rather than just to let enough light in to get the shot. When you start to choose your camera settings on purpose and with your subject in mind, you will be amazed at how fast your photography improves.

Assignment

Depth of Field and Selective Focus

This assignment is about learning to make a photograph with a narrow depth of field. For this assignment, try to get a beautiful photo with selective focus, meaning your subject should be sharp and all else falls out of focus. Photograph a child or children setting your camera on either Portrait mode, if you have it, or Aperture Priority. If you use Aperture Priority, select an aperture (f-stop) that is a small number, such as f/4.0 or lower. If you focus on your subject, that f-stop ensures a narrower depth of field. You will see the difference in a portrait taken with these settings compared with auto focus, where everything tends to be sharp.

These cherubic sisters shown here in their morning garb on the window seat were photographed with a narrow depth of field to blur out the potentially distracting details in the window, as well as create a more painterly look. Taken at ISO 500, f/2.8, and 1/60 second.

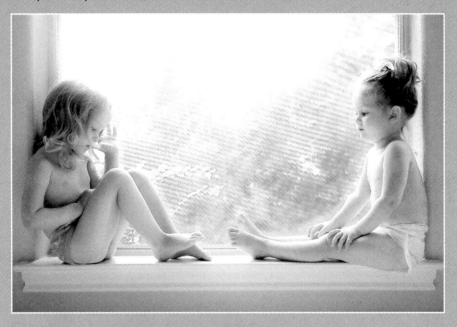

©Natalija Brunner / www.daidalorange.com

Remember to visit www.pwsbooks.com after you complete this assignment and share your favorite photo! It's a community of enthusiastic photographers and a great place to view what other readers have created. You can also post comments, read encouraging suggestions, and get feedback.

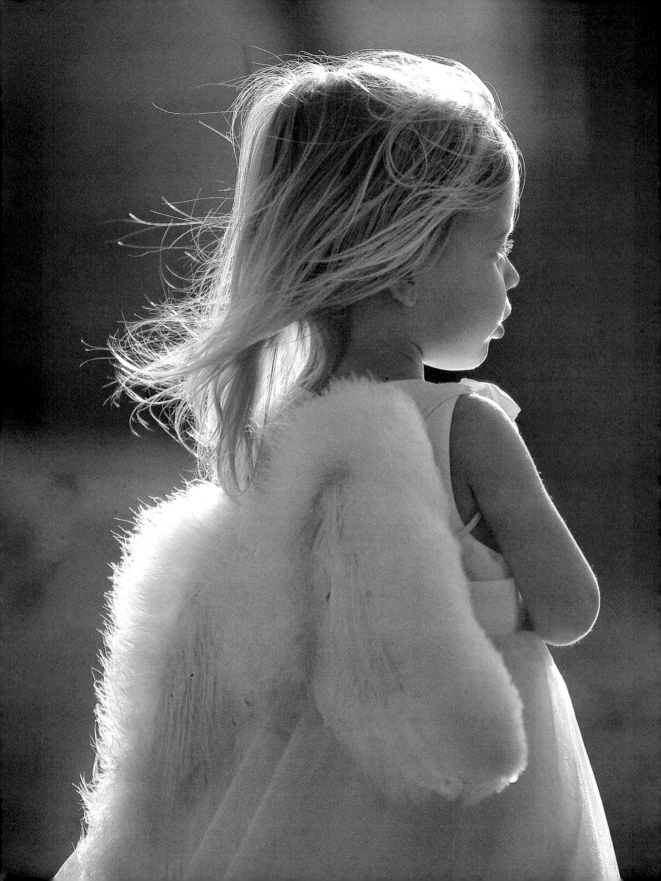

©Mary Schannen / www.melangephoto.com

Learning to see light not only improves the way your photos look, but it also (and more importantly) changes how your photographs *feel*. Used correctly, light can add an emotional element to an otherwise ordinary photograph.

To create dramatic and sensitive photographs, you must simply *fall in love* with light. Slow down and look at the light around you, right now, this minute. Perhaps you are near a window with diffused light spilling into the room. Or perhaps you are reading by the soft glow of a table lamp. Look at the objects in the room and see how their shadows are cast by the angle of the light falling on them. Once you start noticing, you will begin to see the effect of light everywhere you go. It changes your life, whether you have a camera in hand or not. You begin to see how light reveals itself in a soft glow or diagonally, illuminating the shapes and forms of everything before you. You see the light manifest mood, drama, and dreaminess. You might notice how warm, afternoon light tends to exaggerate color, while the light of dawn, just before the sun crests the horizon, tends to diminish or soften color.

LEARNING TO SEE LIGHT

Ruth Bernhard, a renowned photographer who died in 2007 at the age of 101, once said, "Light is my inspiration, my paint, and brush. It is as vital as the model herself. Profoundly significant, it caresses the essential superlative curves and lines. Light I acknowledge as the energy upon which all life on this planet depends." Students would spend the first day in one of Bernhard's workshops without a camera. Her purpose: to engage them with light.

quote   "Light is the Holy Grail of photography." ~Randy Romano

As clouds passed overhead or the sun backlit a flower, students began to see the world in a completely new way: a world full of light and shadow, reflection, and texture. What Bernhard's students realized was that their lives would be forever enhanced, with or without a camera in hand, just by learning to look at light. Much like as you would with a meditation, slowing down and taking the time to observe, really seeing the beauty and grace of your surroundings, are the first steps to capturing unique and stunning images.

Light itself can be the focal point of an image, as in 3-1, where the warm light of early evening created a halo on the head of this little girl.

Learning to use light in a sculptural and emotional way when photographing children takes attention, presence, and practice. Take time to observe the effects of light in your environment and then watch closely how that same light falls on the children in your life.

If you have observed children in their environment for any length of time, you might have noticed how velvety-soft their skin appears when they are sitting by a bedroom window, or the golden halo effect of the light in their hair as they run around the playground; how those big, brown eyes seem to catch the light just right when they are sitting in their highchair in your well-lit breakfast nook, or when they are up to their neck in bubbles in the big, garden tub with the glass block window just above. All of these situations will open your eyes to the possibilities of photographing children using light to convey your feelings about them and that moment in time.

Consider the next two photos, both of the same child. Typically, when photographing children indoors, the temptation is to let the flash do its thing and get the shot, but there might be a

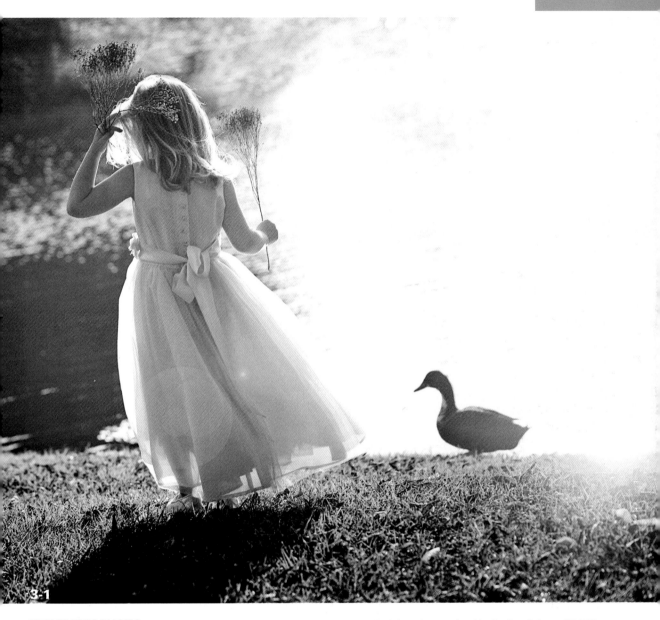

3-1

ABOUT THIS PHOTO *The late afternoon created a stunning rim light on the girl in pink as she meandered by the river. Taken at ISO 3230, f/4.0, and 1/500 second.* ©Mary Schannen / www.melangephoto.com

better way. The photo in 3-2 was taken using on-camera flash. You can see how the flash washed out the skin tones in the image and left a harsh shadow around the little girl. Moving her to a doorway with natural light spilling through, as

in 3-3, allows the light to wrap around and bathe her, revealing the texture of her skin and, more importantly, lending a completely different emotional feel to the image.

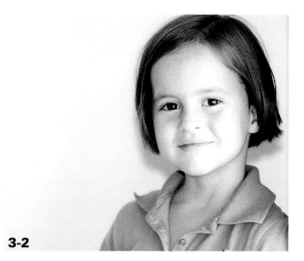

3-2

ABOUT THIS PHOTO *On-camera flash washes out skin tones and makes for harsh shadows. Taken at ISO 200, f/2.8, and 1/250 second. ©Allison Tyler Jones / www.atjphoto.com*

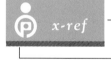

tip

If you are a beginner, you may want to start out with your camera mode set to Automatic. This way, you can concentrate on seeing light. As you complete the assignments throughout this book, you will want to put into practice what you are learning; camera settings are included in the image captions for those who are practicing with their cameras and for those who have a more advanced understanding of their cameras and want more technical information.

It may seem that photographing outdoors is easier because there is so much light, but remember that quantity isn't as important as quality. The photo in 3-4 was taken in direct sunlight, making everyone squint and causing harsh shadows on their faces. The photo in 3-5 was shot after considering where the light was coming from and finding open shade to photograph. Moving the family to an area with open shade allows everyone to have natural expressions and gives an entirely different feel to the image. Isn't it amazing the difference light can make?

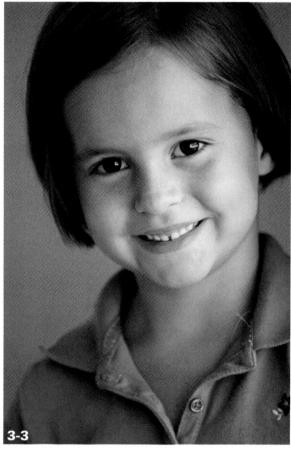

3-3

ABOUT THIS PHOTO *Placing the child inside a doorway with natural light allows the light to wrap around the girl's face, showing the texture of her skin. Taken at ISO 200, f/2.8, and 1/250 second. ©Allison Tyler Jones / www.atjphoto.com*

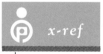

x-ref

Chapter 4 explores manipulating or adding light to a scene.

x-ref

Chapter 5 explores composition and an explanation of the Rule of Thirds.

ABOUT THIS PHOTO *The family has been positioned in harsh, direct sunlight, causing everyone to squint and the expressions to be less than ideal. Taken at ISO 100, f/3.5, and 1/800 second. ©Allison Tyler Jones / www.atjphoto.com*

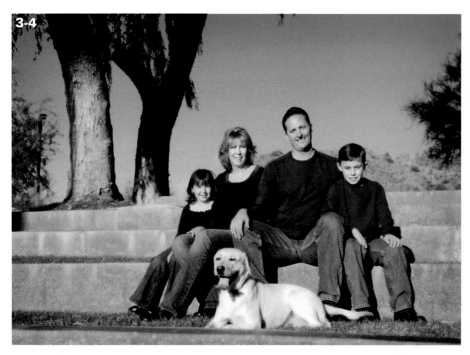

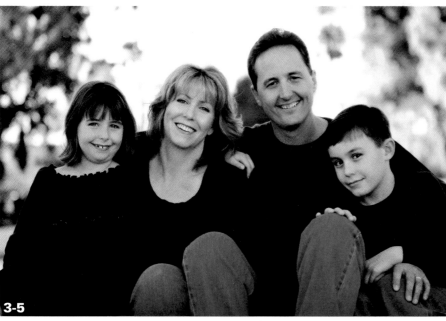

ABOUT THIS PHOTO *Moving the family to an area with open shade softens the light and allows for more natural expressions. Taken at ISO 100, f/2.8, and 1/125 second. ©Allison Tyler Jones / www.atjphoto.com*

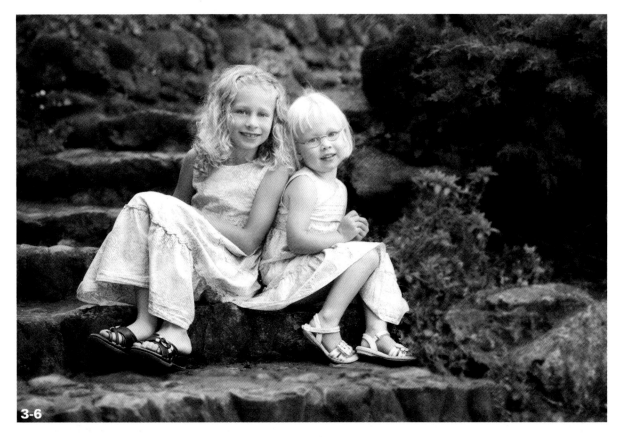

3-6

ABOUT THIS PHOTO *I was thrilled that the soft afternoon light enabled me to use these old steps in front of the beach home that the family has had for generations. The body language of the girls suggests support and connection. Taken at ISO 400, f/4.0, and 1/160 second. ©Ginny Felch / www.photographingchildren.com*

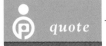 *quote*

"In the right light, at the right time, everything is extraordinary."
~Aaron Rose

AVAILABLE LIGHT

Many of the images throughout this book show children outdoors captured in beautiful light and natural settings, such as in 3-6, where the sisters sit comfortably on the old steps in front of their home. All the photos in this chapter were taken using available light. Available light is just what it sounds like: no flash or reflectors are used, just the existing light in the environment.

Of course, not all available light is great for photographing, but over time and as you peruse this book and photographs, you will begin to recognize that elusive but desirable quality. Available light that is flattering or provides contour or mood, is what you ultimately want to learn to see and to orchestrate. Available light is usually not direct sunlight.

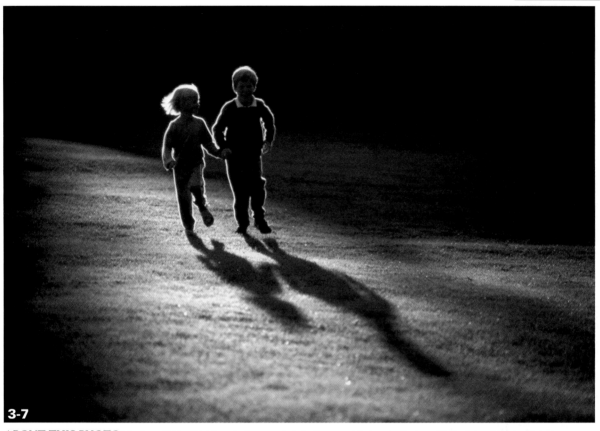

3-7

ABOUT THIS PHOTO *The beautiful backlighting, the long, angled shadows, and the heads aligning with the Rule of Thirds, all pay homage to these frolicking children. Taken at ISO 200, f/8.0, and 1/125 second.* ©Sherman Hines

> **tip**
>
> Check sunrise and sunset times for your local area on www.sunrise sunset.com, and try your own photo shoot at about 30 minutes before and after sunrise, or an hour before sunset. Watch carefully how the light changes as the sun moves higher or lower in the sky and what effect that has on the lighting of the child you are photographing.

The sun hitting the blond hair of the little boy and girl in 3-7 gave the subjects an angelic quality and set them apart from the background, while at the same time throwing their shadows ahead of them. Even though there is only a suggestion of their faces, their parents know who they are!

The dramatic deluge of filtered light from an attic window inspired the photographer to encourage her son to play freely in 3-8 and 3-9. In 3-10, the photographer reversed the formula for the light and captured the children peeking through the window.

Next, I'll show you a practical look at different kinds of lighting situations that you can explore for photographing children.

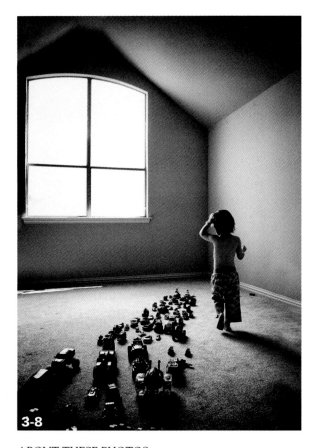

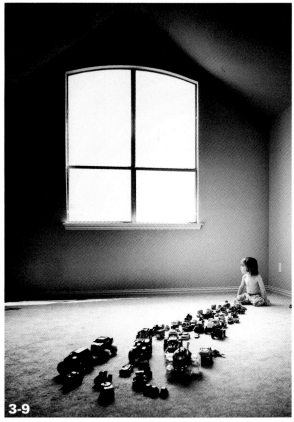

ABOUT THESE PHOTOS *The attic window light and the uncluttered background in 3-8 and 3-9 provided dramatic and story-telling images of a child at play. 3-8 was taken at ISO 1000, f/2.8, and 1/500 second; 3-9 at ISO 100, f/2.8, and 1/30 second. ©Mary Schannen / www.melangephoto.com*

THE SWEET LIGHT: DAWN AND TWILIGHT

Many great photographers only create images during the sweet light, which is the light that occurs at dawn and twilight. This light can be cool in the morning and warm in the evening, each creating its own mood and atmosphere. Because the light is at a greater angle, and often diffused by the atmosphere, a warm and soft glow is more likely (see 3-11 and 3-12).

Light is known to affect mood; you might notice the quiet hush that occurs at dawn and twilight, among both man and nature. What a delightful time to be with a child in a photographic session. The lighting and the atmosphere lend themselves so beautifully to an exploration of nature and lively conversations.

One of the challenges of working in this light is that it is fleeting. Just as you are enjoying and making use of the light, it can disappear, often causing frustration. You must learn to work quickly and spontaneously. After missing your opportunities a few times, you realize just how transient this gift of light can be; but when you see the difference it makes in your photographs, you will seek it.

USING REFLECTIONS AND SHADOWS

While you are observing light, pay attention to reflections and shadows in the environment. You can use both as a dynamic element of design, adding that something extra to your photograph. Reflections can be found in obvious places, such as in window glass or mirrors but can also be found in less obvious places, such as in rain puddles or the wash of the tide on a sandy beach.

When the sun is at an angle with morning or afternoon light, it creates angular or distorted shadows that can add interest and drama. Shadows speak of time passing, which captures the viewer's imagination. Shadows and reflections can help you tell a story while adding dimension to your images.

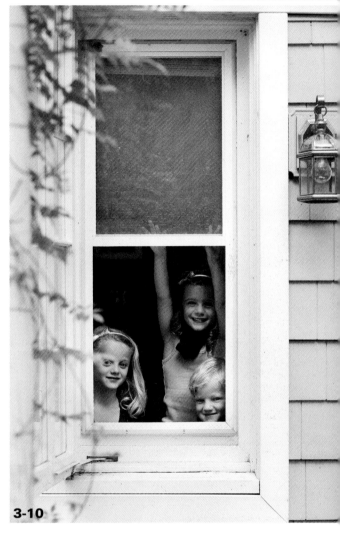

3-10

ABOUT THIS PHOTO *The available light outside of the house illuminated the children in the window. The dark background behind them offsets their cheery brightness. Taken at ISO 200, f/3.5, and 1/400 second. ©Jen Sherrick / www.jensherrickphotography.com*

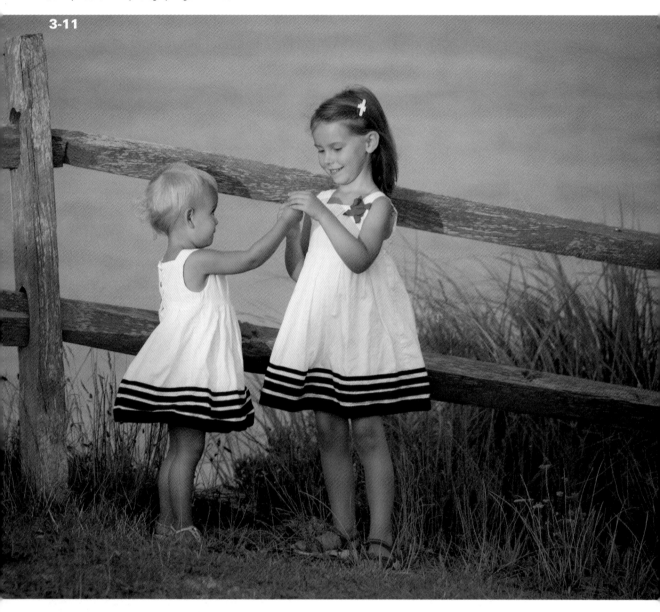

3-11

REFLECTIONS

A puddle on a rainy day can tell a story, such as the story of the little boy under the umbrella shown in 3-13.

Reflections of the subject in water or in windows yield a distorted but painterly quality that adds an artistic touch to the photograph.

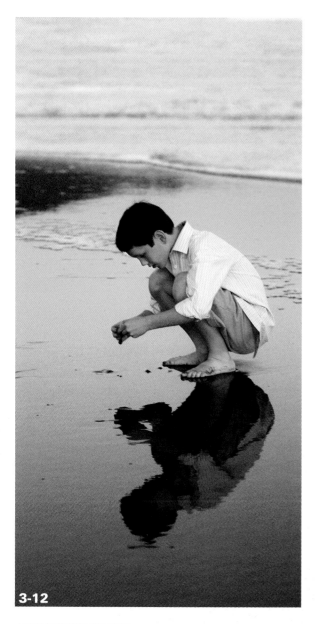

3-12

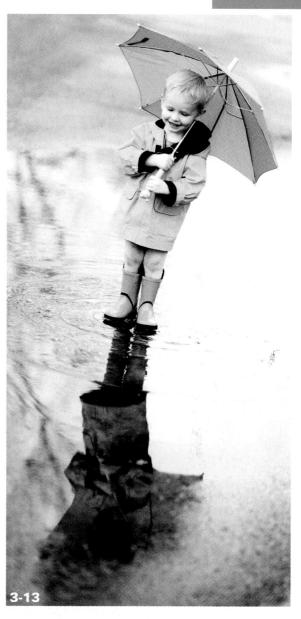

3-13

ABOUT THIS PHOTO *Moments after sunset provided a placid and pleasing environment for this boy to seek treasures. I was very pleased with the warm light and the smooth water's reflection. Taken at ISO 400, f/5.0, and 1/125 second. ©Ginny Felch / www.photographingchildren.com*

ABOUT THIS PHOTO *The reflections add depth and dimension to a photo of a little boy considering his mirror image on a rainy day. Taken at ISO 200, f/2.0, and 1/1600 second. ©Stacy Wasmuth / www.bluecandyphotography.com*

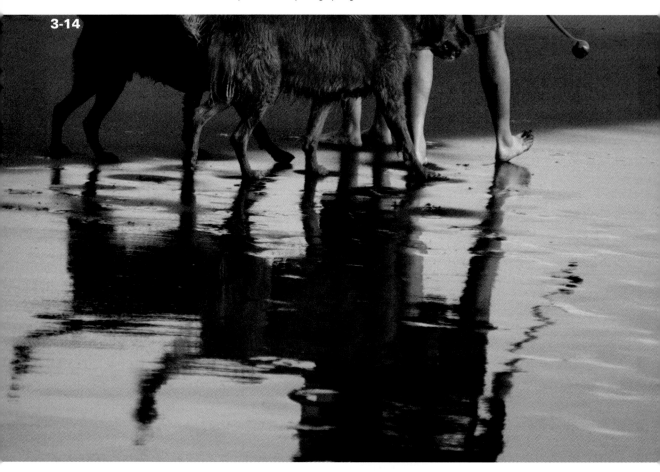

3-14

note When photographing children in a wooded setting, pay attention to the mottled light cast by the movement of leaves in the trees above. Either move your subject and use the light creatively and intentionally, or try the fill flash technique discussed in Chapter 4 to even out the shadows.

tip Those of you with compact digital cameras should check your manual for information on your flash settings. Does your camera allow you to turn the flash off or set it to a lower setting? This control is helpful as you learn to explore light.

I love to photograph at low tide on a beach taking advantage of reflections (as in 3-14). The added color, texture, and design can be other elements of your composition that catch the eye. The beauty of reflections is that they suggest the bigger picture without having to show every detail, leaving the viewer's mind to fill in the rest and create his or her own story about that image.

When using the soft light coming from a window, pay attention to your subject's reflection on the glass. If her head is turned toward the

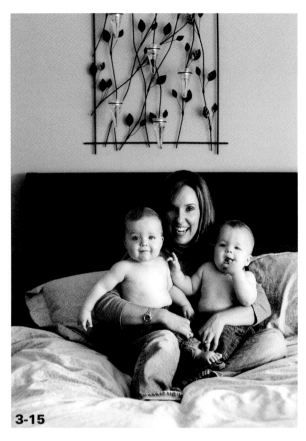

3-15

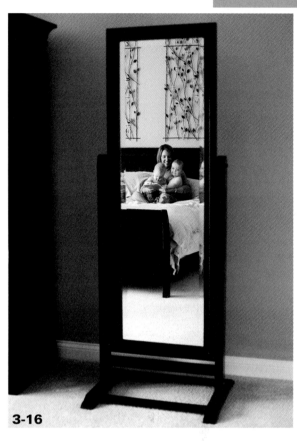

3-16

ABOUT THESE PHOTOS *The classic subject of mother and children, shown in 3-15, is given a modern twist by shooting into a mirror in the mom's bedroom in 3-16. Taken at ISO 600, f/2.8, and 1/250 second. ©Stacy Wasmuth / www.bluecandyphotography.com*

light, you might not be able to see facial details, except for what is reflected back to you. Again, a reflected image is slightly distorted, washed-out, and dreamy looking.

Using reflection as a visual metaphor, you deepen the meaning of your photograph by allowing the viewer to register the obvious and then look a bit closer, see the reflection, and ponder what else is there.

You could also take the reflection idea very literally. Look for mirrors or windows in your environment and take the same shots two ways, as in 3-15 and 3-16.

Babies love to look at other babies, even when that baby is their own reflection! Take advantage of their curiosity by placing a mirror within their reach, as in 3-17, and then watch what happens.

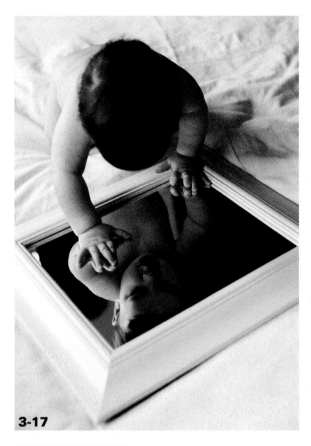

3-17

ABOUT THIS PHOTO *Because babies are naturally curious about other babies, let them play with a mirror while you take advantage of the sweet reflections of babyhood. Taken at ISO 400, f/2.8, and 1/320 second. ©Stacy Wasmuth / www.bluecandyphotography.com*

SHADOWS

When you are first learning photography, it is tempting to avoid shadows for fear that your subject won't be properly illuminated. Don't be afraid to make a few mistakes and explore how shadows can creatively affect the photos you take; the payoffs are worth it.

You may first want to explore the shadows that fall on the child you are photographing. Shadows created by light coming through a set

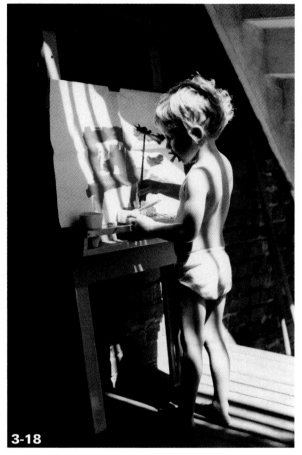

3-18

ABOUT THIS PHOTO *My little artist at work on a sunny morning seems embraced by the shadowed light as he concentrates on his colors. Even his cherished pacifier adds a bit to the story. Taken at ISO 200, f/5.6, and 1/125 second. ©Ginny Felch / www.photographingchildren.com*

of stairs, as in 3-18, or through anything that creates patterns make for an interesting element in a photograph.

On sunny days, the play of light and shadow can cast shadows that emphasize the shape or profile of the subject, as in 3-19. In 3-20, the shadow enhances the story of the photograph, adding mood and drama.

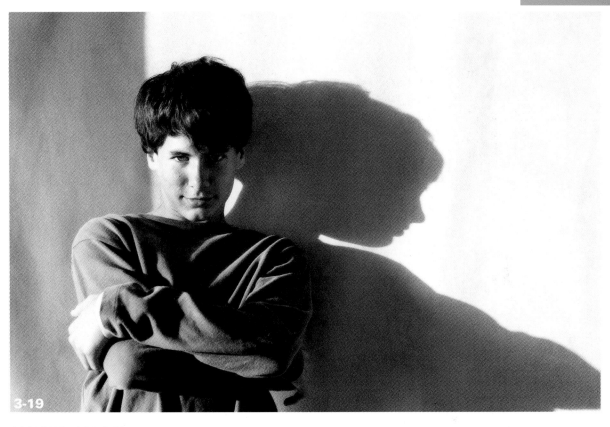

3-19

ABOUT THIS PHOTO *The bold, angular light and shadow give this young man a confident look. After they are drawn straight into his eyes, your eyes move toward the distinctive shadow on the wall. Taken at ISO 400, f/5.6, and 1/200 second. ©Scarlett Photography / www.photographybyscarlett.com*

Shadows can provide a very strong graphic element in a photograph, as in 3-20, where the strong diagonal shadows lead the viewer's eye in to the engaging family at sunset.

PHOTOGRAPHING IN FOG OR WITH OVERCAST SKIES

While many residents of beach communities relish hot, sunny days, some photographers are thrilled when the fog rolls in so they can take advantage of the other-worldly feeling that shooting in foggy

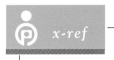

x-ref

For more technical information on aperture and f-stop, see Chapter 2.

light brings to their photos. Foggy skies provide a soft, flattering light that can allow photographers to photograph all day long.

FOGGY DAYS

On foggy days, the light is soft; the colors are monochromatic or pastel, and there is less contrast. Fog can be light, thick, high, low, and

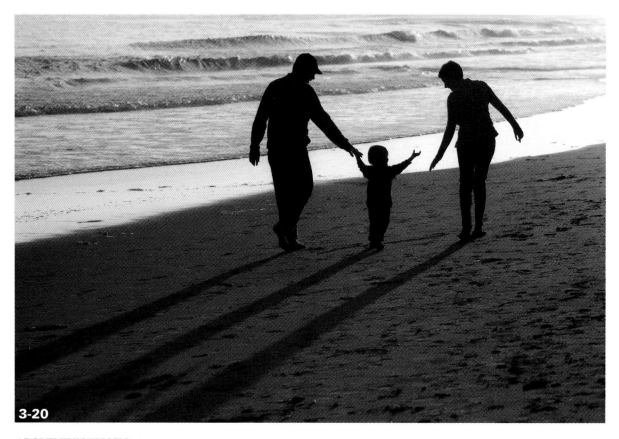

3-20

ABOUT THIS PHOTO *This silhouetted family photographed at sunset is even more dramatic and compelling because of the angle of the shadows. I love the way my grandson is reaching out to his mommy. Many photographs were made of their walk, and this one really spoke to me. Taken at ISO 400, f/5.6, and 1/1250 second. ©Ginny Felch / www.photographingchildren.com*

change by the minute. Its unpredictability adds to its mystery. To use fog to your advantage, you want to avoid high fog because it doesn't create the beautiful haze needed to cut the contrast in the setting. Look for a low, dense fog that obscures the surrounding hills or vegetation.

Fog behaves differently during the various seasons so you may start out your day with perfect fog but by the time the children show up you might be stuck with harsh sun. It's the chance you take when relying on Mother Nature to help with lighting. But when the weather cooperates

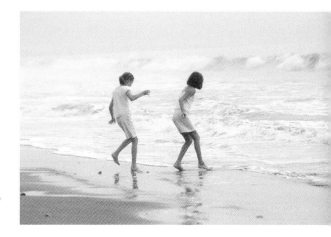

and fog envelops your subjects in a glowing, even light, children can frolic and play and you do not have to worry about from which direction the light is coming. This adds a sense of freedom to your work.

If it is a very foggy day, the available light may not be bright enough to work in until about 10 or 11 o'clock in the morning. In the afternoon, don't wait until too late, or the fog can become gloomy and you won't have the light you need. As with all things photographic, experimentation is the key.

Keep in mind that a lot of fog can create a low-light situation that might cause your flash to engage on your camera. That will really change your outcome. Don't forget — you don't want to use a flash in fog because, among other things, the water droplets reflect the light and end up looking like dots on your image. Photographs of scenes that appear more painterly in this kind of

light are considered high-key photographs, light subjects against a light background, as in 3-21 and 3-22. If you plan correctly and have the children wear lighter clothing, the darkest elements in the photograph are the skin tones, which really draw attention to the children. The background and even the clothing are more subdued. All is in a relative wash of light.

OVERCAST SKIES

Similar to fog, the mood created by overcast skies can be soft and romantic. Because the light is more subdued and has less contrast, it is much easier to achieve lighting with no harsh shadows or overly-bright highlights. This more forgiving light frees you up to concentrate on composition and the expressions of the children in your photograph.

Although overcast skies provide more evenly dispersed lighting than direct sun, photographing in the middle of the day, with light coming from overhead, can cause harsh shadows under the eyes. The next section addresses getting the light at the correct angle to your subject.

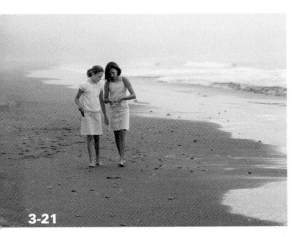

3-21

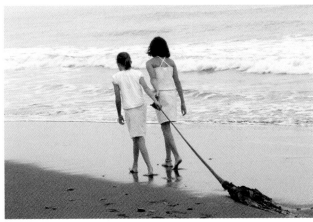

ABOUT THESE PHOTOS *This series of three photographs of two sisters playing at the beach shows a unique relationship between the girls and their environment. The pastel tones of the clothing that we carefully chose are pleasing to the eye and give the portrait a painterly look. Taken at ISO 400, f/16, and 1/250 second. ©Ginny Felch / www.photographingchildren.com*

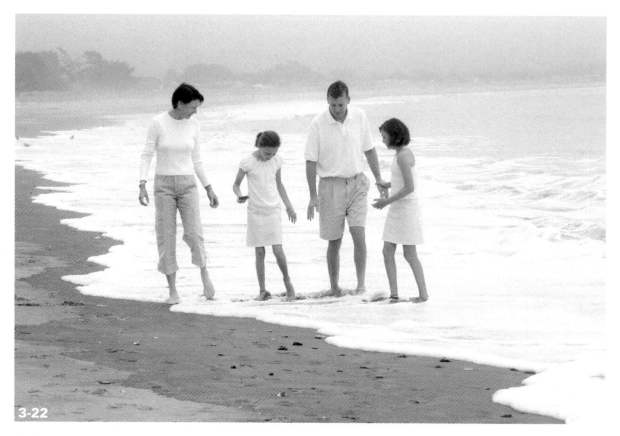

3-22

ABOUT THIS PHOTO *The foggy day and monochromatic tones set off this family as they interact at the beach. The foggy background delivers a monochromatic and moody image. I love the movement and natural pose of this family. Taken at ISO 400, f/11, and 1/250 second. ©Ginny Felch / www.photographingchildren.com*

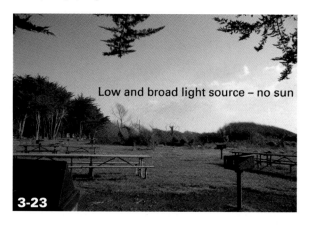

Low and broad light source - no sun

3-23

ABOUT THIS PHOTO *This view shows a low and broad light source that I always seek for portraits — the sky with no sun. Taken at ISO 640, f/5.6, and 1/2500 second. ©Ginny Felch / www.photographing children.com*

FINDING CONTOURING LIGHT

Contouring lighting gives a dimensional look to an otherwise flat piece of paper — your photographic print. That quality of illumination ideally gives three times as much light to one side of the face than the other, or a 3:1 lighting ratio. Don't panic now; this is not a math quiz! It is a matter of learning to see the light, subtle as it might be, fall on a face.

You can do one very helpful exercise that demonstrates the sculptural or contouring effect of light on a sunny, cloudy, or overcast day. Ideally, you

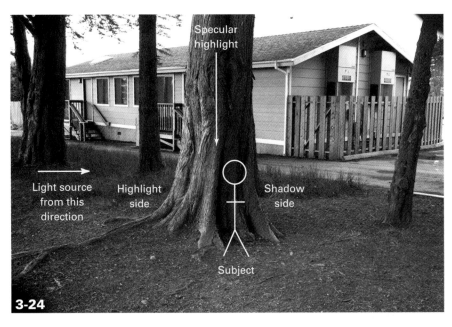

3-24

ABOUT THIS PHOTO *This background was chosen because of the sculptural light (see the highlight and shadow side of trunk) on the tree. Even though there is clutter from the building and tree, I isolated the subject and tree in my camera's viewfinder. Taken at ISO 640, f/5.6, and 1/200 second. ©Ginny Felch / www.photographingchildren.com*

find a spot on the edge of a forest or meadow with trees. Your light source is a low and broad sky without direct sun, as in 3-23.

In this exercise, you evaluate the light on the trees as you search for a location to photograph. See if you can find an area with light falling more brightly on one side than another and look for the *specular highlight*, (that is, the bright line dividing the highlight from the shadow) as in 3-24. Don't worry if the location seems crowded with objects that you don't want in your final image. As you can see, you can focus on your subject and eliminate the distracting details.

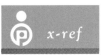 *x-ref*

Reflectors and other tools used to manipulate light are discussed in depth in Chapter 4.

If you place a face in that location, as shown in 3-25, you see similar light flowing on it, and the specular highlight can be placed on the subject's nose. The portrait of Daisy reveals the same light on her face that formerly appeared on the tree. She was asked to turn her head until the light appeared there and the little triangle of light appeared on her left cheek. One side of your subject's face should have about three times the amount of light on it than the other. If you turn her face just right, you see a little triangle of light on the other cheek before the shadow falls off the face. Study the illustrations and then go out in the field and practice.

This is really an exercise about observing light, so that you can see the subtle differences between light and shadow and use it as you want for illuminating your subjects. It can take years to learn to discern this subtlety.

ABOUT THIS PHOTO *The highlight and shadow side give Daisy's face a more dimensional or sculpted appearance. Notice the specular high-light (brightest line of light) that comes down her nose to add contour to her face. Can you see the subtle triangle of light on her left cheek? Taken at ISO 640, f/5.6, and 1/200 second. ©Ginny Felch / www.photographingchildren.com*

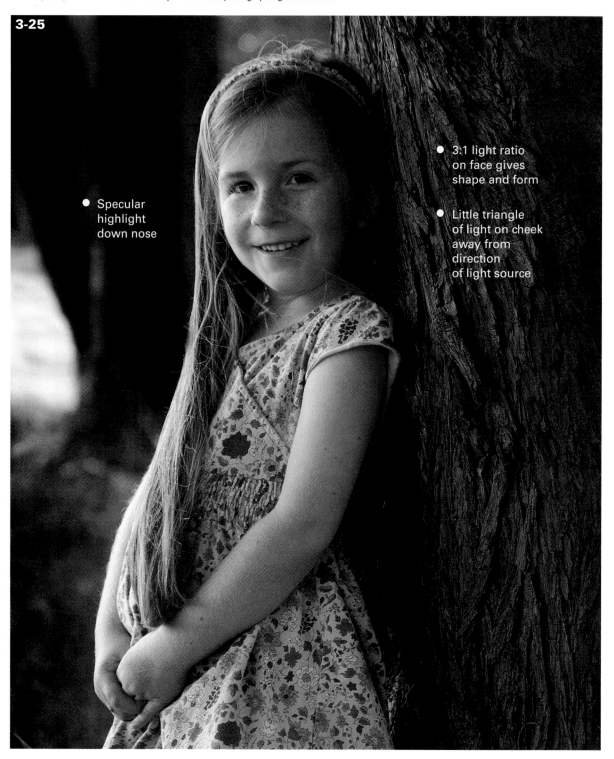

3-25

● Specular
highlight
down nose

● 3:1 light ratio
on face gives
shape and form

● Little triangle
of light on cheek
away from
direction
of light source

USING SOFT WINDOW LIGHT

Indirect light that flows in through a window (particularly a window facing north) is an exquisite source of flattering, soft light to use when photographing children. Although northern light is known to be ideal because of the lack of direct sun, you will find light on an overcast day just as acceptable. Using indirect light rather than sunlight is important when using windows as your source.

The exception to this would be if you choose to use direct sun shining through a window to create an image with more contrast. Naturally, this

would not produce a soft and diffuse, shadowless light. Also, the closer your subject is to the window, the more harsh the light can be.

Experimentation and your own artistic point of view will serve you well as you learn to use window light. However, a few things help you to control it and use it more effectively. In 3-26, you can see the direction of the light better if you are in a room that doesn't have other windows bringing in distracting light. This gives you much better control.

The images shown in 3-27 and 3-28 are examples of soft, directional light coming from nearby windows. The children look cherubic with the side light contouring their soft faces.

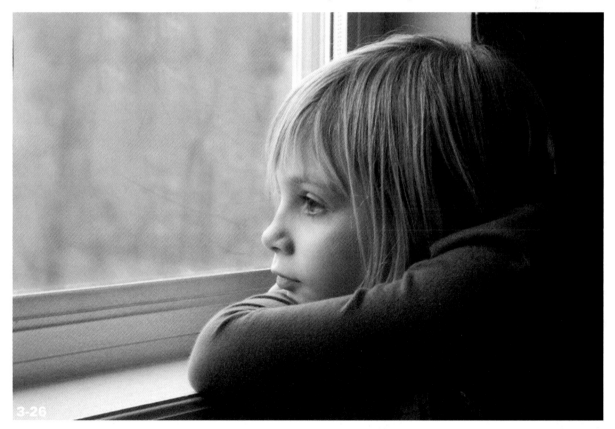

ABOUT THIS PHOTO *Olivia's beautiful profile is caressed by window light, and the colors are soft and harmonious. Her expression relaxes her facial muscles, adding to the velvety look of her skin. Taken at ISO 1600, f/16, and 1/25 second. ©Kim Spilker*

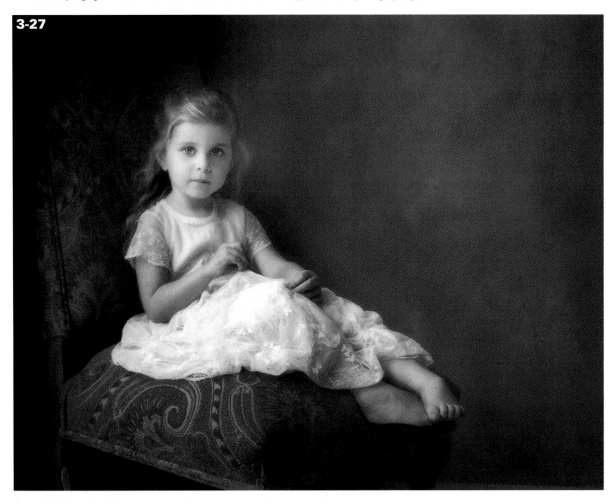

3-27

Of course, you might wish to practice first: Photograph an adult or very cooperative child so that you have the chance to really look at the light by moving the subject and walking around her.

Experiment with having your subject very close to the window and then farther away, as you observe the subtle changes in how the light contours her face. Take a look at the background, making sure it is uncluttered and falls into shadow. To start with, don't use the window as the background. See how the light comes through

and highlights the side of the face closest to the window. The other side of the face falls into shadow, and as you turn the face slowly toward the light source, you see how the light gives the face shape.

As explained earlier in the chapter, ideal contouring light on a face approximates a 3:1 ratio of light to shadow. This means that there is three times the light on the area of the face closest to the window than on the shadow area of the face. Adjust your subject until you see a subtle triangular shape

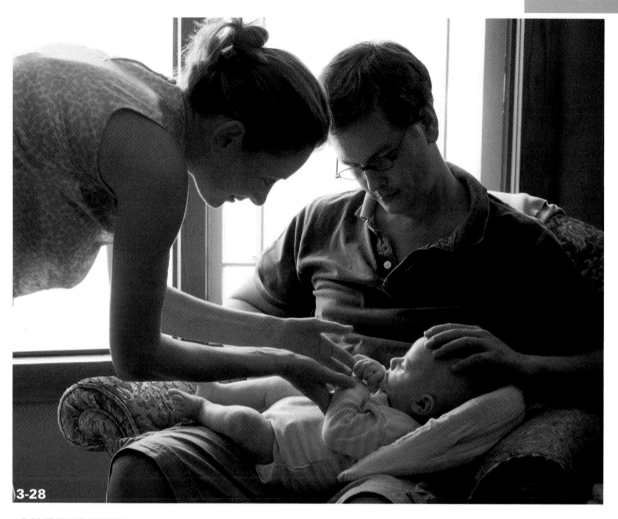

3-28

ABOUT THIS PHOTO *A fleeting, quiet moment in the life of my grandson was captured in the late afternoon window light, which beams in beautifully on his face. Taken at ISO 1250, f/5.6, and 1/125 second. ©Ginny Felch / www.photographingchildren.com*

of light falling on the cheeks of the shadow side, as in 3-29. Again, this helps to model the face, giving it shape, depth, and texture.

If you feel that the light coming through is too bright or strong, you can hang sheer curtains or a white bed sheet over the window to diffuse the light. If the shadows are too dark on the shadow side of your subject's face, you may want to add fill light with a reflector of some kind (you can even use a large piece of white cardboard) on that side. This catches the light coming in through the window, and you can reflect or bounce it back into the shadows. Sometimes, this technique can be used to create a little glint of light in the eyes called *catch lights*, which can make your subject's eyes come alive.

Above all, experiment. Now that you have some of the basics regarding window light down, put them into practice: Move your subject, turn your

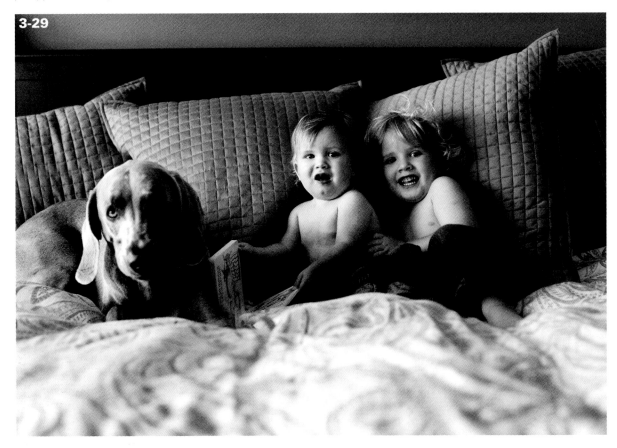

3-29

subject, walk around her, have her look at you, look out the window, look away from the window, and so on. Take a photograph from a standing position, then at the same level as the subject's eyes, and then from below. You get to decide what appeals to you; that is the beauty of it. Don't forget to look for those beautiful reflections in the window.

KNOWING WHEN TO COMPROMISE

As you might have gathered by now, the inspired and intentional use of light when photographing children has an enormous visual and emotional

impact on your final image, as in 3-30. It is something to seek and to recognize. But what if the light isn't perfect or something great is happening and there is no unusual light to be found?

At these times it is helpful to remember the work of renowned photographer Henri Cartier-Bresson, who is famous for what he termed the *decisive moment*, which is that fraction of a second when visual and narrative elements come together, and reveal the intention or attitude of the photographer.

Children's photographers can learn a great deal about observing those decisive moments by further researching his work. Cartier-Bresson's *decisive*

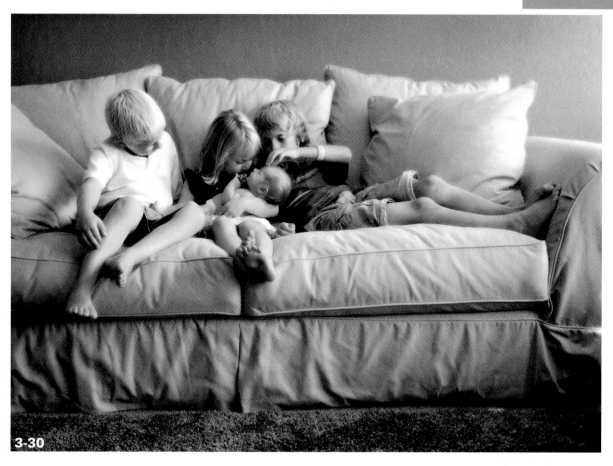

3-30

ABOUT THIS PHOTO *Learning to notice light in your environment allows you to use that light to tell a story, such as how the warmth of the window light in this photo of siblings welcoming their new baby sister matches the subjects' emotions. Taken at ISO 800, f/5.0, and 1/125 second.* ©*Allison Tyler Jones / www.atjphoto.com*

moment can be elusive, but it is worth striving for that moment when expression, light, and composition all fall together in one glorious moment. As you progress, you figure out exactly when that is. When it happens, simply express gratitude and run with it.

Is all else a compromise? Absolutely not! If you capture a marvelous expression or a great composition and your lighting isn't spectacular, you can still make a successful portrait.

You have a secret now embedded in your deepest creative recesses that enables you to recognize when you see dramatic light and you also have some clues as to where you might start looking.

Children's portraiture will always be an art of the soul and of the heart. First, keep the child and his or her personality and well-being in mind; then using the tools of light and shadow, convey the mood and emotion you want the viewer to feel about this child.

Assignment

And Then There Was Light!

For this assignment, choose one of the lighting situations described in this chapter. Choose one that inspired you or caught your attention as you were reading along, so that you enjoy the process of discovery. Create a portrait of a child or children using light. In this photograph, make a statement about light and your use of it. Make sure that your flash is turned off or that you set your ISO high enough so the flash does not fire so that you can see and use the available light in the setting.

My example, in this photograph of my grandson, a large window to his left provides a soft directional light, giving his face shape, form, and texture. I favor window light if the quality is as nice as it is here. Taken at ISO 400, f/4.0, and 1/60 second.

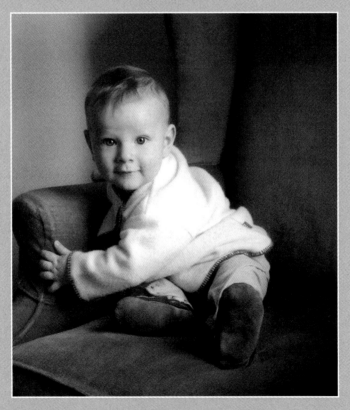

©Ginny Felch / www.photographingchildren.com

Remember to visit www.pwsbooks.com after you complete this assignment and share your favorite photo! It's a community of enthusiastic photographers and a great place to view what other readers have created. You can also post comments, read encouraging suggestions, and get feedback.

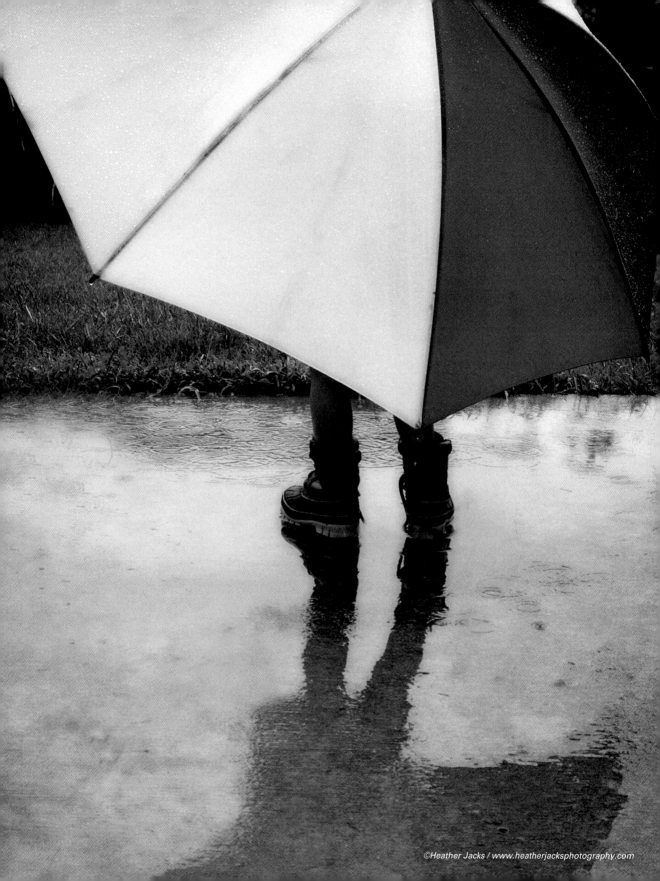

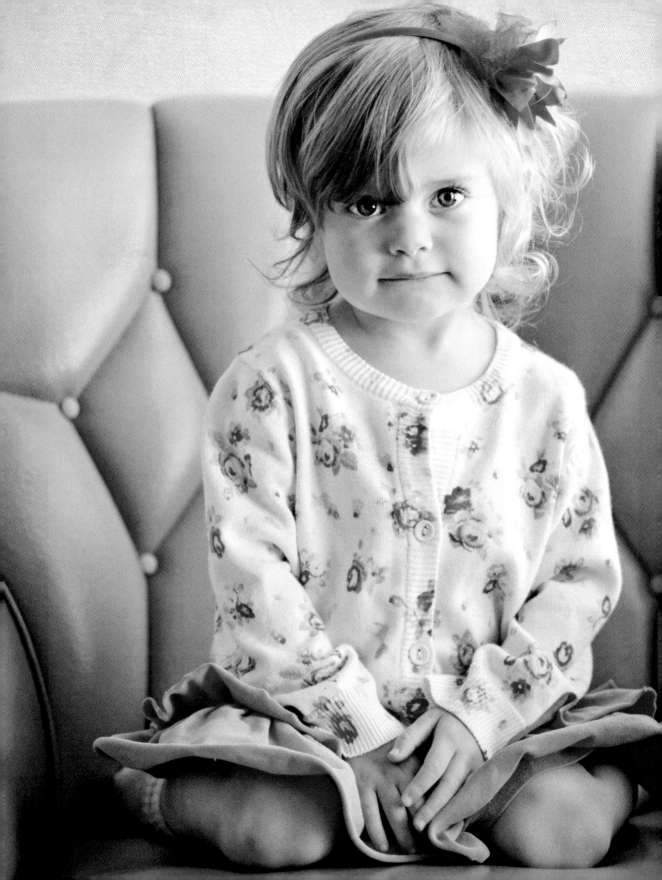

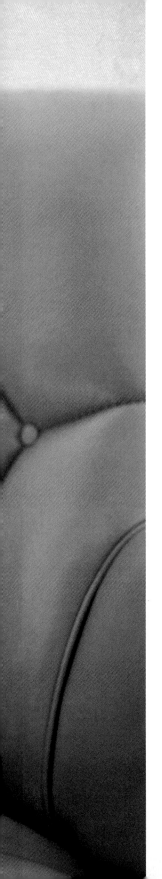

©Valeria Spring / www.theredballoonphotography.com

When it comes to resplendent light, natural light wins, hands down, and, in a perfect world, it would be forever sunny, and all windows would face north to capture that beautiful quality. Unfortunately, we live in a world with all sorts of weather, a sun that sets, and windows that may not face the optimal direction. What's a children's photographer to do?

Kids are not going to stand around waiting for you to fiddle with your camera and lighting. You've got to work quickly and effectively without too much fuss. Luckily, many intrepid photographers have gone before you and figured out helpful and simple tricks for manipulating whatever lighting situation you may find yourself in.

INDIRECT LIGHT

Beginning photographers are so often concerned with finding light in enough quantity to make a good exposure that they don't stop to consider the quality of that light and its effect on the child they are photographing. When you start to see how the quality of light can work for you, you will start to use different types of lighting on purpose to create a certain look or convey an emotion.

Indirect light is the light you have been learning to see and use. The light you find coming through the windows of your home or on your front porch can be soft and beautiful because the light is indirect, meaning it isn't coming straight from the source.

Indirect light has been bounced off of, blocked by, or diffused through something. The light may be bouncing off the concrete walkway up to the house or the house across the street or, possibly,

tip If you need to find a place to take some photos that has nice, indirect light and you don't have a porch, try your garage.

the light has been diffused by a window. Indirect light creates a soft light with no harsh line between light and shadow. It's hard to see where the light stops and the shadow starts, and that makes for beautiful photographs.

PORCHES OR OVERHANGS

In the previous chapter, you learned about window light, but windows aren't the only places to find gorgeous light. Beautiful, soft light might be as close as your front porch.

Porches block the direct, overhead light, leaving a huge window of light in which to shoot your subject. Porches are particularly great places to photograph children because the lighting usually remains constant across the length of the porch and the overhang prevents shadows under the eyes, as in 4-1.

OPEN SHADE

Open shade is an ideal place to find indirect light. By definition, open shade means there is nothing blocking the light from overhead, but the direct light is being blocked by either cloud cover or something on either side of your subject.

Open shade can be found under a tree (as in 4-2), with a low and broad sky as a light source, as diagrammed in Chapter 3. You can find another exquisite source of open shade in a meadow on an overcast day, as in 4-3.

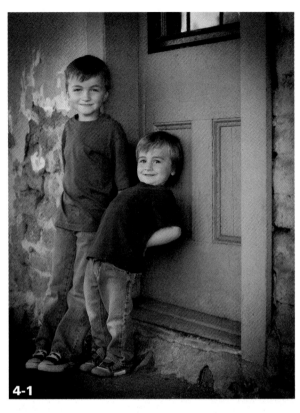

4-1

ABOUT THIS PHOTO *Two brothers leaning against an old Spanish mission are beautifully illuminated by indirect available light. Because of the overhang, notice how there are no shadows under their penetrating eyes. I always take advantage of an overhang to avoid shadows under the eyes. Taken at ISO 400, f/4.5, and 1/60 second. ©Ginny Felch / www.photographingchildren.com*

DIRECT LIGHT

Direct light is just what it sounds like: It comes directly from the light source to your subject with nothing in between. It can be very hard, harsh, and potentially unflattering unless used with care. You probably have a lot of pictures that have been ruined by direct light — overflashed, too bright, or glaring sun photos with ghostly or squinting subjects.

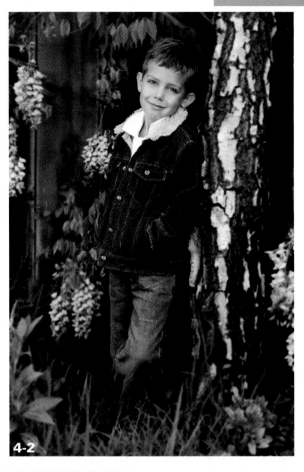

4-2

ABOUT THIS PHOTO *I love the textures of the tree and flora, which make a great, rustic surrounding for this portrait of a young boy. Notice the quality of light because of the tree overhang, and the indirect available light, highlighting his skin and eyes. Taken at ISO 400, f/2.5, and 1/250 second. ©Ginny Felch / www.photographingchildren.com*

note
If you are a beginner, your best bet is to start out finding and using indirect light first. When you're comfortable there, stretch your wings and experiment with direct light. You will have more immediate success, giving you the confidence to move on to more challenging lighting situations.

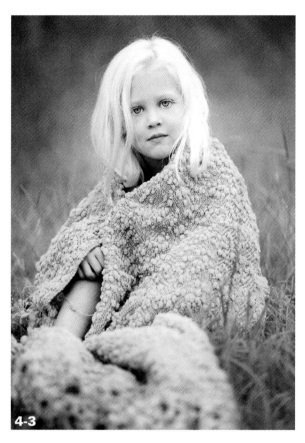

4-3

ABOUT THIS PHOTO *Photographing in a meadow on an overcast day created lovely soft tones. The colors pop because of the contrast with the gray, flat light. All in all, a pastel look is created. Taken at ISO 100, f/2.8, and 1/100 second. ©Wendi Hiller / www.wendihiller photography.com*

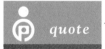 *quote*

"I have seized the light. I have arrested its flight." ~Louis Daguerre

DIRECT SUN

The sun is the most common source for direct light. If you shoot during midday in harsh, direct sun, the shadows are very distinct with a hard line around them, and it's almost impossible for your subjects not to squint. The photo in 4-4 is a prime example of what not to do. The sun is so

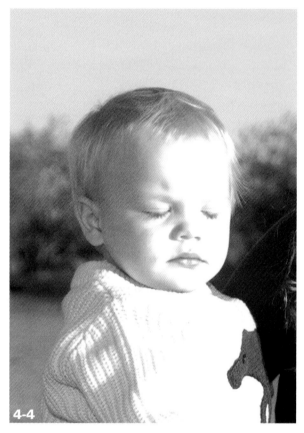

4-4

ABOUT THIS PHOTO *Shooting in harsh, direct sun can be a challenge. Very often it results in photos of squinting children with little or no highlight detail. Taken at ISO 100, f/2.8, and 1/25 second. ©Allison Tyler Jones / www.atjphoto.com*

bright the little boy can barely open his eyes! The shadows are harsh, and the highlights are too bright, leaving little detail.

Negatives aside, direct light can be used to great effect when used correctly. For beginners, it's important to pay attention to the direction from which the light is shining. Planning to shoot earlier or later in the day allows you to work with the sun at an angle to your subject. This gives you more options for positioning your subject. In 4-5, the photographer waited until the bright sun had set; the light is warmer and softer and extremely flattering.

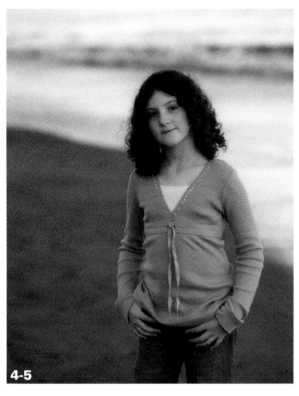

4-5

ABOUT THIS PHOTO *No squinting necessary after the sun sets. I always seek out the sweet light and take advantage of it. Taken at ISO 400, f/4.5, and 1/60 second. ©GinnyFelch / www.photographingchildren.com*

CREATING A HALO: USING RIM OR BACK LIGHT

Have you ever been looking at someone, and the low sun behind him creates a light on the rim of his hair? This is a simple example of what is called *rim light* or *back light*. Studio photographers emulate this exquisite light by actually placing a strobe behind their subjects. This is just another way to give depth, definition, and drama to an image and helps to separate the subject from the background. Rim or back light illuminates and separates the hair and head from the background, as in 4-6. Rim lighting also adds an emotional element to an image.

 x-ref

Halo or rim lighting requires careful metering to be successful. For more information, see Chapter 3.

Working with this type light can be tricky, requiring you to practice everything you learned about exposure in Chapter 2. The best back light occurs either in the morning or late afternoon when the angle of the sun is low, just when sweet light appears. The higher the sun is in the sky, the brighter the light is on the back of the child's head. If the back light is too bright, you may lose all the detail in your highlights.

To really make this technique work, be sure you have enough ambient light (which is the available light in the scene) coming from behind you, so that the faces of your subjects are illuminated properly. Sometimes photographers bring along a small metallic reflector that they use to catch the light of the sun behind the subjects and reflect it back onto their faces. You can also use back light to create dramatic silhouettes by leaving out the reflector and exposing your image for the background instead of the foreground.

TO USE FLASH OR NOT TO USE FLASH

Learning to control the flash output of your camera could be the best thing you ever do for your photos. Consult your manual to see if you can adjust your flash output to half power or even turn it completely off. It is almost always a mistake to use your on-camera flash as the main light. After looking at the not-so-flattering images you have captured using just flash, you may think that you never want to use it again, but there are times when flash has its uses, as in the before and after images in 4-7.

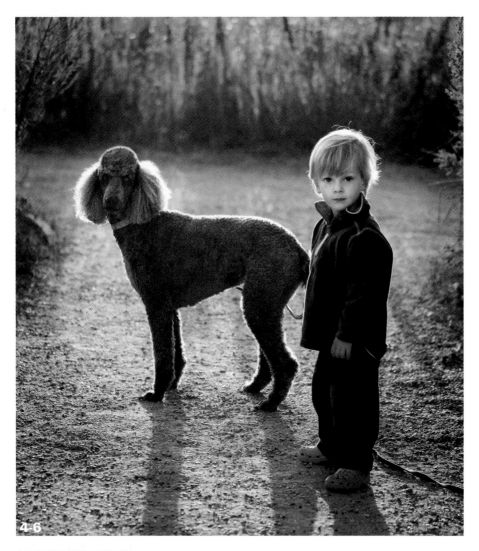

4-6

ABOUT THIS PHOTO *Late afternoon sun going down behind the dune grasses illuminates the back of my grandson and his favorite dog (my Gracie) on an evening walk on the coast. The mood that is created is sweet, which adds to the story-telling effect. Taken at ISO 400, f/3.5, and 1/1000 second. ©Ginny Felch / www. photographingchildren.com*

CONCEPT OF MAIN LIGHT AND FILL

A basic tenet of lighting theory is learning which light will be your main light and which light, if any, will be your fill light. The main light is the light that provides the primary illumination of your subject. The fill light does just what its name implies: It fills in the shadow areas to one degree or another. The main light is the most important light because it determines from which direction

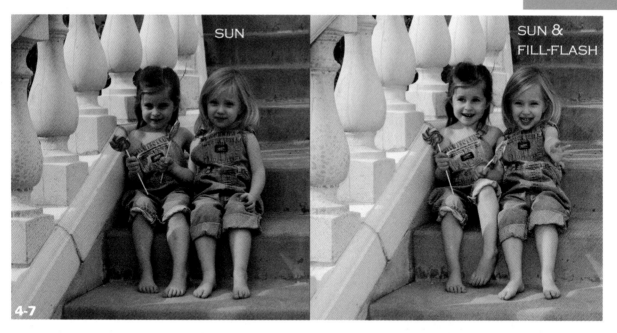

SUN

SUN & FILL-FLASH

4-7

ABOUT THIS PHOTO *This photograph shows a before and after example of how fill flash can be used. The midday sun coming in from the side provided the main light, which produced splotchy skin tones and "raccoon eyes," or shadows beneath the eyes, and made the little girls squint. This is not an ideal time to photograph, but if you must, fill-flash can help. I usually avoid light like this because I prefer not to use flash. Taken at ISO 200, f/9.0, and 1/320 second in Program mode with auxiliary flash set to TTL (through-the-lens). ©Ginny Felch / www.photographingchildren.com*

your subject is lit, which, in turn determines how the shadows fall on the child. You then can add fill light to fill in those shadowy or darker areas. A reflector to one side could act as a fill light, which you learn about later in this chapter, but you can also use a flash as a fill light. Used as a fill light or bounced or diffused in some way, flash can provide a portable source of beautiful light.

BOUNCE IT

If you have an auxiliary flash unit for your camera (often called a *speedlight*) you may find that bouncing your flash off a nearby wall, a ceiling, or even a piece of white cardboard that you have taped at an angle to your flash unit almost always yields better results than straight-on flash.

Auxiliary flashes typically have heads that swivel and allow you to point the flash unit to a wall or ceiling that allows the light to bounce, softly illuminating the child you are photographing.

Some professionals have come up with great formulae to use a fill-flash, so that they are not fiddling with equipment when they are on the move. You might want to try your own formula, like shooting in Program mode and moving your exposure compensation up or down.

Photographer and entrepreneur Gary Fong has developed some very useful attachments for an auxiliary flash called Lightsphere (www. garyfongstore.com). You can see his tutorials for getting excellent results with fill-flash.

WHAT ABOUT ON-CAMERA FLASH? On-camera flash is another common source of direct light. However, if you think about it, on-camera flash is kind of like turning on the high beams of your car to illuminate your subject. You'll get the shot, but does the lighting convey the mood you were going for?

As discussed in Chapter 3, using on-camera flash as your only light source flattens your subject and causes harsh shadows to fall behind them. It is also often the cause of red-eye. Unless there is no other option, it is best to avoid using your on-camera flash as your main light.

DIFFUSE IT

Diffusing your flash means placing some type of material between your flash unit and the subject so the light is softened, eliminating harsh shadows and washed-out skin tones.

Diffusing your flash is the easiest method for all types of flash units whether they are on-camera or auxiliary units. There are many light modifiers for flash units on the market, but some of the best are also the cheapest. One or two pieces of tracing vellum taped across the front of your flash can soften the light enough to keep your subject from looking like a deer in the headlights.

DIRECTION OF LIGHT

Whether you are working with direct or indirect light, the direction from which the light is shining onto your subject greatly affects the look of your photograph. Luckily, kids look good in just about any light so they are the perfect subjects on which to experiment with different lighting directions and patterns.

FLATTER: USING FLAT OR FRONT LIGHTING

It's no accident that just about every cosmetic ad you've ever seen is lit using front or flat lighting, which is lighting from the direct front of your subject. Placing your subject face-on to the light source is most flattering because this lighting pattern creates a shadowless light that disguises all the texture or imperfections in the skin.

For photographing children, however, there is another benefit to flat lighting. The broad light source needed to create a flat lighting pattern is usually broad enough to allow your little subjects to roam around a bit while still in nice light, like this little girl on her front porch in 4-8.

CONTOUR: USING REMBRANDT OR 3-D LIGHTING

Contouring with light, as shown in Chapter 3, requires that the subject be positioned so that the light is coming in from one side. The light then wraps around the face of the subject giving more dimension to the face, as in 4-9. This type of lighting, commonly referred to as *Rembrandt lighting*, is named after the master Dutch painter who often painted by window light.

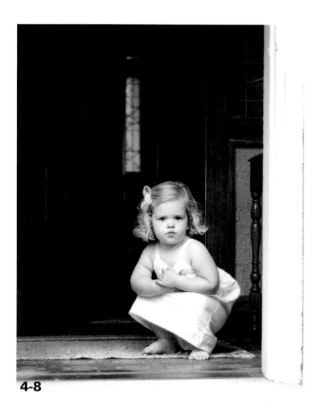

4-8

ABOUT THIS PHOTO *This sweet little girl has a lot of great light to roam in on her front porch. The indirect light is coming from in front of her, providing soft, flat illumination of her face. Taken at ISO 250, f/1.8, and 1/1250 second. ©Melani Sikma / www.melaniesphotos.com*

Rembrandt lighting is achieved by placing your subject at a 45-degree angle to your indirect light source, such as a single window in a room. The light then plays over the face of the subject, creating light on one side of the face and shadow on the other, giving it contour. It also highlights the texture of the skin, hair, and clothing of the subject, lending a three-dimensional look — the feeling that you can almost reach out and touch them.

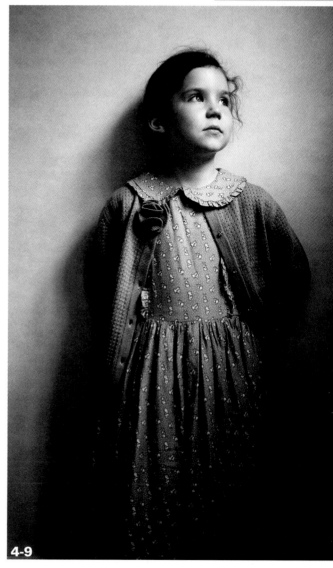

4-9

ABOUT THIS PHOTO *This very soft and moody portrait of a child was made in a true Rembrandt style, where the light comes from above and the side. You can see the contouring of light on her face, giving it dimension and texture. Taken at ISO 500, f/3.2, and 1/400 second. ©Ken Sharp / www.kensharp.com*

LIGHT MODIFIERS

There are so many cool gadgets on the market geared toward modifying light in one way or another, but when all is said and done, they can all be put into one of three basic categories: reflectors, diffusers, or gobos.

REFLECTORS

Reflectors are the most commonly used light modifier in the photographic world. A reflector is any reflective surface used to reflect light onto your subject. You would use a reflector when the light is a bit too dim on one side of your subject or to correct unflattering shadows on the face; or you might use a reflector to throw a bit more light into any image. Reflectors can be found in the environment, such as a white wall reflecting onto your subject, or they can be commercial reflectors manufactured specifically for photography and found in your local camera store.

tip If you're not sure you want to spend the money on a commercial reflector, try using a piece of white foam core or poster board from your local art supply store. You could even use someone wearing a white T-shirt as a reflector if you're really desperate.

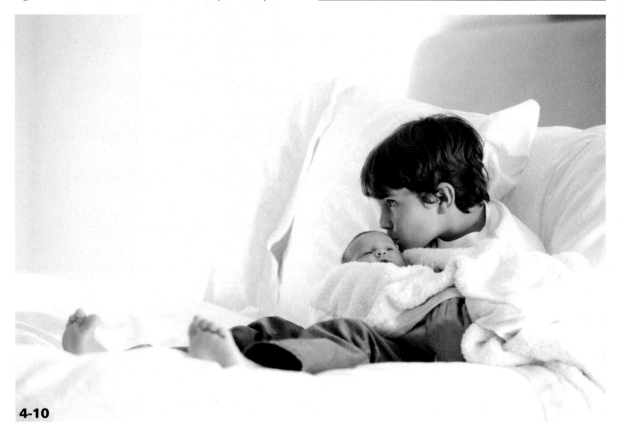

4-10

ABOUT THIS PHOTO *The white sheets on the bed make for gorgeous, reflective light. Taken at ISO 400, f/3.2, and 1/125 second. ©Allison Tyler Jones / www.atjphoto.com*

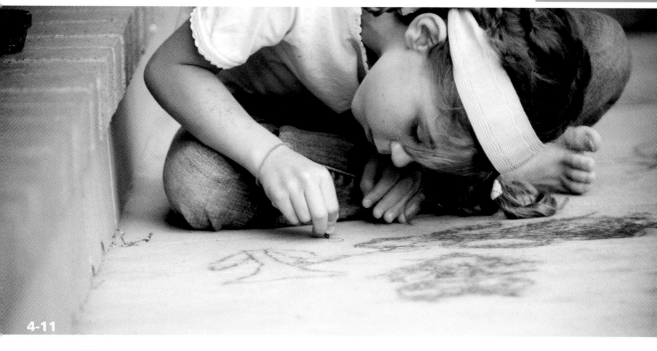

4-11

ABOUT THIS PHOTO *The light bouncing off the pavement in front of this little girl's home provides a gorgeous, even illumination of her sweet face. Taken at ISO 400, f/2.8, and 1/400 second. ©Allison Tyler Jones / www.atjphoto.com*

Reflectors are everywhere, like in the new sibling relationship in 4-10. The photographer used the white sheets and duvet cover on the parents' bed as well as the white clothing they were wearing as reflectors to help add light into the image. Even a natural surface, such as the pavement beneath the girl in 4-11, can act as a reflector to help gently light your photos.

You can purchase commercial photographic reflectors, which are very handy for reflecting light into too-shadowy areas of your subject's face. Often reflectors come with other materials, such as gobos (which are explained later). A popular reflector style is a two-sided, collapsible reflector, as demonstrated by the young lady in

4-12, 4-13, and 4-14. You can find them with different options, such as white on one side and gold on the other, or silver on one side and gold on the other.

A white reflector doesn't add any colorcast into the image and provides a soft fill light into the shadow side of your subject. A silver side is more specular and can give a bit more punch to an image, which is essential when you are working in low light or shooting at sunset and losing light fast. The gold side is great for warming up skin tones in photos taken in shade (which can tend to be bluish in color) or during overcast days. A little experimentation will determine your favorite.

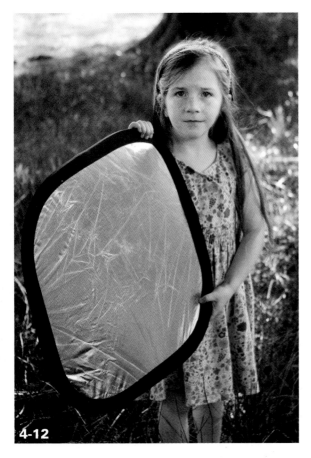
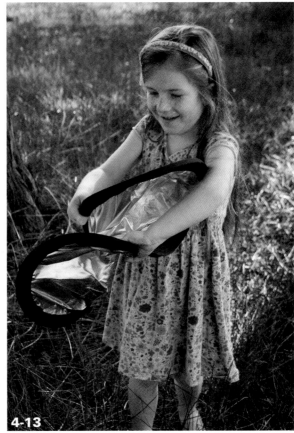

4-12

4-13

ABOUT THESE PHOTOS *Commercial photographic reflectors come in different shapes and sizes. They are great when lighting is less than ideal and fold up easily to stow with your camera gear. My pal Daisy is seen here demonstrating how easy it is to open and close. ©Ginny Felch / www.photographingchildren.com*

DIFFUSERS

Diffusers are made to diffuse, or spread out, the light that is shining onto your subject, making the light less harsh and more flattering. When all you have is harsh, direct light, a diffuser can be your best friend. Pop it into a window or have someone hold it between the harsh light and your subject and you'll be amazed at the difference, as demonstrated in 4-15, 4-16, and 4-17. A diffuser can be a commercial product (similar to the reflector shown in the previous series of images),

or you can use a panel of translucent drapes or a white sheet to diffuse the light between its source and your subject.

GOBOS OR SUBTRACTIVE LIGHTING

Sometimes you don't want to reflect or diffuse the light, you just want to block it altogether and that's where gobos come in. *Gobos* are light-blocking devices; the name comes from "go-between." You place a gobo between the light

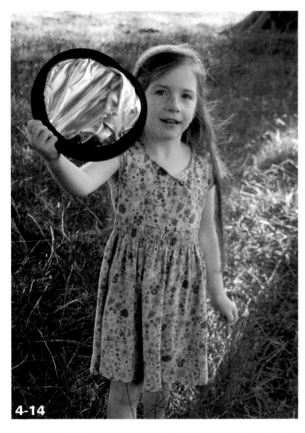

4-14

source and the camera or the light source and the subject. Many of the reflector kits mentioned previously have a black side that works really well for blocking stray light.

Why would you want to block the light when you've spent so much time trying to find it in the first place? Maybe you are trying for the halo light mentioned earlier, but the sun is causing flare spots on your lens; in this instance, you can have someone stand holding the gobo to block the light from hitting your lens. Or maybe there is just too much light all around, and you have envisioned a more subdued, moody look to your

image. Blocking the light from one side of your subject will give you more of a Rembrandt-like look.

COLOR TEMPERATURE OR WHITE BALANCE

Color temperature refers to the color of light in an image. For example, you have likely noticed that when you photograph indoors and your flash does not fire, the image has an almost orange cast to it. Perhaps you have photographed a subject on an overcast day or on the shady side of a building and found the image to have a bluish tinge to it. Both of these scenarios highlight the importance of understanding how color temperature can affect your images.

Film photographers have long struggled with color temperature in their images, requiring special films or filters to correct the colorcasts created by different types of indoor and natural lighting situations. Digital has eased this dilemma by giving us the gift of white balance, but you have to know how to use it in order to take advantage of it.

If you've experimented at all with your digital camera, you might find that Auto white balance doesn't take care of everything. Photos with weird colorcasts to them (too yellow, too blue, greenish, and so on) mean that your white balance settings aren't working the way you'd like them to. Check your manual or the menus on your camera to see if you can manually set the white balance to accommodate the type of light you are shooting in.

x-ref For more about hard and soft light, or light in general, see Chapter 3.

Following are a few examples of lighting situations that might play tricks on your Auto white balance, requiring you to choose a specific white balance setting on your camera.

- **Daylight.** By default, digital camera settings are geared to daylight photography. Daylight is considered neutral as far as color temperature is concerned — not too cool or too warm. Real life is different, however. Place a child on the shady side of the house and you might have an image with a decidedly blue cast. Shooting during the sweet light of early evening often casts a very yellow tone onto your subject. Check your white balance settings for Shade or Full Sun options and experiment with them until you come up with a result you like.

- **Flash.** The flash on your camera is balanced to daylight color temperature. This allows you to use your flash as a remedy for lighting situations with extreme colorcasts. Using your flash might be your best option if you are having colorcast problems with your images and don't have custom white balance settings for your camera. For example, when you are stuck in a school gym with horrible fluorescent lighting, your flash is probably your best bet.

- **Fluorescent.** Shooting under fluorescent light makes for sickly, greenish skin tones. If your Auto white balance setting isn't handling it

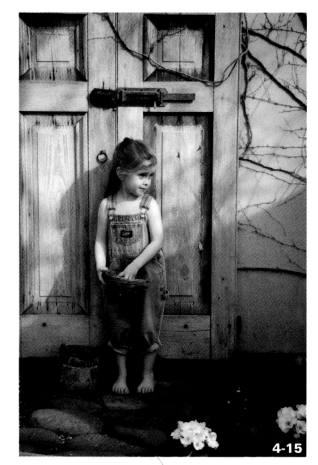

4-15

tip

If purchasing a studio strobe setup is not in your budget, you may want to experiment with halogen or tungsten garage lights from your local hardware store. Use caution, particularly with children, because these lights are very hot. For additional information on setting up your own economical home studio go to www.diyphotography.net.

well, switch to the Fluorescent setting in the White Balance menu on your camera, usually denoted by a mini fluorescent tube icon.

- **Tungsten.** Tungsten lighting is just a fancy name for the regular bulbs in your lamps at home. Tungsten or incandescent lights give off an almost orange light that you can use to great effect when photographing your Christmas tree lights or if you are looking for that warm look, as in 4-18. If not, adjust your white balance to the Tungsten setting, usually denoted by a small light bulb icon.

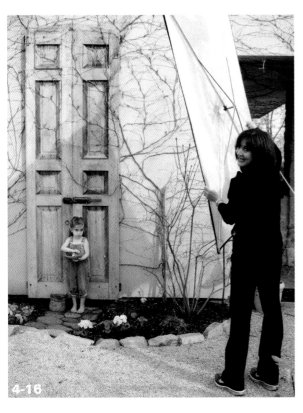

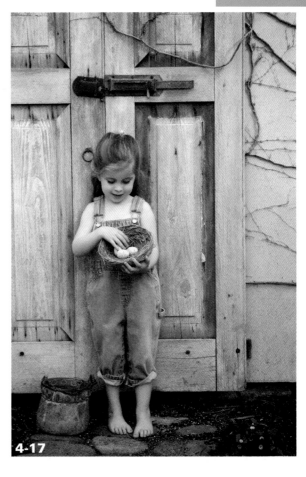

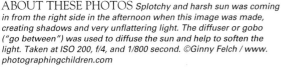

ABOUT THESE PHOTOS *Splotchy and harsh sun was coming in from the right side in the afternoon when this image was made, creating shadows and very unflattering light. The diffuser or gobo ("go between") was used to diffuse the sun and help to soften the light. Taken at ISO 200, f/4, and 1/800 second. ©Ginny Felch / www. photographingchildren.com*

WHAT ABOUT RED EYE? Red eye happens because the photographer is using on-camera flash in a darkened setting. The subject's pupils are more dilated so when the flash fires, the light reflects off the retina of your subject and shows up in your photo as red eye. Because most on-camera flashes are very close to the camera lens, the angle of the flash is too close to the angle of the lens, allowing the light to more readily reflect off the retina.

How to avoid it? Try the red-eye reduction setting on your camera if you have one. If not, you might try raising the ambient light in the room by turning on more lights, which will close down the pupils of your subject, reducing the chance for red eye. If neither of these tips works and you do a lot of shooting in dark environments, you may want to consider a dedicated flash unit for your camera. Flash units typically sit higher on the camera, increasing the angle between flash and lens, thereby eliminating the red-eye problem.

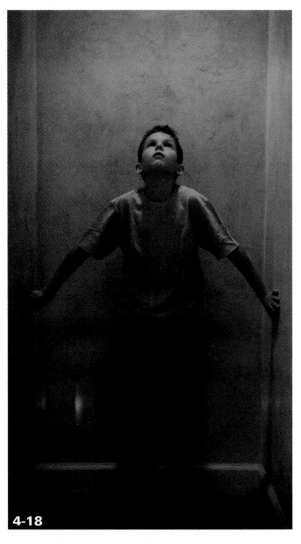

4-18

ABOUT THIS PHOTO *Using regular tungsten or incandescent lighting casts a very warm glow on your subject that can be used for effect, as in this photo of a young boy in his home. Taken at ISO 1250, f/2.8, and 1/125 second. ©Allison Tyler Jones / www.atjphoto.com*

> **note** Although it seems counterintuitive, the closer the light source is to your subject, the softer the light appears. The farther you move the light away, the harsher it becomes.

- **Shade.** Shooting on the shady side of a building or under a tree during daylight hours can cause your images to be very bluish in color, as in 4-19. Select the Shade setting in your White Balance menu, usually denoted by a little house icon showing shade to one side. The Shade setting offsets the color cast and results in a more pleasing image, as in 4-20.

- **Custom White Balance.** Check your camera manual to see if your camera has a setting for Custom White Balance. This is the manual version of setting your preset white balance options. Most cameras require a white card or some kind of white balance tool (such as Expo Imaging's Expo Disc) to aid in setting a custom white balance. Setting a custom white balance might be a bit advanced if you are just starting out, but it is good to know it is available.

BASIC STUDIO LIGHTING

Studio lighting may seem mysterious and complicated but if you think about the big studio lights as oversized flash units or big windows, you might feel a bit less intimidated. Studio flash was created so that photographers could shoot at any time of day, in any weather, and still get natural-looking results. Studio lighting also gives the photographer much more control over the lighting. Photographing children in a studio has its distinct advantages. Some photographers find it a bit easier to corral kids in the enclosed space of a studio. The quality of light produced by studio strobes tends to be a bit more sparkly than natural light, and because these lights are essentially big flash units, they can freeze action very well.

Everything you have learned up to this point is applicable in studio. Do you want the light to be hard or soft? Which direction do you want the

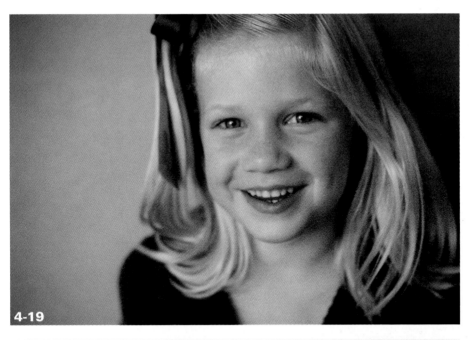

4-19

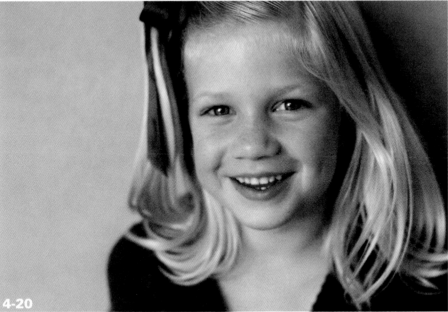

4-20

ABOUT THESE PHOTOS *In 4-19, the little girl was photographed on the shady side of a building. The shade plus the blue color of the surrounding walls made for a bluish cast to the image. Taken at ISO 400, f/2.0, and 1/250 second on Auto white balance. In 4-20, you see the same image with the colorcast corrected with the white balance set to Shade mode. ©Allison Tyler Jones / www.atjphoto.com*

light to come from? Are you looking for a flat lighting pattern or a more dimensional, contoured look?

ONE-LIGHT SETUP

Within a studio shoot, you can achieve a lot with just the basics: a single light and a reflector. The single light provides the main light, and the reflector fills in the shadows, keeping them from becoming too harsh and dark. This is the easiest and one of the most economical lighting setups if you are just starting out.

In 4-21, you can see that the flash head, in this case a monolight, has a large soft box attached to the front. A monolight is a flash head that has all the controls and power source built in to the head of the flash unit. Monolights are often less expensive than flash heads that require a power pack to run them. A soft box is a big black fabric box with a translucent front that acts as a diffuser, keeping the light from becoming too direct and harsh. The translucent material on the front of the box spreads out the harsh light from the monolight creating a large, diffused light source. Also, note how close the light setup is to the subject.

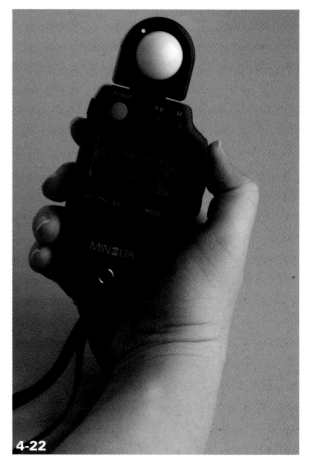

4-21

4-22

ABOUT THIS PHOTO *The main light is fitted with a 4 x 6-inch soft box that creates a large area of soft, even light. On the right side is a reflector to keep the right side of the child's face from becoming too dark. ©Allison Tyler Jones / www.atjphoto.com*

ABOUT THIS PHOTO *A flash meter is a vital tool to ensure proper exposure of your studio flash images. ©Allison Tyler Jones / www.atjphoto.com*

Keeping the light close keeps the light soft. On the other side of the subject is a big silver reflector that throws light back into the face of the child being photographed keeping the shadows from becoming too dark on the right side of his face.

METERING

Monolights are fitted with modeling lights, which gives you an idea of how the light will fall on the subject. The actual illumination of the child, however, is done by the powerful flash inside the monolight unit. Because you can't see how the flash turns out until the photo is taken, it's a good idea to have a flash meter (4-22) that allows you to measure the light and get a starting point for

properly exposing your image. Using a flash meter that is tied into your monolight either by a cord or a wireless device, measure the light and set your camera manually to the settings recorded by the flash meter.

THE FINAL RESULT

The final result of a setup similar to what is illustrated in 4-21 shows just how simple it is to create a pocket of gorgeous light to photograph children in, as shown in 4-23. You might also notice that the big chairs are white, which catches the light and bounces it back into the child's face. Big chairs are also a good place to corral wild and wiggly kids for a quick photograph!

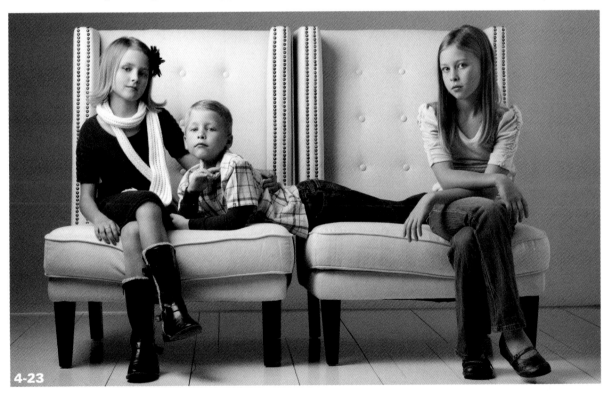

4-23

ABOUT THIS PHOTO *The final result of this lighting setup, using two chairs for this sibling portrait. Taken at ISO 250, f/10.0, and 1/200 second.* ©Allison Tyler Jones / www.atjphoto.com

Studio photography doesn't have to produce the overposed, boring pictures of years gone by. The studio is a perfect place to, literally, do a study of and explore the personalities of your subjects. With no distractions in the environment, expressions and relationships are all you have to concentrate on, as demonstrated in 4-24.

Learning to manipulate the light no matter where you are shooting will build your confidence as a photographer. Every professional photographer knows that you rarely happen upon the ideal lighting situation; instead, you have to work with what you're given, and sometimes it's that problem-solving that results in some of the best images you ever take.

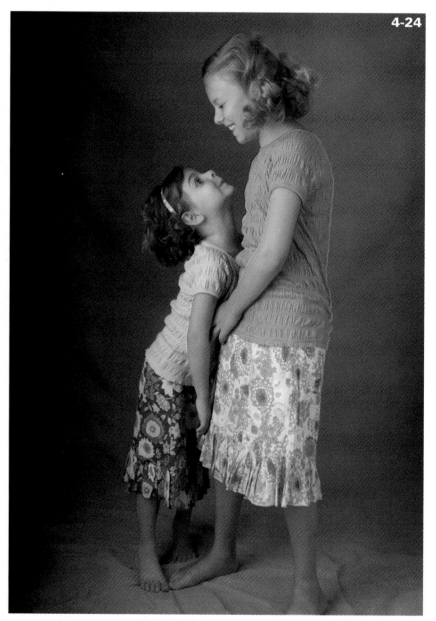

4-24

ABOUT THIS PHOTO *This photo perfectly illustrates the personality and relationship between these two sisters. This was shot with the lighting setup outlined earlier in the chapter. Taken at ISO 100, f/2.8, and 1/250 second. ©Allison Tyler Jones / www.atjphoto.com*

Assignment

Manipulating the Light

Choose one of the lighting situations described in the chapter and try to work out the lighting to best flatter your subject. You may want to experiment using a single window to light your subject or try using rim lighting to separate your subject from the background. Just try one of them and focus all your attention on the lighting and how it is falling on your subject. Walk all the way around the child you are photographing, taking photographs from different directions and documenting how the light falls from different angles. Examine the results once you are finished and determine which lighting patterns most reflect your individual style.

In this image, I chose to use late afternoon sun at an angle, creating a halo effect on my grandson's hair. This light really adds to the mood of the photograph. Taken at ISO 400, f/5.6, and 1/320 second.

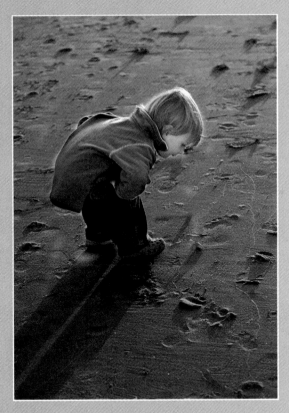

©Ginny Felch / www.photographingchildren.com

 Remember to visit www.pwsbooks.com after you complete this assignment and share your favorite photo! It's a community of enthusiastic photographers and a great place to view what other readers have created. You can also post comments, read encouraging suggestions, and get feedback.

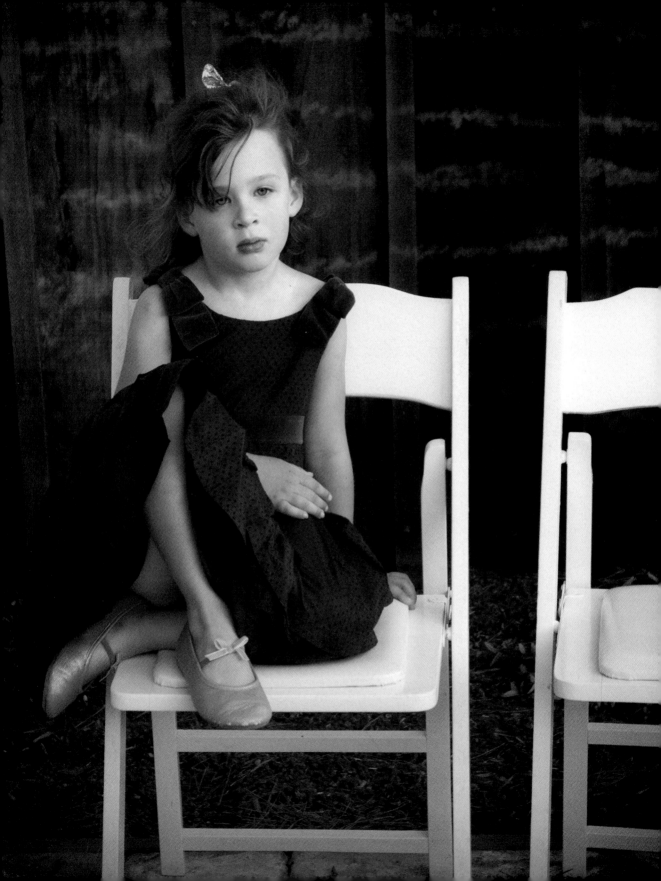

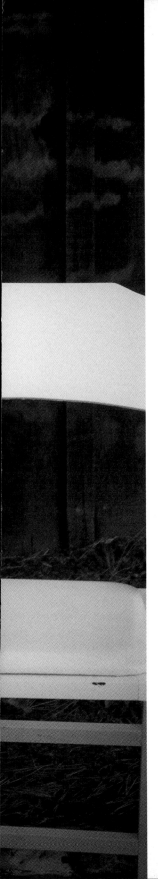

Composition refers to the arrangement of the elements in a photograph to create a pleasing whole. At its very essence, composition is a decision about what to include and, just as important, what to leave out of any given photograph. The human eye appreciates order of some sort and visual paths to follow. As a photographer, your decisions about composition can help lead your viewer's eye to what is most important in your photograph.

Composition in photography is perhaps the most subjective element of all. For some photographers, composition is unconscious or second nature; their sense of balance and emphasis comes naturally. Other photographers come from an art or painting background and can apply their experience with basic composition and graphic elements. Even if you don't have an art background, you can study and learn composition. It will take a great deal of observation and developing your eye. Learning some basic guidelines will help you simplify and improve your photography immediately. When you have a firm grasp of the guidelines you will be able to bend them a little, maybe even break a rule or two.

Start paying attention to the work of other photographers and painters. Where do your eyes land first? Was that the intention of the photographer, or was it an accident or a lack of attention to detail? The most common mistakes that amateur photographers make are not honing in on the subject and allowing distracting elements in the environment to lead the eye away from the most important elements in the photograph. Keep an eye out for clutter!

FROM A SNAPSHOT TO A FINE PORTRAIT

A photograph that reveals even one element of thoughtful composition can stand out in the crowds of snapshots filling up computers, hard drives, and online galleries. And why is that? What is the difference between a snapshot and a portrait? While many other factors, such as lighting or background, are relevant, the greatest difference between a snapshot and a portrait is how the image is composed. The point of composition in portrait photography of children is to draw the viewer's eye naturally to the child — plain and simple. Beyond that, you can use composition to create a feeling or tell a story. What often differentiates a snapshot from a fine portrait is that a snapshot includes too much information, or has too much clutter.

Painters don't have to worry about an errant garden hose in the background, or a palm tree growing out of their subject's head; if these types of objects appear in a scene, painters simply leave them out. Our cameras, however, capture everything we point them at. And because amateur photographers are more often concerned with capturing the subject, they often neglect to notice that they have also captured distracting elements in the background of their photos.

Before you even hold your camera up to your eye, take a good look at the background. Make it right before you take your exposure and don't rely on fixing it later in an image-editing software program. This is the habit of a good photographer. If what you are seeing through your viewfinder isn't pleasing, move around the subject and watch for changes in light and composition until you get the portrait you want. Finding the best light and composition will vastly improve your photograph.

FOCUS ON FEELING

A good place to start when you are learning composition is with a feeling. What do you feel about this child you are photographing? What do you want to convey about his or her personality?

Are you trying to convey a message that is bigger than just this child, a feeling about childhood in general? Is it the word *wonder* that inspires you when photographing a baby peering through the window, as in 5-1? Sometimes starting with a word in your mind allows you to make a choice about what you include or exclude from the frame.

Once you have an idea about the feeling you want to convey, many of the decisions about composition will flow from that initial idea.

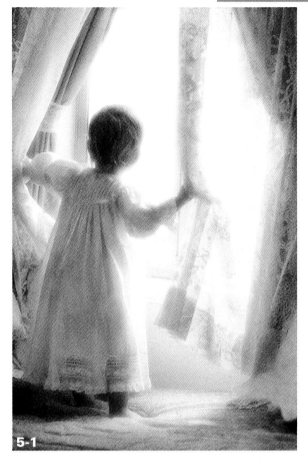

5-1

ABOUT THIS PHOTO *I captured this spontaneous moment soon after the mom left the room to answer the telephone. At the time, I was using Fujicolor 1600 film to add grain to add a painterly effect. Taken at ISO 400, f/4, and 1/125 second. ©Ginny Felch / www. photographingchildren.com*

KEEPING IT SIMPLE

Anne Geddes, a photographer famous for her photograph of babies as flowers, said, "The hardest thing in photography is to create a simple image." Keeping it simple means showing only what tells the story and nothing else. A good starting place for learning to keep it simple is to get close to your subject — really, really close.

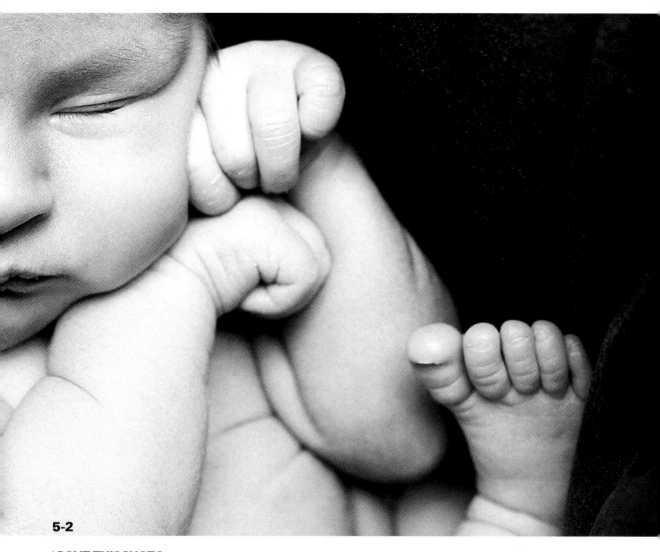

5-2

ABOUT THIS PHOTO *Zooming in close and getting just pieces of your subject can sometimes tell a larger story about miracles and new life. Taken at ISO 320, f/3.2, and 1/250 second. ©Stacy Wasmuth / www.bluecandyphotography.com*

tip A good photographic practice is to check the four edges of your viewfinder before you click the shutter every time. Do you see anything in the background that is detracting from your subject? Does it look like something is growing out of your subject's head? Changing your position or the position of your subject might be all that's needed to simplify the background and improve your photograph.

Zoom in and get just the face or the bits and pieces that tell the story. In 5-2, a photo of a newborn baby, there is no doubt what the subject of this photo is. This photo could be titled "New" because it highlights features that are unique to a newborn baby: the curled-up body, the wrinkles on the hands and toes.

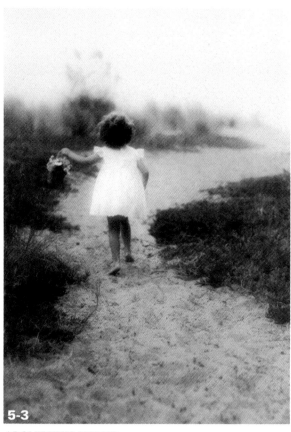

5-3

ABOUT THIS PHOTO *This simple composition of a little girl walking up a foggy dune path toward the sea resonates with the idyllic nature of quintessential childhood. I was inspired by my own summers at Cape Cod as a child. Taken at ISO 200, f/4, and 1/250 second using 1600 Fujicolor film (changed to sepia in post production). ©Ginny Felch / www.photographingchildren.com*

WATCH YOUR BACKGROUNDS

You know the expression about real estate: "Location, location, location!" Well, part of your quest is indeed to find a location that is free from distracting elements, as in 5-3.

The worst distractions in any image can most commonly be found in the background, behind your subject. When you first start out, it's easy to become so focused on the child that you don't even see what is behind him or her that might be distracting from the subject.

Distracting items such as tree branches going in awkward directions, bright splotchy leaves or holes of sunlight, fences, flowers, poles, furniture, and so on, can combine to clutter up an otherwise beautiful portrait.

The photo of a young family at the beach in winter in 5-4 is a perfect example of watching your background. The photographer has been careful to isolate the family against the dunes, sky, and sea, which combined create a perfect pastel hue that offsets the rich winter colors of the family's clothing.

When it comes to backgrounds, watch out for dark things in light places and light things in dark places. Squinting while looking at the background immediately isolates distracting bright or dark spots. Watch especially for bright or dark spots directly behind and around your subjects that can take the eye away from your intended focus.

USING NEGATIVE SPACE

Including negative space (space in your image where the subject doesn't appear) in a composition makes great use of the concept of simplicity, and also enhances the story. A little girl standing in the lower corner of expansive grass or a beach might look hopeful, mysterious, or even lonely. Be certain you are telling the story you want. Of course, you can leave the interpretation to the eyes and heart of the viewer, but you can shape the reactions with your compositions.

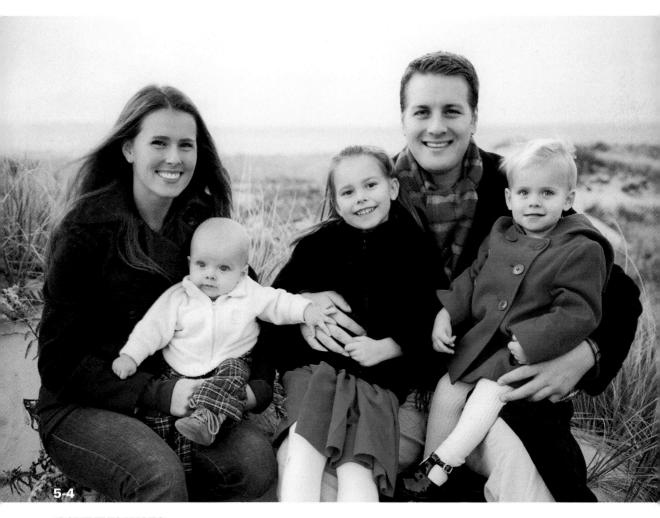

5-4

Negative space can emphasize the child, as in 5-5, or it can give a child space to roam, as in 5-6. Negative space works kind of like a wall with only one picture hanging on it; you can't help but notice that one picture. Using negative space in the composition of a photograph simplifies the composition and draws your attention to the child.

FRAMING THE IMAGE

Even though digital editing makes it easier to crop and remove clutter in the background, it is a much better practice to learn to crop in the camera by intentionally framing the image to begin with, rather than relying on cropping later. It is good training in observation to look carefully through the lens, create a pleasing composition,

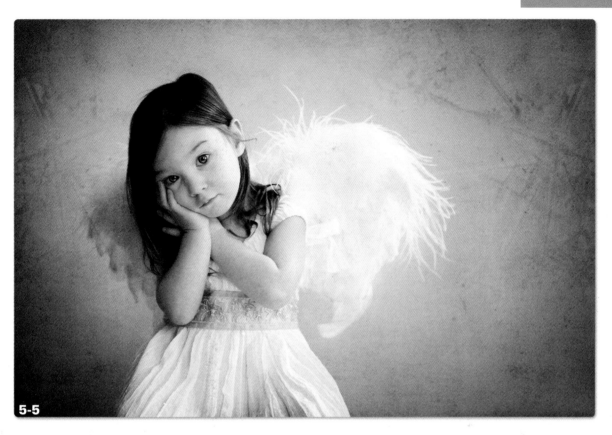

5-5

ABOUT THIS PHOTO *Placing the child slightly off center in a very simple background holds the viewer's attention on this lovely angel child. Taken at ISO 500, f/2.8, and 1/200 second. © Leah Profancik / www.leahprofancik.com*

and to keep an eye out for hot spots (bright high-lights such as shiny leaves, or other distractions and clutter). If after you zoom the lens in and out and walk around the subject if necessary, you still can't avoid certain obstacles, consider using some of the techniques discussed in Chapter 2 for throwing the background out of focus by adjust-ing the depth of field. If all else fails, you might be able to remove any remaining distractions in post-production.

GENERAL FRAMING GUIDELINES

Learning to frame your images while you are cap-turing them will improve your sense of composi-tion immediately. You can benefit from the experience of photographers who have gone before you and made all the mistakes. The follow-ing are some tried and true guidelines for framing your photo when working with children:

■ **Hold the camera at the child's eye level.** This means you may need to stoop, bend, or kneel. Not only does this make the child feel

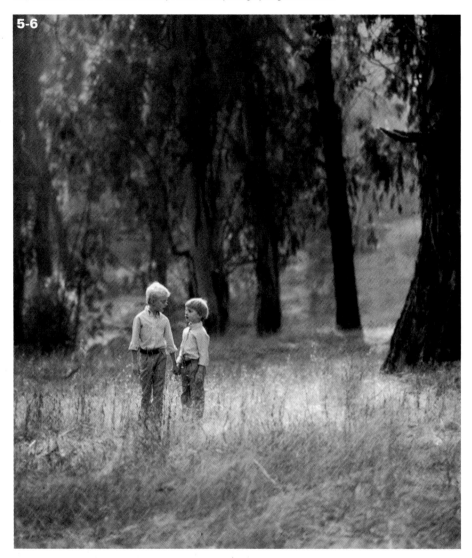

5-6

more comfortable, but it creates a much more pleasing image because this angle helps elimi-nate lens distortion (also known as big head, little feet syndrome, demonstrated by 5-7), while at the same time imparting a sense of dignity and respect to children, as in 5-8, who are often photographed from above. If you are fortunate to have a newer camera with displays that swivel, take advantage of not having the camera between your face and the child. That might improve the "connection" with the subject.

■ **Never crop at the hands or feet.** Either crop in close to the head and shoulders, move out and crop below the hands, or back off

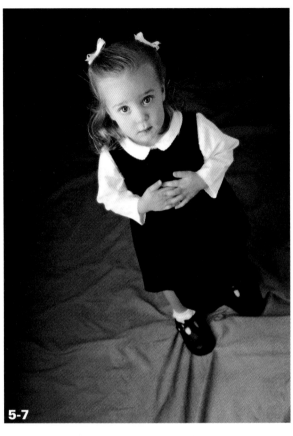

5-7

ABOUT THIS PHOTO *This is how children are often photographed: from a standing position, looking down on them. This angle makes heads appear larger and feet tiny. Taken at ISO 100, f/2.8, and 1/250 second. ©Allison Tyler Jones / www.atjphoto.com*

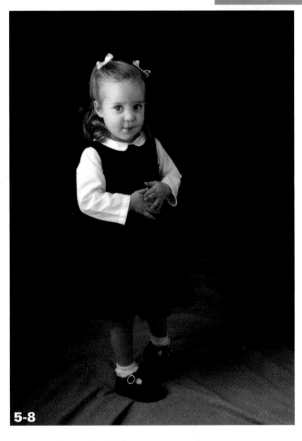

5-8

ABOUT THIS PHOTO *Photographing a child straight on requires you to position the camera at the child's waist height, but the results are worth it. The proportions of the child's body are correct, and there is a sense of dignity that is lacking in 5-7. Taken at ISO 100, f/2.8, and 1/250 second. ©Allison Tyler Jones / www.atjphoto.com*

> **x-ref** The environment where you choose to photograph can dramatically affect the style of your photography. Different styles are explored in Chapter 6.

completely and include the whole body. Cropping at the joints (wrists, ankles, hips, or knees) generally makes for an awkward-looking photograph. Children's hands and feet are sweet and should be included if possible. There are more examples of better cropping in Chapter 10.

■ **As a general rule, don't place your subject in the very center of the photograph.** Refer to the general composition guidelines discussed later in the chapter in the section on the Rule of Thirds. Exceptions to this are frequently made, but it is all too common for beginners to place the subject right smack in the middle of the frame.

■ **Leave plenty of growing room around the child in the image, above the head or in the foreground.** It is comforting visually to create a sense of space.

- **If a horizon line is visible, be sure it is straight.** This is one of the most common errors photographers make, particularly at the beach. The exception would be, of course, if you choose a slanted horizon for a contemporary composition.

- **Look carefully to see whether distracting elements are in the background.** Look for hot spots, trees growing out of heads, wires, and so on; if you see distracting elements, move around until they are gone if possible or crop in close to simplify the image.

- **If you are photographing children in profile, try to leave more space in front of their line of vision, as though they have some space to look into.** This also applies to photos of children walking across the horizon line; give them space to walk into.

A well-composed photograph is one in which every element has earned a right to be included.

FRAMES WITHIN THE FRAME

Employing simplicity in the design of a child's portrait includes using certain strong elements, such as archways, windows, and doorways, to literally frame your subject within the frame of your viewfinder. Remember, all design elements should lead to, illuminate, or enhance your subjects. Finding

appealing frames in the environment to highlight an important part of your image can hold the viewer's attention.

Arbors, gates, curving trees, and foliage can create a natural vignette to surround and showcase your subject as well. If the background is generally light,

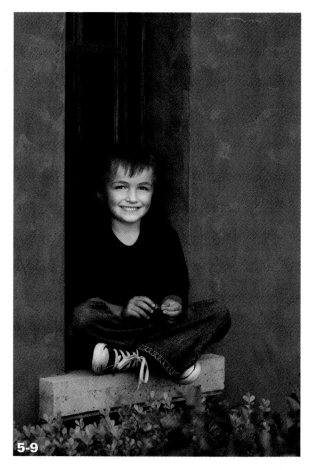

5-9

ABOUT THIS PHOTO *The vivid adobe winery window frames this little boy perfectly and even adds a bit of color to his cheeks. I love the way he found a comfortable and natural position. Taken at ISO 400, f/4.5, and 1/200 second. ©Ginny Felch / www.photographingchildren.com*

a darker shape that subtly or distinctly surrounds the subject can be extremely effective. Consider the pleasing shapes in the environment that you can use as a frame, particularly circles, ovals, squares, and rectangles.

Paying attention to what is beyond, behind, or surrounding your subject can make a world of difference in adding drama and focus to your photographs. Your eyes become trained to notice these elements as you pay attention and observe. After you become more experienced and spontaneous, you can take chances with new locations that you haven't previewed. Many children's photographers use the same locations over and over

because it is safe, and it is easy to understand why: There is already so much unpredictability when working with children. However, the more experienced and observant you are, the more you can take the risk of exploring new territory, with the possibility of great serendipity. This results in great leaps and bounds creatively.

Psychologically, framing can make a statement as well. A bold or rugged rectangular frame adds strength and structure to the image, as in 5-9 and 5-10. Making these choices carefully and thoughtfully will result in making stronger images that leave no doubt as to what you're trying to say.

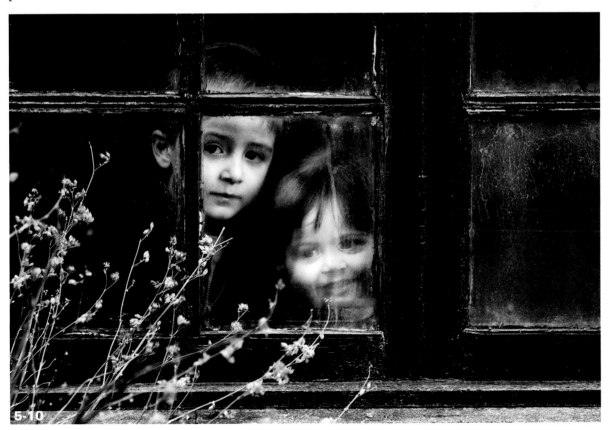

5-10

ABOUT THIS PHOTO *The bold and dramatic framing of two children seen peeking through a window pane provides a dynamic photograph. Keeping them relatively small in the composition with the angle of the weeds pointing towards the subjects helps to keep the viewer's eyes in just the right place. Taken at ISO 400, f/2.8, and 1/125 second. ©Ken Sharp / www.kensharp.com*

DISCOVERING THE GOLDEN RECTANGLE: DIVINE PROPORTION Another interesting compositional shape or formula is the golden rectangle, Golden Ratio, or divine proportion. This concept dates back to the ancient Greeks. If you think of the shape of the nautilus shell, with the outward spiraling-shape within the space of a rectangle, you might begin to comprehend the Golden Ratio. You might also find it inspiring to do a web search for Henri Cartier-Bresson and browse through his images. Try this exercise: Observe the direction of your glance as you scan the compositions. I found it rather breathtaking to see his consistent use of divine proportion.

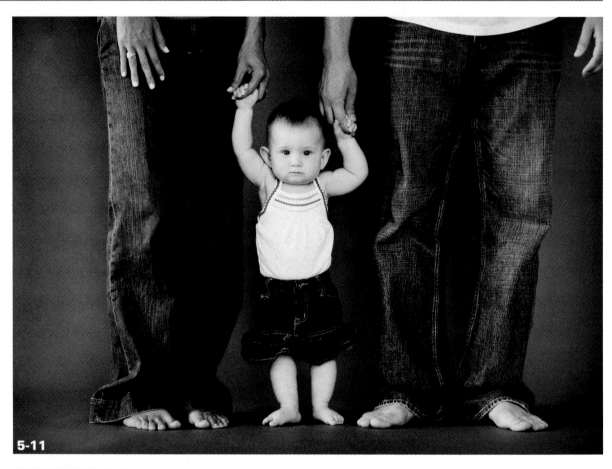

5-11

ABOUT THIS PHOTO *You don't need to see the whole parent to know that this is an image about a family. Use the height difference of adults and children to your advantage and frame a toddler using the legs of her parents as a backdrop. Taken at ISO 500, f/2.0, and 1/250 second. ©Leah Profancik / www.leahprofancik.com*

quote

"When you are dealing with a child, keep all your wits about you, and sit on the floor." ~Austin O'Malley

PARENTS AS PROPS

Adding parents to the photograph can help your composition in a variety of ways. It allows the child to feel more comfortable while being photographed and adds a storytelling element to your image, as in 5-11. Having one of the parents hold a newborn tenderly can make a photography session go smoothly, as in 5-12.

THE RULE OF THIRDS

For centuries, artists and architects have been guided by the Rule of Thirds, which is thought to have derived from the Greek Golden Ratio. The Rule of Thirds is just a technique for learning to position the elements within a photograph in a pleasing way, which is a great starting point when learning about composition.

The Rule of Thirds, as applied in photographic terms, takes into account that the format of a camera's viewfinder is usually rectangular in shape and

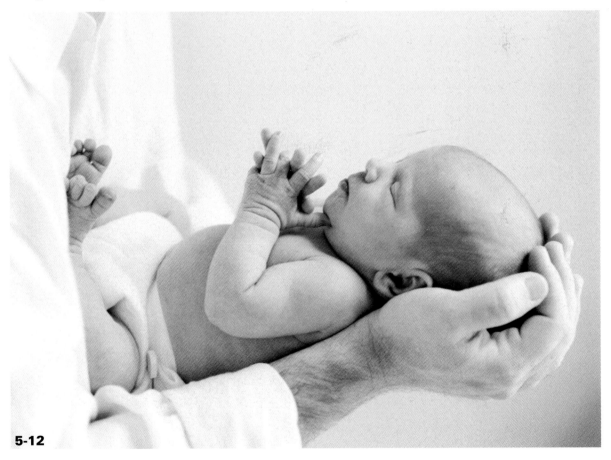

5-12

ABOUT THIS PHOTO *Such tenderness and security are evoked as the dad cradles his newborn. The father's arms frame the baby, and also provide a diagonal lead-in to the baby's face. Taken at ISO 500, f/5.6, and 1/60 second. ©Theresa Smerud / www.theresasmerud.com*

ABOUT THIS FIGURE *The diagram shows the Rule of Thirds so that you can see where the lines intersect. Those intersections are where you want to place your subjects in this kind of composition. The circles indicate placement possibilities.*

5-13

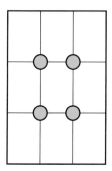

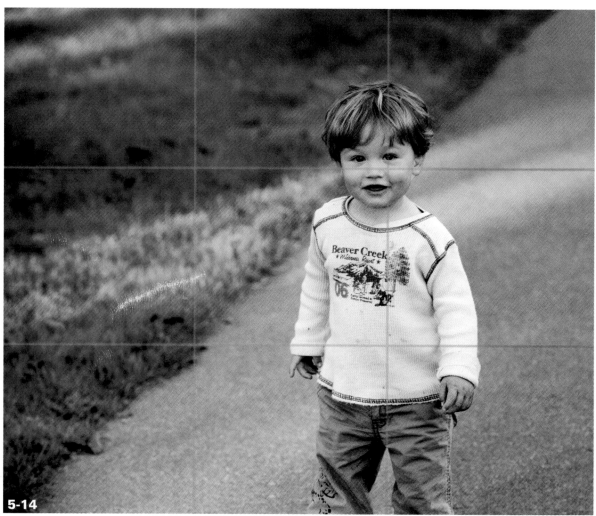

5-14

ABOUT THIS PHOTO *This bright and expressive child comes right to you on the diagonal path; notice the diagram showing that I placed his head in one of the four points of interest. Taken at ISO 800, f/5.0, and 1/400 second. ©Ginny Felch / www.photographingchildren.com*

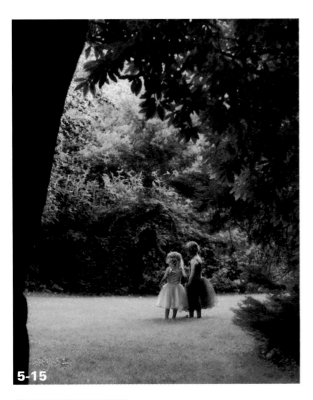

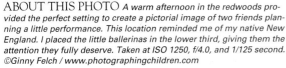

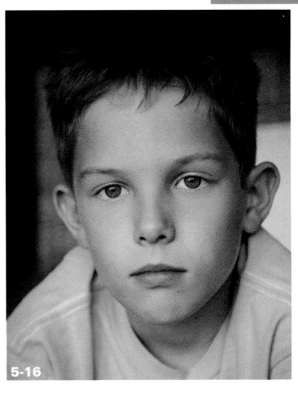

ABOUT THIS PHOTO *A warm afternoon in the redwoods provided the perfect setting to create a pictorial image of two friends planning a little performance. This location reminded me of my native New England. I placed the little ballerinas in the lower third, giving them the attention they fully deserve. Taken at ISO 1250, f/4.0, and 1/125 second. ©Ginny Felch / www.photographingchildren.com*

ABOUT THIS PHOTO *When photographing a close-up of a child's face it is best not to have the child's eyes at dead center, which makes the forehead appear too large and gives a static appearance to the image. Taken at ISO 400, f/2.8, and 1/125 second. ©Allison Tyler Jones / www.atjphoto.com*

that placing your subject in certain areas of that area can make the difference between an average or a dynamic photo. You can use this screen horizontally (landscape) or vertically (portrait), as in 5-13. Divide the viewfinder into thirds both horizontally and vertically (see 5-14). The points where these lines intersect are points where you can place your subject or parts of your subject to create tension, energy, and interest.

Often, one of the first things you hear as a photographer is, "Don't center your subject." Or, "Don't center your horizon." Try centering a few photos and then retake them using the Rule of Thirds.

Once you compare them, it becomes clear that centering the subject often creates a static effect — think twice before using that composition.

These guidelines are a wonderful starting point to start thinking about composition and noticing where the eye flows. The way to find your own

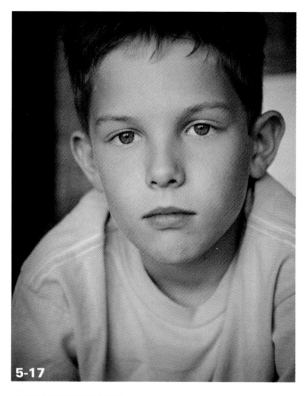

5-17

ABOUT THIS PHOTO *Placing the eyes of your subject in the upper third of the frame creates a more dynamic composition. Taken at ISO 400, f/2.8, and 1/125 second. ©Allison Tyler Jones / www.atjphoto.com*

impact the Rule of Thirds can have on a simple headshot by comparing 5-16 and 5-17. In 5-17 the placement of the boy's eyes is more dynamic, keeping your attention longer.

USING LINES

Lines are everywhere, from the curves of a child's profile to the lines in the horizon or a pathway through the woods. Learning to see lines and shapes when creating images can open a whole new way of photographing your subject, allowing you to direct the attention of the viewer exactly where you want it to be.

PARALLEL LINES

A useful visual dynamic in composition is learning to see parallel lines in your photographs. This is particularly useful in nature or landscape portraits, where visual lines are often formed by horizontal planes created by land and sky. A literal translation of this dynamic would be a view of the beach, in which the sand might form one line, the dark and textured water forms the second line, and the sky forms the third parallel line. You don't always have to think in thirds, but the composition can be more pleasing, less static, and more balanced if you use parallel lines in uneven numbers.

In general, seeing and using parallel lines, both horizontal and vertical, make for dynamic compositions.

After you become used to seeing the Rule of Thirds proportions in a landscape, start to evaluate and plan how you might use this knowledge in a portrait. You can actually use the spaces

signature, to express your own vision, is to decide every time you click the shutter what it is you feel and how you want to reveal it. Remember, these are merely guidelines to teach a technique.

- **Rule of Thirds in the environment.** The easiest way to begin using the Rule of Thirds is in an environmental shot. It is easy to place your subject in the upper or lower third of the picture and let the environment help tell the story, as I did in 5-15.

- **Rule of Thirds in a headshot.** What if you favor close-ups? How does the Rule of Thirds apply then? You can immediately see the

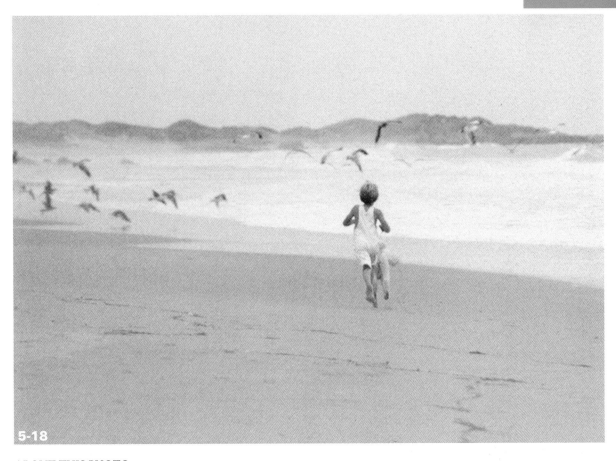

5-18

ABOUT THIS PHOTO *This photograph of my son, Zach running with his dog shows the horizontal parallel lines presented by the beach, sea, and sky. His placement was chosen so he would stand out. Taken at ISO 200, f/16, and 1/250 second. ©Ginny Felch / www.photographingchildren.com*

between the lines to frame the subject(s). You want to be careful not to have one of the lines running through a child's head, for example.

In 5-18, my son, Zach and his dog, Brandy, are running on the beach, and although the lines aren't straight, a sense of direction and framing still exist in the lines created by the sky, the beach, and the sand. I intentionally clicked the shutter when I felt that his head and body would be nicely set apart by the white foam of the sea. The fact that the line of the beach is not straight creates a nice directional line that leads to the

quote

"There is a garden in every childhood, an enchanted place where colors are brighter, the air softer, and the morning more fragrant than ever again." ~Elizabeth Lawrence

subjects. However, notice that the horizon line is straight. The footprints in the foreground show direction as well as add nicely to the texture. You can see here how successfully the composition sets up the story of the photograph.

This image was the first time I ever attempted high-key photography. Proving that things don't always go smoothly, the dog soon ran into the water and came out looking like a drowned rat. Also, Zach was very unhappy wearing his OshKosh overalls, so I actually paid him a dollar.

Trees, columns, and other vertical and parallel objects can give a sense of balance in a photograph. Vertical parallel lines can lend solidity to a photographic composition and suggest stability.

DIAGONAL LINES

Another commonly used principle of design is the diagonal lead-in line. This diagonal can come from such things as a shadow, path, road, swath of light, fence, lined-up objects, and so on, and it can occur anywhere in the photograph that effectively points toward the subject.

Use of diagonals can draw the viewer's eye just where you wish. The diagonal lead-in provided by the light coming through the door adds great energy and direction to the young skateboarder in 5-19. You can also see how the vertical lines of the barn door strongly frame the child.

The diagonal can be taken into consideration in posing children or families. For example, legs or arms can be used as a diagonal leading line. Using walls and walkways, as in 5-20 and 5-21, can lead the viewer's eye to your intended subject.

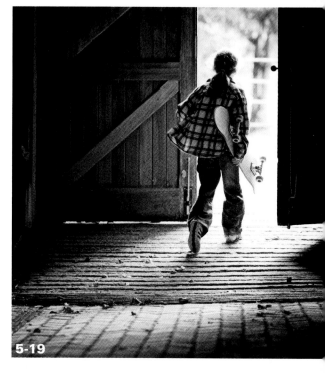

5-19

ABOUT THIS PHOTO *The diagonal light shaft coming from the door, widening in the lower left corner creates a strong diagonal line, which directs the viewer's eye right to the exiting skateboarder. Taken at ISO 400, f/1.8 , and 1/160 second. ©Doreen Kilfeather / www.dkilfeather photography.com*

Taking just a second to see the lines in your surroundings can make an enormous difference in the dynamics of your photographs. If you have children walking on a path, you can always move slightly until the path runs diagonally in your viewing screen.

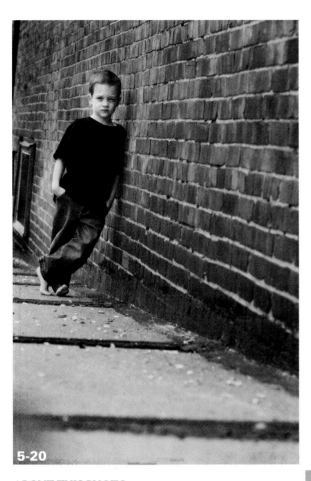

5-20

ABOUT THIS PHOTO *The photographer used the brick pattern on the side of an abandoned building to draw the viewer's eye directly to the little boy. The big wall also provides a sense of scale. Taken at ISO 200, f/5.6, and 1/320 second. ©Jeffrey Woods / www.jwportraitlife.com*

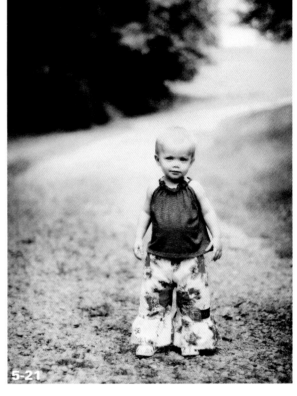

5-21

ABOUT THIS PHOTO *A very fashionable little miss is brought right to us at the bottom of a lovely C-curve in the road. Taken at ISO 400, f/1.4, and 1/8000 second. ©Jen Carver / www.jencarverphotography.com*

> *quote*
>
> "We find delight in the beauty and happiness of children that makes the heart too big for the body." ~Ralph Waldo Emerson

CONVERGING LINES

Converging lines play a similar role in composition to diagonal lines in terms of a powerful lead-in to the subject. These lines are even more commanding, because two diagonal lines come together at one point, giving you direction to the subject. You can see a great example in 5-22, where the lines of the path on the beach frame this playful child who seems to know just where he is going.

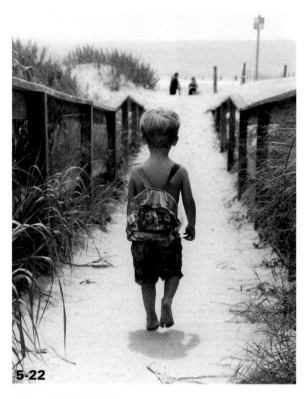

5-22

ABOUT THIS PHOTO *The converging lines of the fence and placement of the little boy lead you to his destination, the beach. Taken at ISO 400, f/4, and 1/250 second (sepia toned in post-production). ©Heather Jacks / www.heatherjacksphotography.com*

S- AND C-CURVES

Straight lines are just one way to add impact to a photograph. Exploring curving lines is one more way to explore lines in your work. Although the diagonal leading line is more direct and perhaps more powerful, a curve is a subtle and gracious way to direct the eye. S-curves and c-curves are very graceful and beautiful compositional elements and can often be found in the environment as well as in the body, posture, or face of the child you are photographing.

Photographing children on curved paths, as in 5-23, can give a sense of freedom adventure, beauty, forward movement, and direction. It offers a way for the viewer to visually enter and

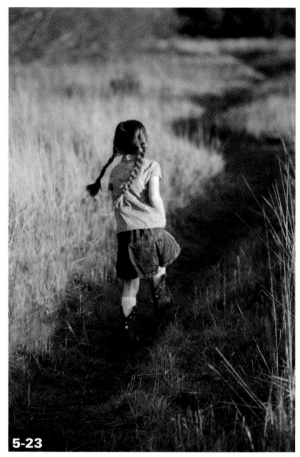

5-23

ABOUT THIS PHOTO *Daisy skips along the coastal path, which forms a wavy S-curve. I placed her in the foreground and left space above her giving her lots of room to move. Taken at ISO 400, f/5.6, and 1/250 second. ©Ginny Felch / www.photographingchildren.com*

leave an image in a pleasing way. Curves can be found on curved beaches, rivers, paths, roads, and so on. They create a sweeping movement toward your subjects if you set them up to do so. You can find a location in just the right light for optimizing the appearance of the curve and have the child just start walking in one direction or another. As she walks, you start to see where the positioning becomes a powerful visual and click the shutter. It becomes a wonderful opportunity for free movement and very spontaneous poses.

Curves are naturally pleasing compositions for creating stunning children's portraits, but curves like those in 5-24, the subtle but strong curve of a father's arm, and 5-25, the line of handprints in the sand, are not always easy to find, so keep your eye out for possibilities.

ABOUT THIS PHOTO
The strong curve of the dad's arm gives a sense of security and connection, framing the sleeping baby. I think that this image has the feeling of a cozy nest. Taken at ISO 400, f/4, and 1/125 second. ©Ginny Felch / www.photographingchildren. com

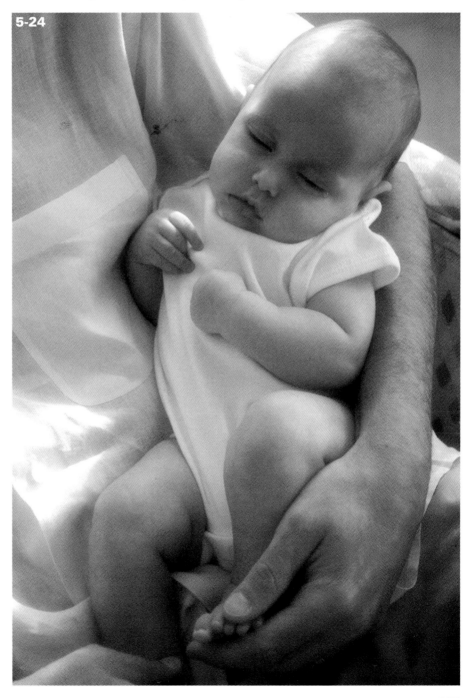

5-24

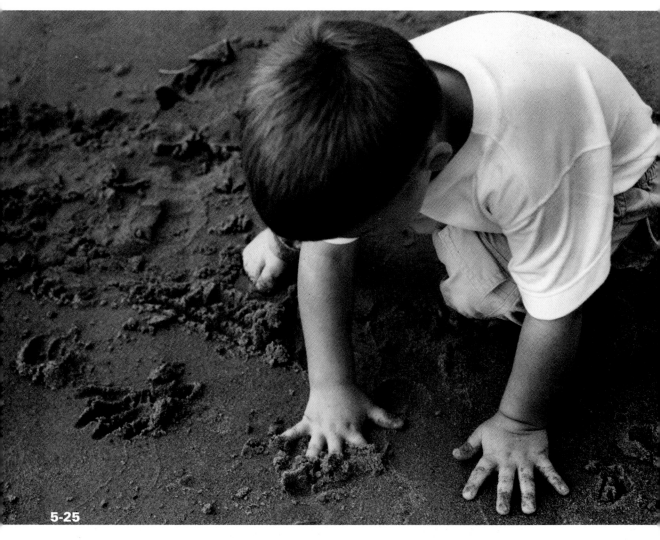

5-25

ABOUT THIS PHOTO *The curved shape of the prints in the sand swirl your eyes to the boy's hands and then up to his shirt and head. Taken at ISO 400, f/4, and 1/250 second. ©Theresa Smerud / www.theresasmerud.com*

Curves in the bodies of your subjects can be hard to see when you are actually taking the photo, but sometimes you'll get lucky and see it after the photo has been taken. Learn to see the curves in the stance of a little ballerina with her hand on her hip or the curve of a sleeping baby's cheek.

BREAKING THE RULES

There is a common and ironic secret that wise photographers hold: You will need to master the rules so that you know when you are breaking them. Studying and learning to apply the rules correctly give you the confidence to stray from the path when the creative urge strikes. You will also sharpen your observational skills, which is a skill all good photographers must have.

It is unfortunate that many photographers have painstakingly learned the rules only to turn out photograph after photograph that adheres to the rules yet leaves the viewer cold. So learn the rules and then take some chances. You'll make a lot of mistakes along the way, but those mistakes often teach you more than your successes ever do. You can create unique styles by playing with the rules and seeing how they work for you.

As you go through the process of learning the rules and looking more analytically at images, you begin to develop an eye for composition. Once you've seen a horizontal line running through a child's head in one of your photos, you'll never again look through your lens and allow that to happen. A lot of practice and a little patience helps you learn from your mistakes.

And, by learning from your mistakes, you can be bolder and take more risks. For example, observe the composition in 5-26. This image has an unconventional composition, yet it is a very powerful and amusing image.

Many professional photographers would say that no image is ever really final. They gather inspiration by continuing to critique, to edit, and to look through the lens or at an image with a new eye. After years of practice and a lot of trial and error, accomplished photographers look through the lens with confidence in their eye and skill. They have learned what works for them, and they can spend their time pursuing more creative images rather than worrying about the rules or techniques.

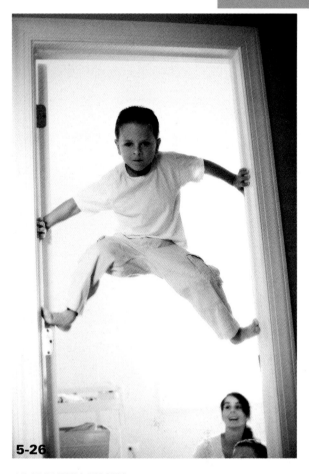

5-26

ABOUT THIS PHOTO *What a photograph of this agile little boy showing off his Spidey abilities. The strong composition employs framing, and his head is placed in a place of impact. Taken at ISO 500, f/2.0, and 1/80 second. ©Marianne Drenthe / www.marmaladephotography.com*

The conscientious choice to break rules that you have learned is a creative choice, as in 5-27. You make this choice perhaps without even thinking of the rules. You click the shutter at the right moment for you, and you love what you see. It might have the subject centered, or it might show the child with a big cheesy grin. The expression might be extraordinary and the lighting only adequate, but somehow it works.

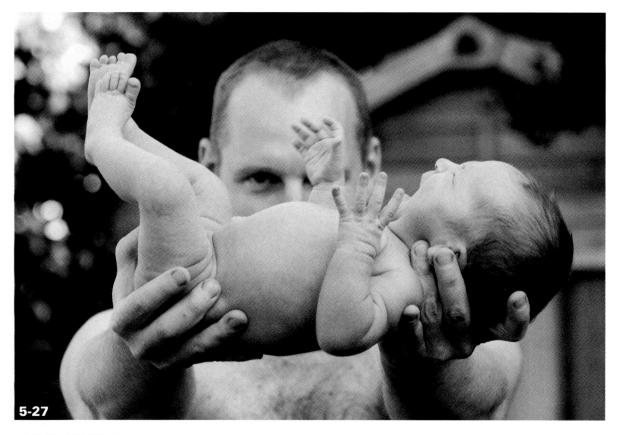

5-27

ABOUT THIS PHOTO *As he keeps an eye on his baby son, this father has a masculine pose that exquisitely breaks all the rules with a powerful result. Taken at ISO 200, f/4.5, and 1/60 second. ©Leslie Chapman*

How often have you been in a situation where you just miss a shot because the light disappears or the child moves? When you take children's portraits, so much is out of control and unpredictable in even the best of circumstances. If you stay open, ready, flexible, and patient, you will be graced with happy accidents, as in the image in 5-28.

Don't be discouraged. Keep your eye to the viewfinder and stay open and spontaneous; those happy accidents may result in some of your favorite images. Learning composition in photography can and should be a lifelong endeavor and an extraordinary path to follow.

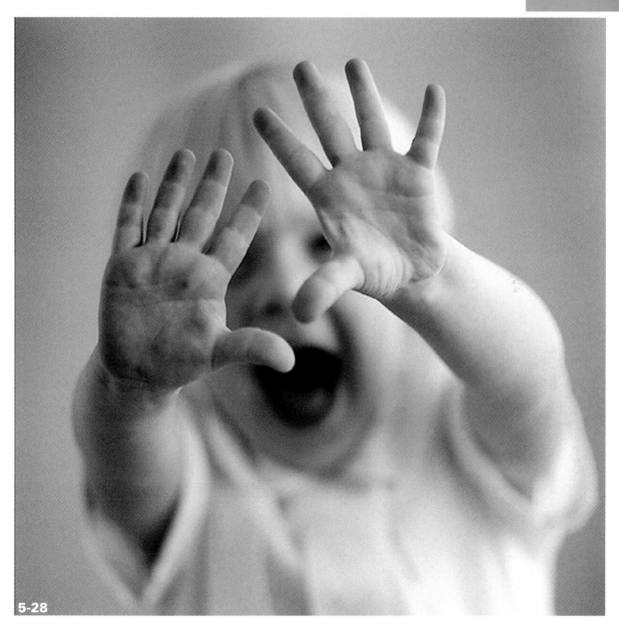

5-28

ABOUT THIS PHOTO *This shot could never have been planned, but the photographer recorded a riotous moment in a toddler's day. Taken at ISO 100, f/1.2, and 1/800 second. ©Scarlett Photography / www.photographybyscarlett.com*

Assignment

Delivering Your Subject

Choose one of the elements from the chapter (for example, C-curve, S-curve, diagonal leading line, Rule of Thirds) and create a strong composition using this element. Be sure that the child, or children, as subject is delivered to the viewer.

This photographer took great advantage of both the Rule of Thirds and negative space to create a contemporary and spontaneous image. This photograph also uses leading lines to great effect. Taken at ISO 200, f/8.0, and 1/800 second using highly creative post-processing (see Chapter 11 for ideas).

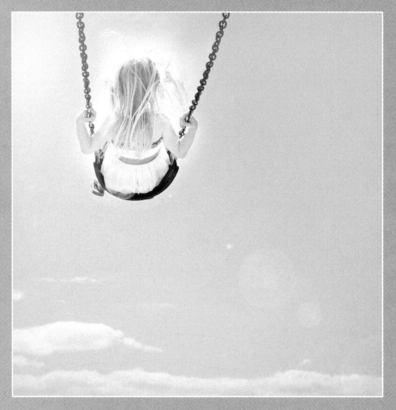

©Valeria Spring / www.theredballoonphotography.com

 Remember to visit www.pwsbooks.com after you complete this assignment and share your favorite photo! It's a community of enthusiastic photographers and a great place to view what other readers have created. You can also post comments, read encouraging suggestions, and get feedback.

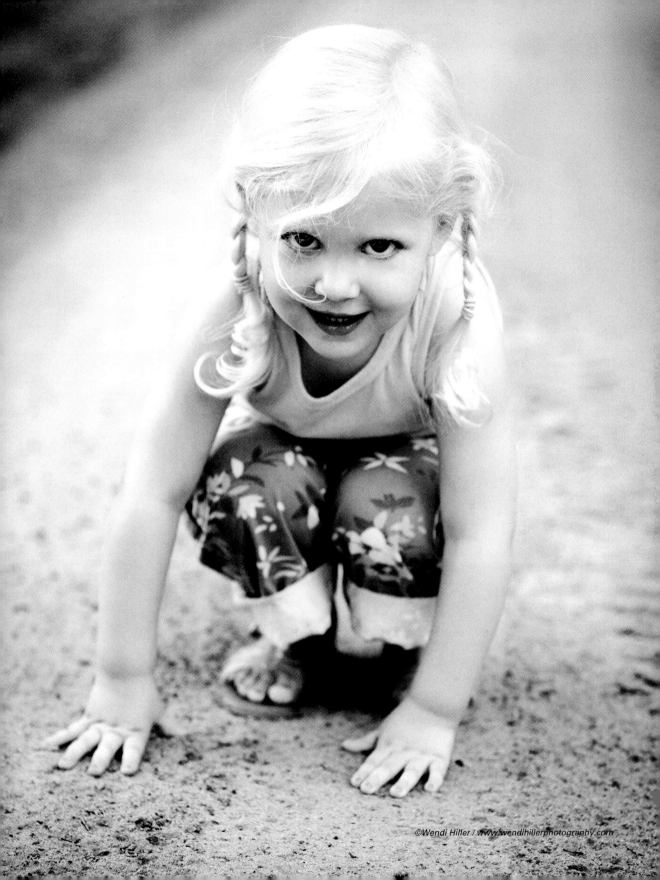

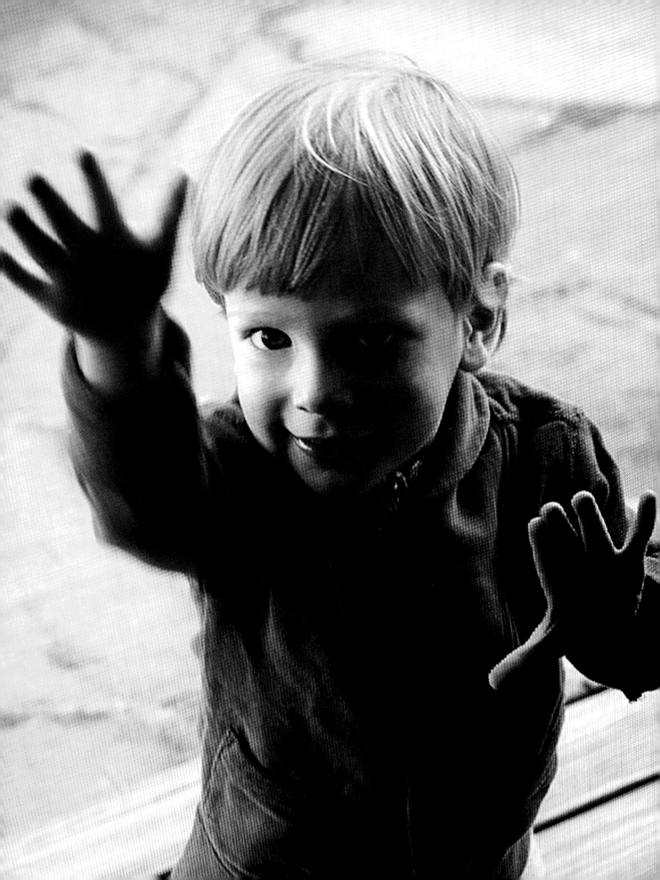

WHAT'S YOUR STYLE?

©Ginny Felch / www.photographingchildren.com

If you asked ten different photographers to photograph the same child in the same setting, you would have ten different interpretations of that same child. Just like the children you photograph, each photographer is unique in his or her view of the world. Some bring a fresh, hip perspective to their work with children, while others prefer to capture childhood in a more timeless, less trendy fashion.

What is your style? Do you have one yet? While most photographic work can't simply be slotted into one category or another, it is helpful to make some broad generalizations when you're starting out to give you a point of departure for your own work.

No matter what style of photography inspires you, it's a good idea to try a little bit of everything when you start out. Learning to experiment with different locations and settings can give your inspiration a boost. This chapter shows you some ways to expand your skills and try some new styles.

> **tip** Start an idea file or bulletin board of photos that you've clipped from magazines and/or bookmark your favorite websites that show photography that inspires you. As your skill level increases, these references give you inspiration for your own work.

CLASSIC AND ROMANTIC

Many parents appreciate portraits that reveal a sense of timelessness. The classic style of child photography has its roots in the paintings of the old masters. Drawing on the style of painters such as Rembrandt, Vermeer, and others, the classic and romantic style of children's portraiture can often be seen as an idealized version of childhood.

IN THE STUDIO

When shooting in the studio, a classic portrait becomes a study of the child you are photographing. There are no distracting elements to take your attention away from the child, leaving only their expressions and gestures to tell the story. In many ways, capturing a storytelling image in the studio can be much more challenging than shooting on location, where you can rely on the environment to render part of the story.

In a photograph that is *low key*, the background is darker and perhaps more colorful, as it would be in a garden or forest. If the clothing is darker as well, your attention again is drawn to the skin tones, or the lightest thing in the photograph, as in 6-1. Classic and romantic styles work well with painted muslin or canvas backgrounds that give a painterly feel to the image.

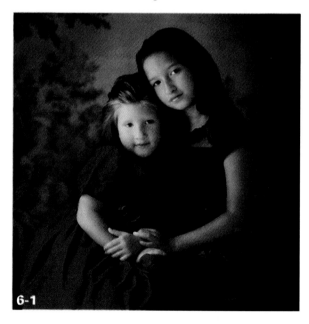

6-1

ABOUT THIS PHOTO *A classical portrait of two sisters was captured in the window light in front of a painted backdrop. The tones of the dresses and the background make a lowkey image. Taken at ISO 400, f/4.0, and 1/30 second.*
©Lizbeth Guerrina / www.paulineandlizbethphotography.com

ABOUT THIS PHOTO *The timeless tapestry on the chair harmonizes with the coloring of this little girl, enhanced by soft window light. Taken at ISO 640, f/5.6, and 1/60 second. ©Theresa Smerud / www.theresasmerud.com*

6-2

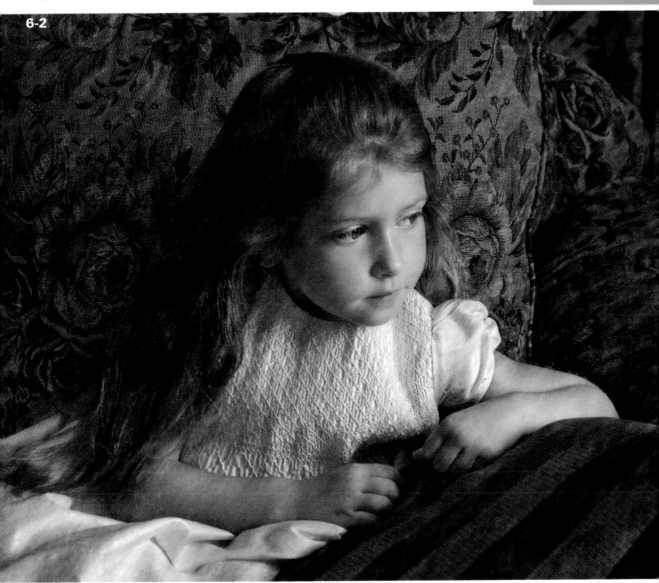

A simple chair and pillow and window light can provide all you need for a portrait, without any worry about wall backdrops (see 6-2). Just be sure to crop in close and avoid any clutter in the background.

ON LOCATION

For classic and romantic portrait styles, seek soft light and a quiet, peaceful location, as in 6-3.

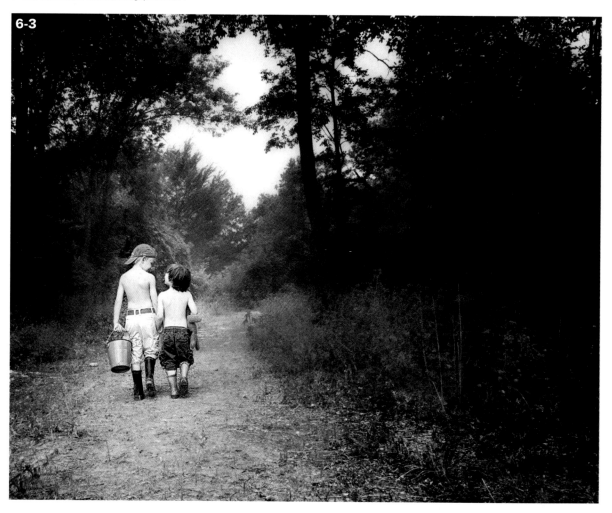

6-3

When children are quiet and wistful, their eyes are often open wide, and their cheeks are soft and full. On the other hand, never let a spontaneous, energetic, or spunky moment, as in 6-4, go unphotographed. Capturing these moments on location allows you to tell a more layered, romantic story.

Photographing on the family's property or at a favorite place adds meaning to the photograph that just isn't possible in a studio environment.

Talk to parents about your desire to work in the best and most dramatic lighting situations you can find, as in 6-5. Usually they aren't as aware as you are of what that actually means, so you need to help them understand so they are cooperative. You are the professional, and they should look to you for guidance.

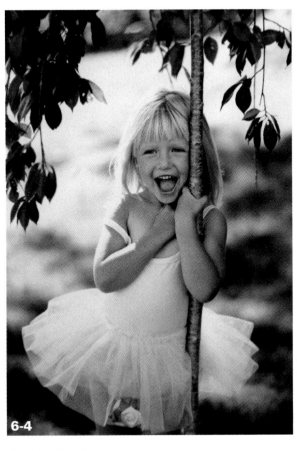

6-4

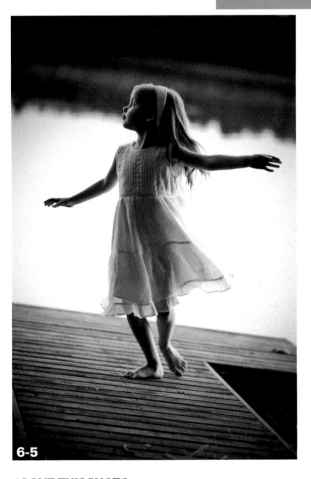

6-5

ABOUT THIS PHOTO *Does it get any better than wearing your tutu on a summer day? This expression begs otherwise! The backlighting and framing by the foliage add to what is already a beautiful image. Taken at ISO 320, f/4.0, and 1/125 second. ©Patrisha McLean / www. patrishamclean.com*

ABOUT THIS PHOTO *The graceful little dancer practices her moves as the setting sun adds a moody backlight. Taken at ISO 100, f/1.8, and1/160 second. ©Andrea Joki / www.ajatonjoki.com*

As you now know, choosing the best location is dependent on high-quality available light. You can't always count on the very best, but you can surely try. Let parents know that late afternoons, when the sun is at an angle, provide beautiful and luminous warm light. Foggy days work really well at the beach.

Visit the location ahead of time to see what you can expect the day of the session. Maybe the parents can go along with you to see what you are looking for and, thus, further collaborate to make a better portrait. Whatever it is you personally want to convey, share it with the parents so you all are in accord with what is going to be created.

THE KEY OF LIGHT Just as music is played in different keys, light can also be keyed to the mood you want to portray. A great deal of latitude exists in-between these examples, but they demonstrate an important point: The faces, eyes, and skin tones of the child are emphasized by choosing clothing and surroundings that suit the mood of the portrait envisioned by the photographer. Parents might have a preference for one style over another, so it helps to show them photographs you have made beforehand that demonstrate the following styles.

A *low-key* portrait is one in which the tones of the image are predominantly dark (or low), leaving the skin tones of your subject as the lightest parts of the image. Typically high in contrast, a low-key image can be very dramatic and moody.

A *high-key* portrait is predominantly light in tone with the skin tones being the darkest parts of the image, allowing them to stand out. Usually low in contrast, a high-key image can be ethereal and romantic.

In almost every major metropolitan area there are botanical and historical gardens and parks. These are good places if you live in an urban area and want to add the feel of nature in your work. Don't overlook buildings or areas with classic architecture to enhance your images. If you live in rural areas, meadows, orchards, and fields are at your disposal. Take advantage! If you are lucky enough to live near the ocean, beaches are a lovely place to photograph children.

CLOTHING

For a classic portrait, you want the clothing to be as timeless and traditional as possible. Distracting logos, plaids, and large stripes can often distract from the child. Solid colors and timeless clothing designs such as white dresses for girls and button-down shirts and jeans for boys leave the emphasis on the child. Avoid huge hair bows and uncomfortable clothing for babies. Babies are often best photographed *au naturel* (with no clothes at all)!

Watch out for shoes as well. Nothing dates a photo faster than ever-changing shoe styles, so when in doubt, have your subjects go barefoot. Children's feet are usually so perfectly round and sweet, but be sure to get the parents' permission first!

In 6-6 you can see that the siblings are dressed in light-colored vintage clothing to add to the timelessness of this photograph. All the decisions in light, composition, and clothing were intentional to create a timeless, enduring photograph.

quote

"When the first baby laughed for the first time, the laugh broke into a thousand pieces, and they all went skipping about, and that was the beginning of the fairies." ~Sir James M. Barrie, in *Peter Pan*

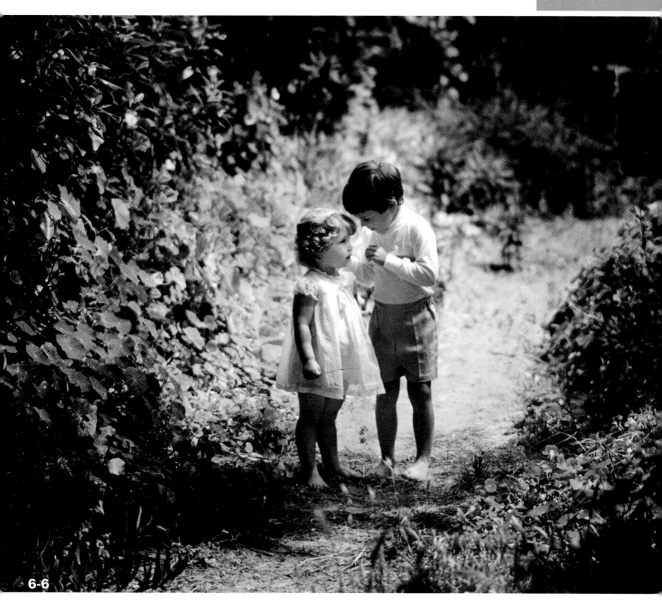

6-6

ABOUT THIS PHOTO *I was probably unconsciously inspired by W. Eugene Smith's photograph "The Walk to Paradise Garden" (1946) when I photographed these cherubs in a nasturtium patch by the beach. The vintage clothing and the vignette of the foliage added aptly to the composition. Taken with film at ISO 160, f/5.6, and 1/100 second. ©Ginny Felch / www.photographingchildren.com*

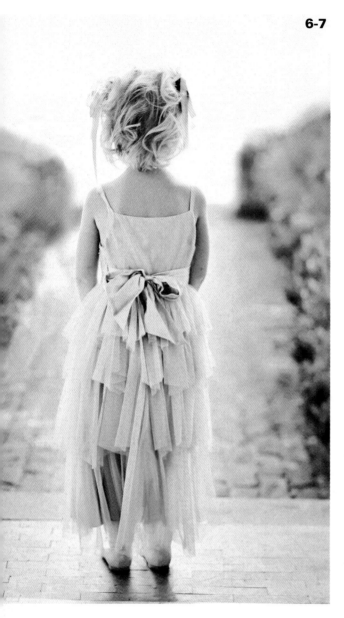

6-7

ABOUT THIS PHOTO *The clothing for a ballet performance inspired the photographer to make use of lovely window light to compose this painterly portrait. The subdued yet vintage clothing could be right off of a movie set; the pastels and the composition draw us in to the possible stories. Taken at ISO 200, f/2.0, and 1/160 second.* ©Abi Campbell / www.abicampbellphotography.com

Clothing should not overwhelm or distract from your subject. In both 6-7 and 6-8 you pay attention to the children, not so much their clothing. If either had been wearing a T-shirt with a big logo or stripes, these images would have had a completely different look.

All the decisions you make, whether it's the location, the lighting, or the clothing you've selected, add or detract from the mood you are trying to convey. Deciding ahead of time what mood you would like to convey in your image is the key.

What are you trying to convey about this child and her personality? What elements in the surrounding environment can you use to support your vision? Do you want an image full of energy and whimsy or is the child more thoughtful and shy?

For example, the soft, contouring light that surrounds this young girl's peaceful countenance in 6-9 causes the viewer to ponder what she might have been thinking when this photo was captured. The mood is serene and thoughtful.

ABOUT THIS PHOTO *Using texture and a straightforward classical composition, this masterly and moody portrait of a boy in the woods evolved. Taken at ISO 800, f/ 2.8, and 1/125 second. ©Jessica Drossin / www.jessicadrossinphotography.com*

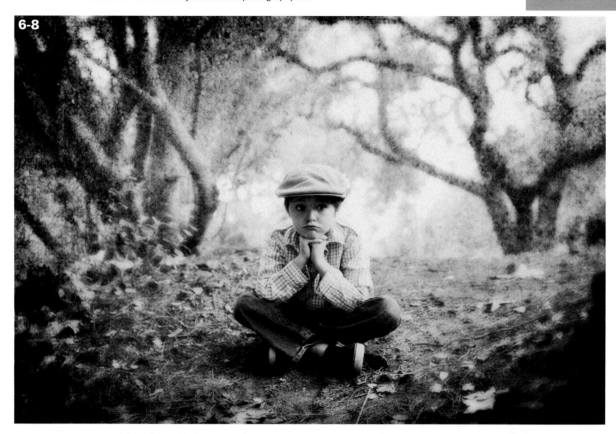

6-8

GENERAL CLOTHING GUIDELINES Parents need to know that the whole idea of fussing about clothing serves but one purpose: The focus should be on the child's beautiful, soft face, not the clothing. That is why it's important to have certain guidelines about clothing, which, when followed by parents, result in great photos. Regardless of your style, the general guidelines here should serve you well.

> Suggest parents avoid bold stripes, plaids or prints, insignias, logos, and so on. Textures work beautifully in sweaters, just in case it's chilly, but be careful that the texture isn't overpowering.

> Have tools handy to fix a child's hair. Ask parents to tell you ahead of time what they do and don't like. You can simply carry a little bottle of spray water and another of light hairspray. You don't want to be in a situation where you have taken a series of great photographs and find out later that mom dislikes her daughter's hair pulled back, or some such disaster.

> If a child has braces, tell parents not to worry. Braces are a rite of passage, and most people will look back with smiles as they remember those times. However, if parents wish, you can decrease the brashness of the metal or even completely remove them in post-production.

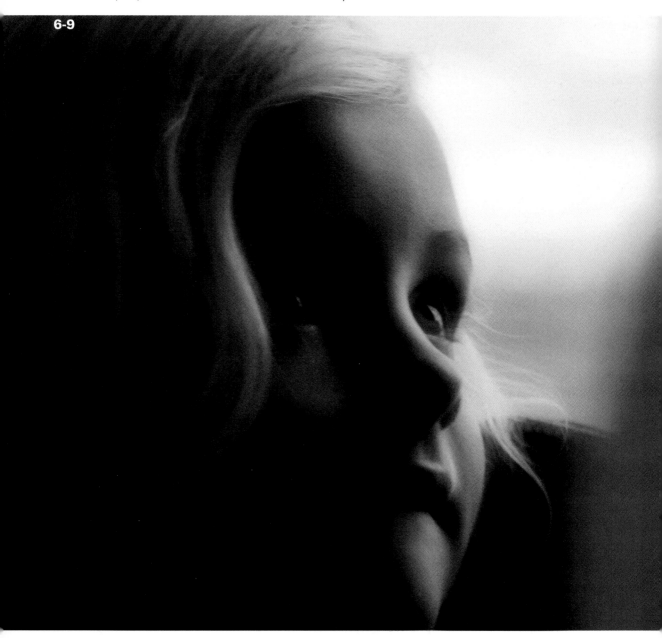

6-9

A tranquil, otherworldly feeling permeates the image of a little explorer at the beach in 6-10. An entirely different mood would have been captured had she been dressed in contemporary colorful clothing. Her gesture with the walking stick suggests that something as formal as a white dress would hardly have been appropriate for this session.

ABOUT THIS PHOTO *This modern, yet classic portrait of a strawberry-blonde adventurer was composed thoughtfully in a C-curve for emphasis. The photographer used her own actions in post-production. Taken at ISO 200, f/4.5, and 1/1250 second. ©Annie Manning / www.paintthemoon.net*

6-10

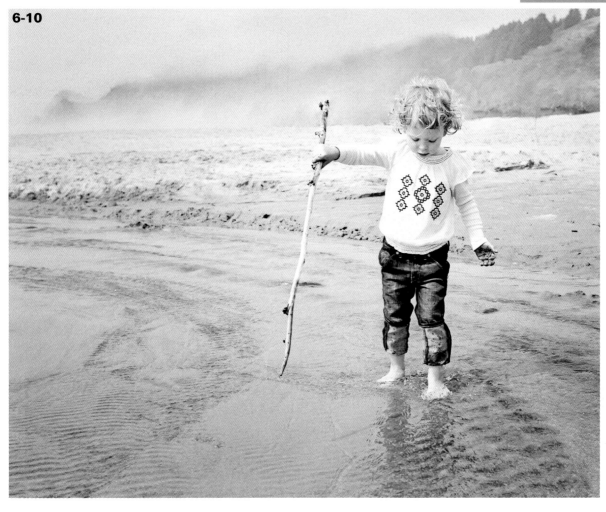

CONTEMPORARY

Contemporary children's portraiture is whatever is trendy and cool at the moment, but even within current trends there is often a strong thread of timelessness. A contemporary style tends to break with tradition. Instead of stylized posing, the idea is to encourage the real, often more animated, personality of the child to come to the forefront. Cropped-off heads and full-out belly laughs are just right for this style of portraiture.

IN THE STUDIO

Studio photography lends itself very well to contemporary portraiture, as much of this style is inspired by magazine advertising. Seamless paper backgrounds work well for a contemporary feel. Inexpensive and available in a wide variety of colors, seamless backgrounds can give you many background choices for much less money than canvas or muslin backdrops.

When attempting a contemporary style in the studio, the idea is to set up the lighting so that a fairly wide area is well lit, allowing the subject a bit of room to move around. As in the photo of two sisters in 6-11, the background doesn't compete for attention, and a fan blows their hair, giving movement to the image.

Sometimes, extreme cropping can give an edgy, contemporary feel to your images. The images in 6-12 and 6-13 both take advantage of negative space, allowing all the focus to fall on the subject. Who says your subject's head has to be in the photo? In 6-13 you get a good sense of these little boys without ever seeing their faces.

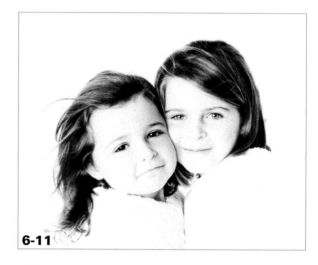

6-11

ABOUT THIS PHOTO *A more contemporary treatment of a sisters' portrait utilizes a white background and fan to provide movement in their hair. Taken at ISO 100, f/2, 2.8, and 1/125 second. ©Jeffrey Woods / www.jwportraitlife.com*

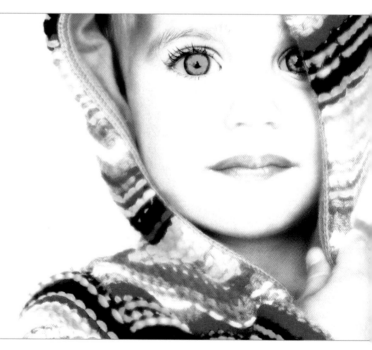

6-12

ABOUT THIS PHOTO *The photographer placed this little girl in the far right of the frame, which adds to the contemporary feel of the image. Taken at ISO 100, f/3.5, and 1/125 second. ©Jeffrey Woods / www.jwportraitlife.com*

ABOUT THIS PHOTO *The sneakers, bruised legs, and cut-offs tell you just as much about these boys as seeing their faces would. Taken at ISO 400, f/1.6, and 1/400 second. ©Cama Cathrae / www.camacathrae.com*

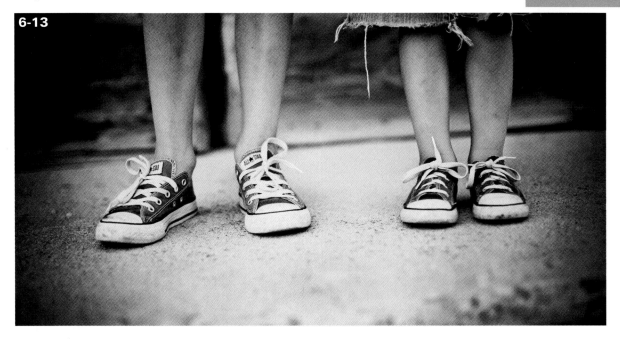

6-13

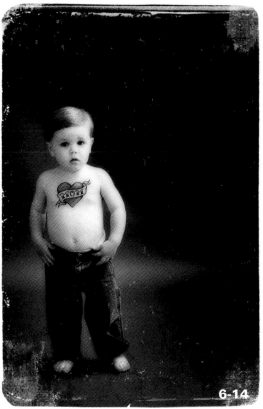

6-14

Sometimes contemporary style consists of turning the traditional style on its head, as in 6-14. The lighting and background just scream classic and romantic. But a topless baby in a pair of jeans with a (Photoshopped, of course) tattoo on his chest is anything but traditional.

ABOUT THIS PHOTO *The background and lighting are traditional, but the pose and treatment are anything but. Taken at ISO 125, f/7.1, and 1/125 second. ©Jeffrey Woods / www.jwportraitlife.com*

In this day of media saturation, we are much more image savvy than ever. Ads on television, in magazines, and on the Internet all influence our taste and style. This girl in 6-15 is very young, but that doesn't prevent her from wanting to look like a super model and express some attitude!

Traditional family portraits rely on careful posing and arrangement of each family member. A contemporary style seeks to get a little closer to reality by allowing the family members to pose themselves and interact with each other in a more natural way, as in 6-16.

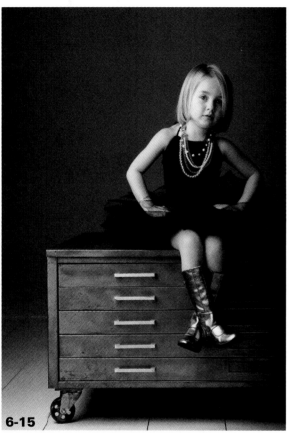

6-15

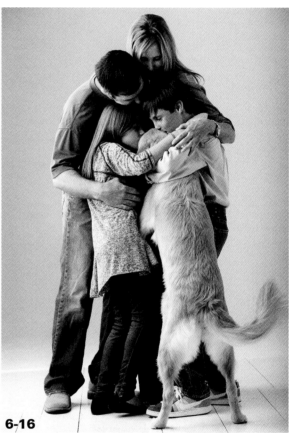

6-16

ABOUT THIS PHOTO *The interaction between the photographer and this sassy and adorable little girl, along with the minimalist setting, just screams out contemporary. Taken at ISO 200, f/9.0, and 1/250 second. ©Allison Tyler Jones / www.atjphoto.com*

ABOUT THIS PHOTO *Inviting the family pooch on the set will always liven up a photo session, and the connection of this family is palpable. Taken at ISO 200, f/5.6, and 1/250 second. ©Allison Tyler Jones / www.atjphoto.com*

ON LOCATION

Any location can work for a contemporary style because the style depends on how the photographer sees the subject more than on the actual location itself. However, you may want to look through this section for ideas on similar locations in your town. As you look through them, you may see how each location could be used in a classic and romantic or a contemporary or photojournalistic way. It all depends on your point of view.

Urban decay is part of the world we live in, and contemporary portraiture is geared to take full advantage of what some might see as old and ugly. An old industrial door adds texture and interest to the background in the image of the young girl in 6-17.

A wall mural acts as an interesting and amusing background for the stylish baby in 6-18. However, kids often just aren't into the "cutesy" that their moms still love. They are just as influenced by images as their parents and they want to look cool. In 6-19 for example, the vibrant blue building acts as a video-like set for this group of friends while the subtle backlight separates them from the background.

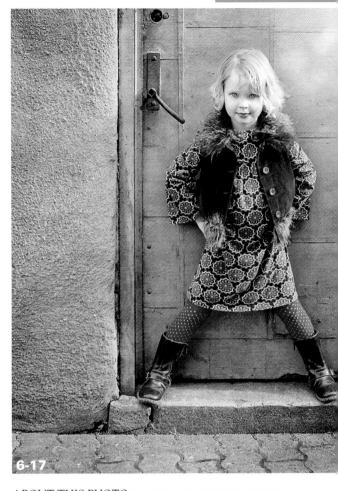

6-17

ABOUT THIS PHOTO *The old farm door and stucco wall add texture and interest to the background while the girl's confident expression conveys her personality. The photographer used her own actions and textures in post-production. Taken at ISO 400, f/2.8, and 1/640 second. ©Annie Manning / www.paintthemoon.net*

> *quote*
>
> "The portrait photographer who understands his work will never seek a formula for success. Those who would simplify portraiture to a few rules and diagrams will serve you pretty cold potatoes, for the vital essence of the good portrait is too elusive to be caught and bottled. Portraiture will always be an art of discovery." ~Edward Weston

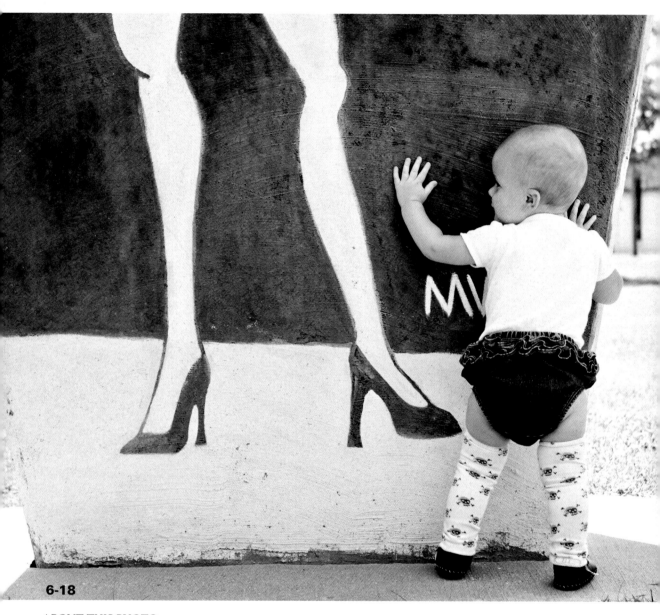

6-18

ABOUT THIS PHOTO *The keen and observing eye of the photographer caught the irony of the fashionable baby in front of a very grown-up poster. Taken at ISO 100, f/5.0, and 1/200 second.* ©Melanie Johnson / www.melaniejohnson.com

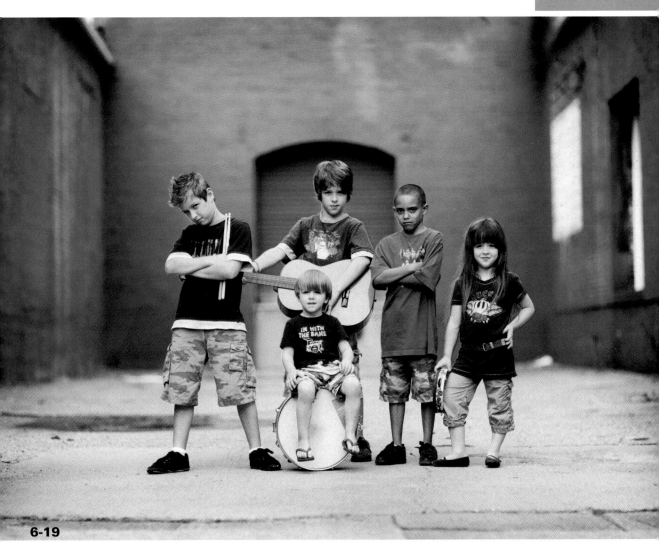

6-19

ABOUT THIS PHOTO *Surely the photographer and performing kids were influenced by contemporary media. Taken at ISO 100, f/1.6, and 1/1000 second. ©Leah Profancik / www.leahprofanicik.com*

Libraries, art centers, and other public buildings (even parking garages) can be great places to capture children and their families. Use the lines in the architecture to frame your subjects or draw attention to them, as in 6-20.

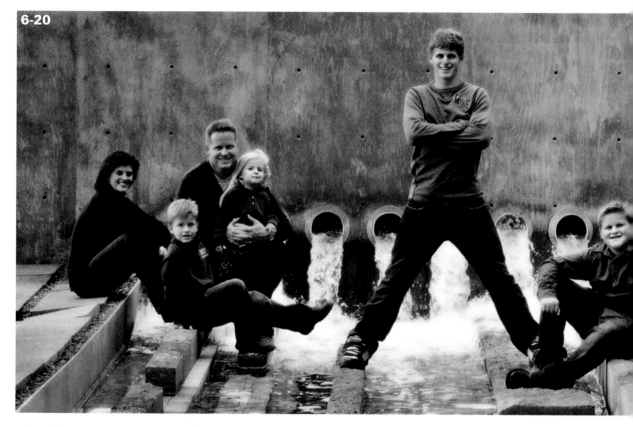

6-20

LIFESTYLE PHOTOGRAPHY

Lifestyle photography has greatly increased in popularity, and has some qualities of a photojournalistic style, giving photographs a more spontaneous, spirited, and unadulterated look and feeling. True photojournalists often act as a fly on the wall, observing and capturing what is happening before their lens for the purpose of telling the news. They don't interfere with their subjects in any way.

Photographs are not set up, there is no wardrobe change or fixing of hair — the photo opportunity presents itself, and the moment is captured.

Lifestyle photography is seldom romantic or timeless; it can be considered contemporary because it is fresh and *of the moment.*

Lifestyle photography borrows elements of true photojournalism with a few key differences. You might plan wardrobe and location, which is obviously not photojournalistic; however, once the setting is established and the subjects are in place, lifestyle photography requires you to get out of the way and let kids be kids. Forget posing or fixing hair as you go, just let them run and be ready with the camera.

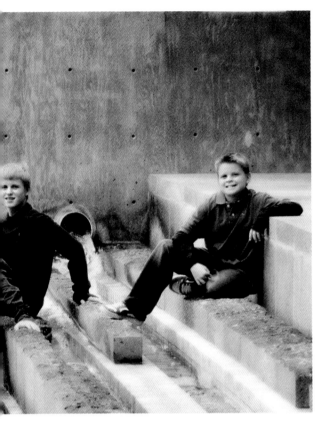

BlendCam, TiltShiftMaker, and Vintage Video Maker, to enhance or embellish the images. Why not keep a journal on your cell phone using the camera, the video, and even the recording devices? That way you can document your family life. There are also apps that serve as actual journals for you to organize your moments methodically.

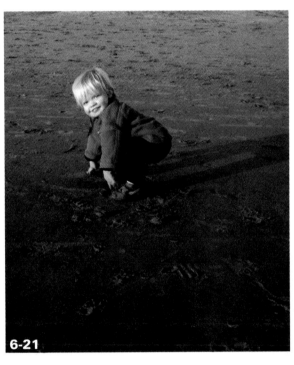

6-21

USING YOUR CELL PHONE'S CAMERA/VIDEO

One way to assure spontaneity and freedom while capturing your children and family is to take advantage of your handy cell phone camera, as in 6-21. These days it seems it will always be at your fingertips, but sometimes we forget we have it in moments that can slip by unrecorded.

Some photographers take this fun quite seriously and use creative apps, such as Hipstamatic, Photoshop, Colorsplash,

ABOUT THIS PHOTO *The always improving quality of cell phone cameras and the spontaneity they afford you give you great opportunities to record precious moments like this one, late in the afternoon at the beach. I cropped it with the iPhone Photoshop Express App. Taken at ISO 70, f/2.8, and 1/180 second. ©Ginny Felch / www. photographingchildren.com*

131

ON LOCATION

As the family documentarian, it can be challenging to capture those spontaneous moments if your kids always want to pose for the camera. The best antidote to this is to keep your camera out and use it often. Before long, these creatures become accustomed to it and go about their business, allowing you to chronicle them in their natural habitat.

Telephoto or zoom lenses come in handy when you want to capture your photograph unobserved, as in 6-22 of a big brother giving a piggyback ride to a sibling. The longer lens allowed the photographer to get in close and simplify a cluttered background by focusing on just the subjects and a blue sky above.

Lenses and their various types are covered in depth in Chapter 9.

ABOUT THIS PHOTO *The expressions on the faces of these siblings tell the story. The little girl adores her older brother, and he adores her but just doesn't want to show it. Taken at ISO 200, f/4.5, and 1/1250 second. ©Jeffrey Woods / www.jwportraitlife.com*

6-22

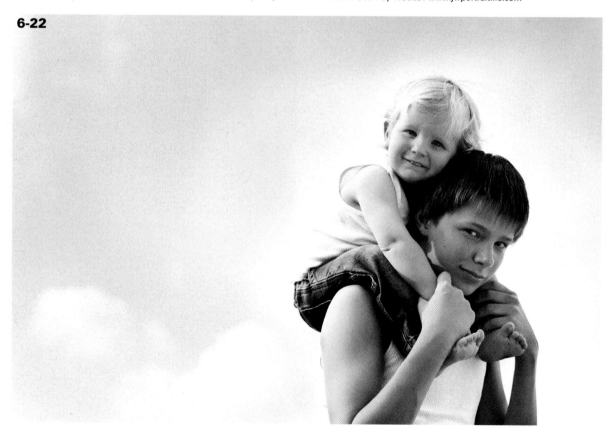

When striving to attain a lifestyle approach, you will want to capture the kids wherever they are, whatever they are doing. Can you imagine if the photographer had waited to shoot until the little girl in 6-23 was sitting up straight in her chair?

Photographing children in their natural environment allows them to be more comfortable, and the images have the added value of triggering memories later in life of their childhood home. With the parents' cooperation, roam around in the home to find ideal or unusual settings and light to add pizzazz to your photos, as in 6-24, 6-25, and 6-26.

ABOUT THIS PHOTO
This photograph gives a great sense of this little girl's personality. Taken at ISO 400, f/2.8, and 1/160 second. ©Stacy Wasmuth / www.bluecandy photography.com

6-23

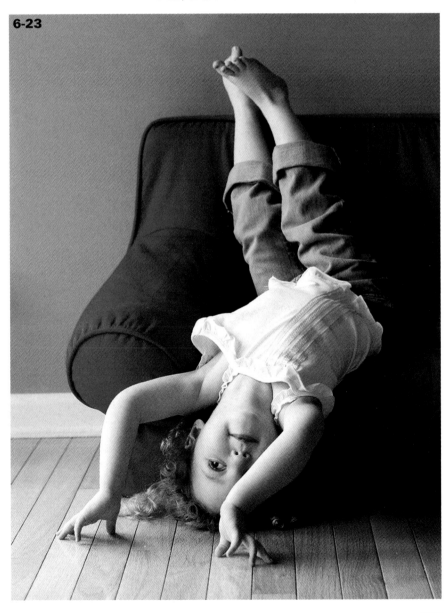

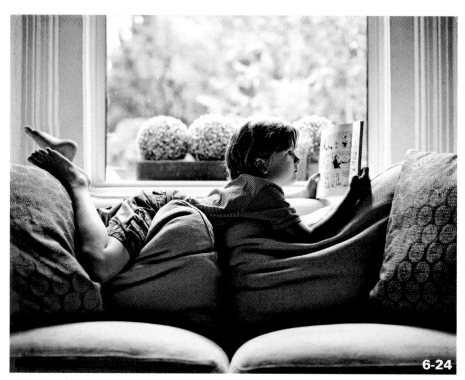

6-24

ABOUT THIS PHOTO
Years from now, this photo will be a reminder of the home where this boy grew up. The natural and comfortable demeanor he shows while reading suggests that the photographer did not interfere or pose him. Taken at ISO 1600, f/1.8, and 1/400 second. ©Doreen Kilfeather / www.dkilfeatherphotography.

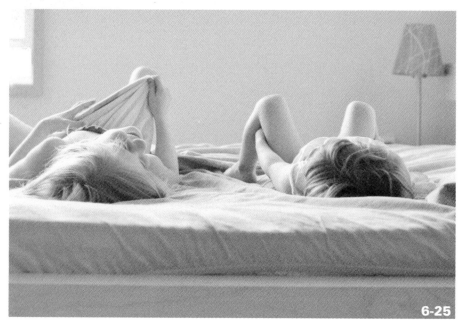

6-25

ABOUT THESE PHOTOS
Kids love to show off their bedrooms, which, in turn, conveys part of their personality. These playful and casual girls just exude comfort as they spend some afternoon time chatting away. The soft pastels and window light, as well as the photographer's post-production skills, tie it all together. Taken at ISO 1250, f/4.5, and 1/80 second. ©Valeria Spring / www.thered balloonphotography.com

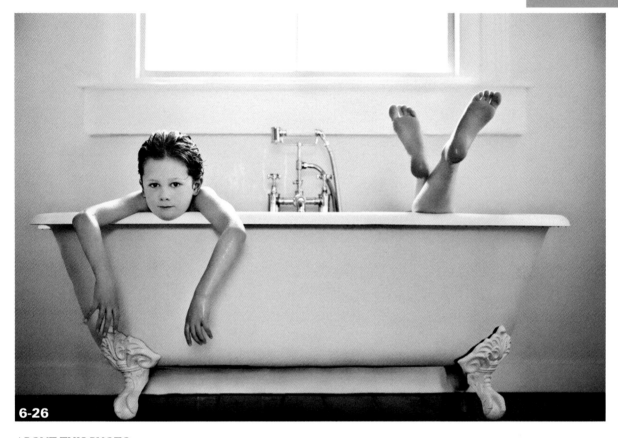

6-26

ABOUT THIS PHOTO *Often times, the family bathroom has some of the best light and reflection in the house. Using it as your location can add fun to the experience and result in a surprising and extraordinary image. Taken at ISO 1000, f/2.2, and 1/60 second. ©Doreen Kilfeather / www.dkilfeatherphotography.com*

MOOD

It's not very realistic to think that you will just happen upon amazing moments and capture them. Sometimes that happens, but most times, it doesn't. That's where a little assisted reality comes in. Put the kids in their environment and then let them have fun. For example, the little boy in 6-27 was easily entertained playing superman on the living room couch. Using available window light helped to give the photographer enough light to catch the action with a fast shutter speed. Giving a child the opportunity to play his favorite everyday games can really enhance the mood and feeling of a photograph.

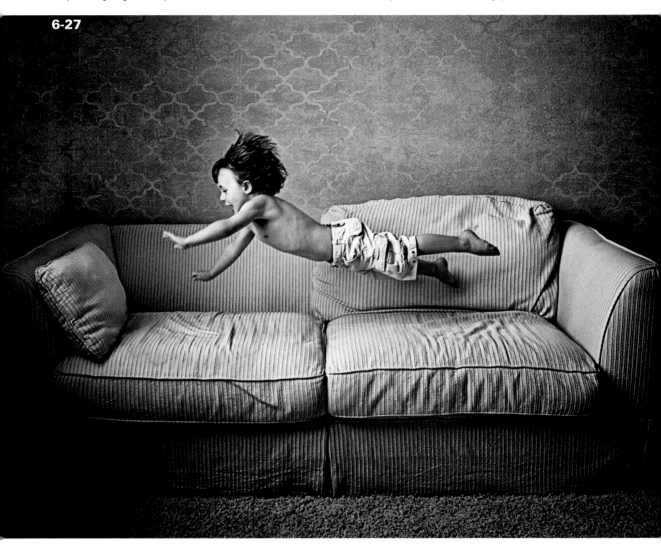

6-27

A foggy beach day highlights the family in 6-28 as they cavort in front of the cave on the Oregon coast. The clothes and setting and lighting were all planned, but the fun and emotion are the real deal.

Another way to portray siblings is by focusing in on only a part of them, as in 6-29. Placing the children on the mom and dad's bed in their light-filled bedroom allows for a new take on a traditional portrait.

ABOUT THIS PHOTO *Finding the right lighting and setting allows the family to be spontaneous and free in their expressions and actions. Taken at ISO 125, f/3.2, and 1/640 second. ©Linda Lapp Murray*

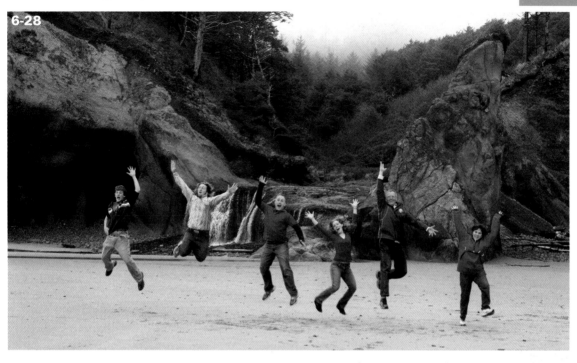

6-28

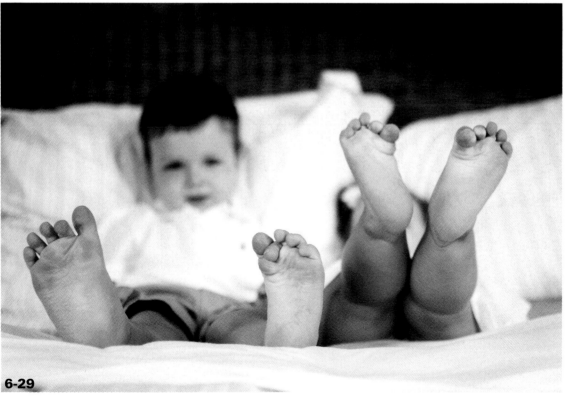

6-29

Cropping in tight to capture the child sharing a mischievous grin while enjoying his snack creates an instant connection with the viewer, as in 6-30.

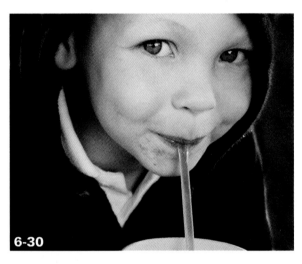

6-30

ABOUT THIS PHOTO *I captured this elfin smile on a ferry with my nephew, and it is emphasized by cropping in close. The darker tones surrounding his face draw your eyes to the place of interest. Taken at ISO 500, f/4, and 1/125 second. ©Ginny Felch / www.photographingchildren.com*

PREPARING PARENTS FOR THEIR CHILD'S PORTRAIT

Whether you are photographing children as a hobby, a passion, or as a career, communicating with the parents of your subjects is an important part of creating a unique and meaningful portrait. Ultimately, your portraits contain a large part of you and your vision, even when you are following parents' wishes. If you are interested in developing your photography as a vocation, both your images and your business will reap the benefits of collaboration and communication.

quote "In the faces of children I have seen a look of wisdom and of kindness expressed with such ease and such certainty that I know it was the expression of the whole race." ~Robert Henri

OUTLINING EXPECTATIONS

It is a good idea to give the parents some idea of what your expectations are for photo sessions. Many professional photographers reveal their philosophy and working style as well as clothing suggestions and other important information on their websites or brochures. Take the time to get an idea of what the parents' goal is for the final result of the photo session. For example, do they want a large wall portrait or just a couple of shots for the annual Christmas card?

This kind of communication works to establish trust in you as an artist and respect for your time and opinions. The clarity of the information up front prevents miscommunication and misunderstandings later. Some photographers place their business forms and policies online, which helps avoid costly and timely mistakes.

The most important thing you can do to prepare parents for an upcoming portrait session is to ask them to play the session down when speaking with their child. Children should come into your time together without feeling the pressure of any expectations. Many of the photographs in this book may look as though the children were perfectly behaved and everything was going according to some master plan, but nothing could be further from the truth.

Everything that you plan and discuss ahead of time is valuable and helpful in order to make a meaningful children's photograph. However, when you work with the highly unpredictable nature of children and weather, both you and the parents need to let go of the exact results.

More often, if both parties (parents and photographer) are savvy to this, photographs are likely turn out better than expected. Surprises that come along won't be frustrating, but creatively challenging.

COLLABORATING WITH PARENTS

Many child photographers prefer to work with the children they photograph one-on-one, with the parent off to one side or in another room completely. One of the main reasons parents want to remain with the child and photographer is that they want to make sure that the children don't exhibit their funny smiles, their little quirks, and so on. The irony is that when the children are separate from parents, these expressions rarely occur. If the parents still insist on being present during a session, you might ask that they stand back, watch quietly for awhile, and perhaps walk away for 45 minutes if they feel comfortable doing so.

Tell the parents that you take pride in evoking expressions from the children, and that is usually possible only without distractions. If you are photographing outside, allow the child to be quiet and listen to the surroundings. Bring the silence to their attention and ask them what they hear. These quiet moments can evoke wonderful, natural, whimsical expressions, as in 6-31. Evoking these moments requires uninterrupted time between photographer and child.

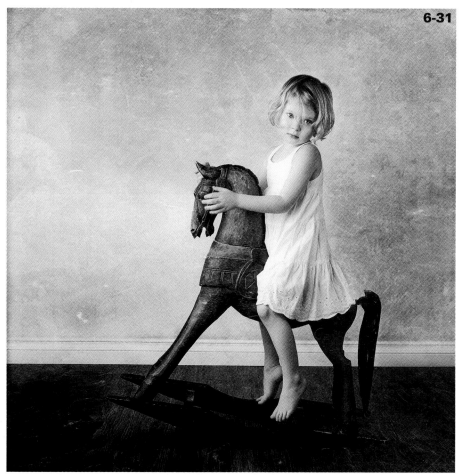

6-31

ABOUT THIS PHOTO
Riding on her old-fashioned rocking horse seems to have evoked memories or fantasies for this little girl, as her expression is far-off and otherworldly. These expressions can only happen when the photographer establishes trust and comfort. The photographer used her own texture and actions in post-production. Taken at ISO 200, f/5.6, and 1/250 second. ©Annie Manning / www.paintthemoon.net

Leave the big, cheesy smiles to the school photographers. If there is a smile or a hint of sweetness, let it be a reaction to something you have said. If you must work with an assistant, which is helpful if there are two or three young children, ask him or her not to distract from the relationship unless requested.

Ask the parents not to prime their kids about smiling or to discuss behavior issues. You should expect children to be children, and the more relaxed and happy they are as they enter the session, the better it all works for everyone. Parents should also try to be relaxed and confident because they can influence the attitude of their children. Tell them they are going to have fun with the photographer, but don't ever fib about what is coming up.

If parents convey confidence and make very little fuss about bringing their kids to you, they can set the tone for the entire session. Always do your best to distract the children during those potentially tender moments.

If you choose to make a career of children's photography, you will experience a wide array of behavior from very good to downright horrible. That's what makes it challenging, fun, and creative for those who love children.

Some children are soothed by having a creature comfort along with them. You might suggest in your communication with parents that they can bring along a blanket, stuffed animal, or favorite toy. Special treats can also be a good idea (always check with parents first). You can offer them during the session, as long as they aren't too messy.

KEEP PHOTOGRAPHING

Inevitably, when you think the session is complete and it's time to pack up and go, something surprising and photo-worthy will happen (as in 6-32), and you won't have your camera in hand. Make it a practice not to put your camera away until you are in your car ready to leave. Moments like this cannot be re-created, no matter how hard you try!

PORTRAIT PLANNING

Sometimes you will be creating individual portraits as well as family portraits. Ask parents to decide beforehand which is more important to them. Try not to go beyond the comfort zone and attention span of the children. That can be a brief period, depending on the ages of the child or children. Better to start off with individual portraits and move on to the groups if time and temperament permit. If you, or the family, prefer the family portrait, do that first.

Many people want to have more natural and unposed photographs. Of course, the more people you have in a portrait, the more posed it tends to be as you try to corral everyone into the frame, unless you have the luxury of scheduling a session during a more natural event (family reunion or picnic). Be sure to communicate that knowledge with parents so they are prepared to see less spontaneity when there are more people in the photograph.

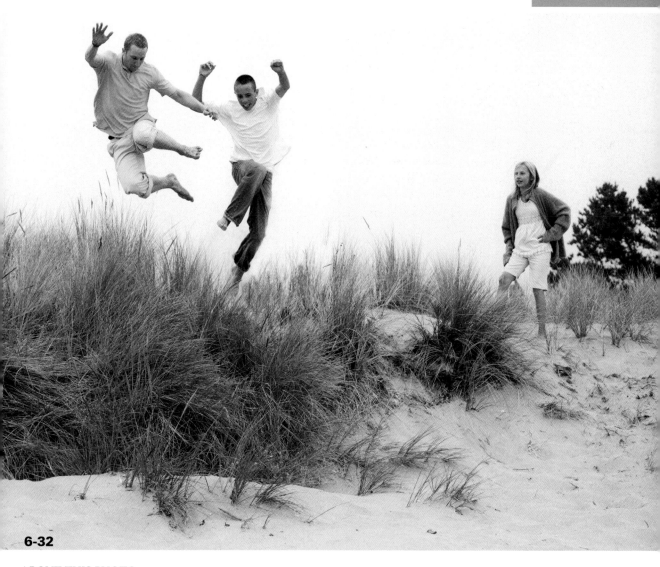

6-32

ABOUT THIS PHOTO *As soon as the extended family portrait was completed, the teens broke out into acrobatics on the sand dunes in celebration. Fortunately, I had not put away my equipment! Taken at ISO 1600, f/7.1, and 1/400 second. ©Ginny Felch / www.photographingchildren.com*

Assignment

Create a Special Portrait

Ask friends with a child if you can create a portrait for them. Communicate your desire to make a special portrait and collaborate with them, with you as their guide. Use the information you learned in this chapter. Post your best image of the child.

I wanted to capture a very special and close relationship between a boy and his cherished puppies, so I chose to crop in tightly to give it an intimate and contemporary feeling. Taken at ISO 500, f/5.0, and 1/100 second.

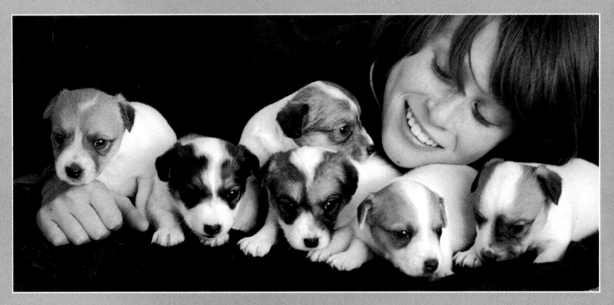

©Ginny Felch / www.photographingchildren.com

 Remember to visit www.pwsbooks.com after you complete this assignment and share your favorite photo! It's a community of enthusiastic photographers and a great place to view what other readers have created. You can also post comments, read encouraging suggestions, and get feedback.

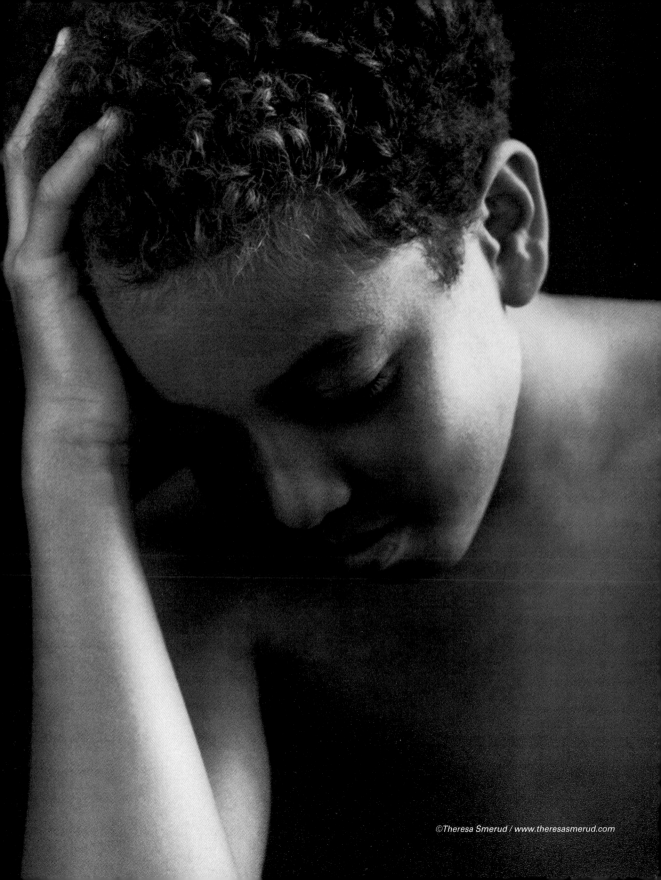

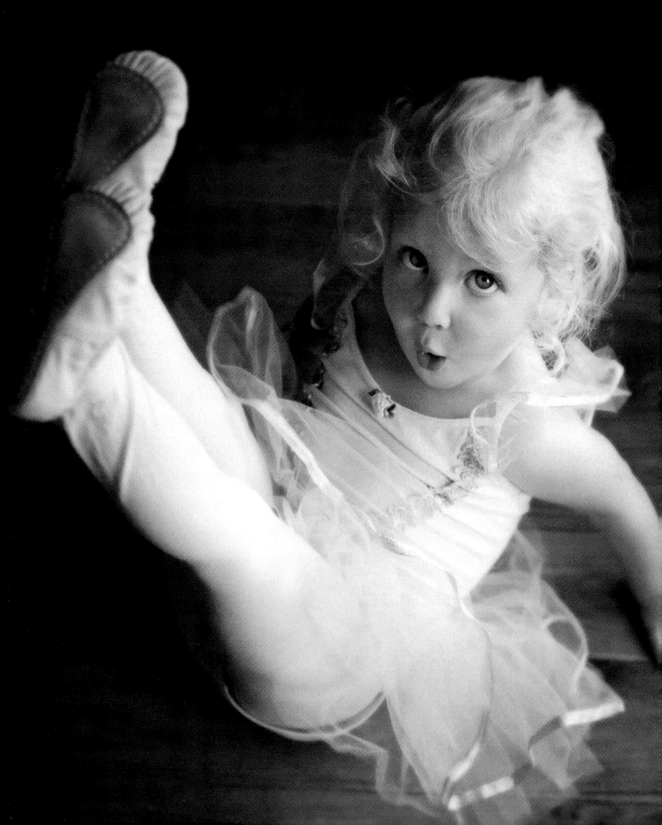

EVOKING EXPRESSION AND EMOTION

©Wendi Hiller / www.wendihillerphotography.com

As you look through photographs, whether they are your own family photographs, a friend's collection, or even magazine images, you intuitively flip through them at a certain pace. Every so often you might come across one that stops you, slows you down, and invites you to explore or engage more deeply. It might make you smile, think for a minute, or take you back to a place in time. What a wonderful exercise this is to hone your own observation skills and to see what pulls

you in. The chances are very good that the photograph that stops you or slows you down contains something profound or alluring in the expression, mood, and emotion. This is particularly true in children's photography. Children's expressions and emotions are usually close to the surface and readily available. As a children's photographer, you just need to be there, to witness, and to capture, what is offered so freely.

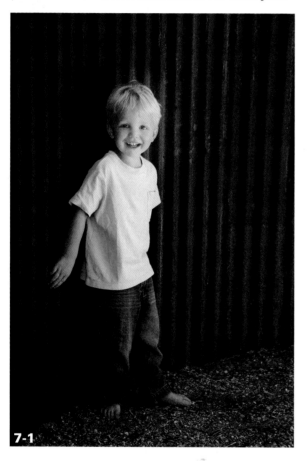

7-1

ABOUT THIS PHOTO *The energy and spirit of this sparkling little guy flows in this image, and the warmth of the contemporary metal wall adds an appropriate glow. Taken at ISO 800, f/7.1, and 1/80 second. ©Ginny Felch / www.photographingchildren.com*

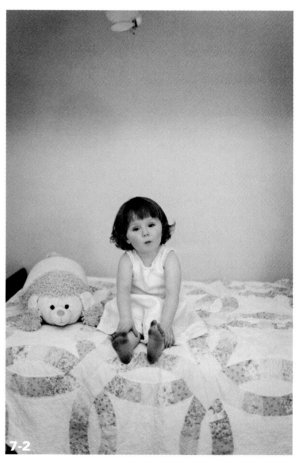

7-2

ABOUT THIS PHOTO *Pictured with a distinctive toy and quilt, this girl's body language and expression are very natural and characteristic of her age. Her dirty feet help tell the story. Taken at ISO 400, f/1.8, and 1/80 second. ©Marianne Drenthe / www.marmaladephotography.com*

"I think that emotional content is an image's most important element, regardless of the photographic technique. Much of the work I see these days lacks the emotional impact to draw a reaction from viewers, or remain in their hearts. ~Anne Geddes

The great advantage of digital photography over film (yes, film is still used) is that you can be spontaneous and capture special moments and a child's natural enthusiasm, as in 7-1 and 7-2, without the high cost of processing. The technology offers you the opportunity to learn as you photograph, and reviewing the immediate results allows you to erase and try again. For those who learned to photograph with film, this convenience is really a dream come true.

OBSERVING EMOTIONS AND MOODS

When photographing children, the elements of expression, emotion, and mood are of utmost importance. Some expressions or moods you might observe include:

- Busy or preoccupied
- Curiosity
- Daydreaming
- Delight
- Engagement
- Flirtatiousness
- Frustration (as in 7-3)
- Intrigue
- Involvement
- Joy (as in 7-4)

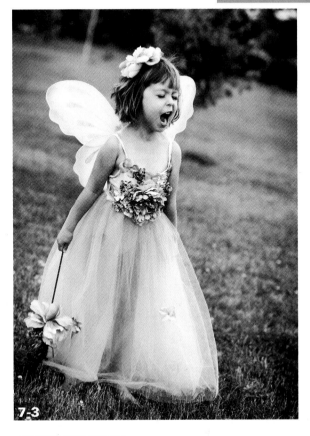

7-3

ABOUT THIS PHOTO *Even a wee temper tantrum can make a memorable and amusing photograph for the archives. Taken at ISO 640, f/2.8, and 1/250 second. ©Jen Sherrick / www.jensherrickphotography.com*

- Observing
- Playfulness
- Pouting (7-5)
- Restfulness, peacefulness, sleepiness
- Surprise
- Tenderness
- Thoughtfulness

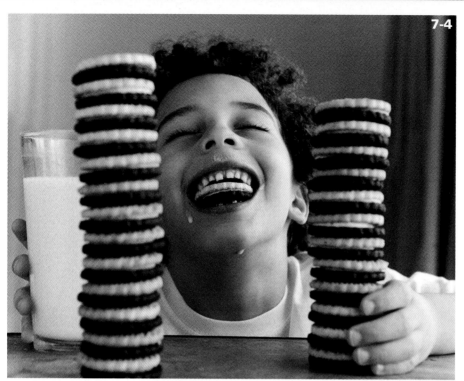

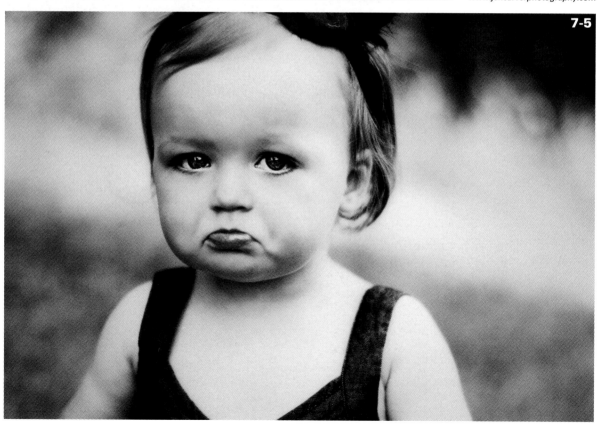

7-5

quote "You are the camera, your eyes are the shutters. What you absorb through them is what you paint, and it's you that is mixing the colors, not the camera." ~Richard F. Barber

VISUALIZATION

If you are a parent, you have probably stumbled on many instances when you wish you had a camera in your hand. How many times have you looked in the rearview mirror of your car and seen the soft, round cheeks of your sleeping toddler in the backseat. Wouldn't it be great if all you had to do was blink and a photo would be recorded with all the emotion you were feeling about that person at the moment? Actually, practice in visualizing these moments makes it far more likely that you can capture them in the future. As you go about your day and see children around you, compose and mentally click off a few frames; it will make you a better photographer when you actually get the camera in your hands.

In an ideal world, you would just come upon "the moment" and photograph it, but those kinds of happy accidents are few and far between. It is more likely that you either won't have your camera with you, or that the moment you turn toward the subject, all spontaneity dissolves, and the magic moment disappears, only to become another beautiful memory.

If you've ever tried to recreate a moment just to get the photo, you know that, most of the time, it just doesn't work. However, you can remember the feeling of that moment and try to pull it out of your bag of tricks for the next time.

Take your camera, even if it's your cell phone's camera, everywhere you go with your child, and you will have opportunities galore to capture innumerable precious moments. Your kids will think of the camera as part of their daily life. They will quit mugging and go about their business, which is exactly what you want.

The following sections explore ways to encourage, create, and capture these magic moments while photographing children.

REVEALING THE EYES: GATEWAY TO THE SOUL

The anonymous quote varies: Eyes are the gateway to the soul, the mirror of the soul, or the windows of the soul. The concept remains the same and is paramount when photographing children. In portraiture, the face is the most expressive part of the body, and of the face, the eyes are most important. You might be forgiven if you get any other part of the image out of focus, though not the eyes. Pay close attention to how the light is illuminating the child's eyes as well. Look for the *catchlights* — the little white reflections in the eyes that show life and sparkle. Very often it's just a matter of turning the child to get the light just right in his or her eyes.

When school photographers and, in fact, most photographers and parents, choose to show children with big, squinty-eyed grins, it makes everyone feel good. The universal appeal of a happy child can't be disputed, but at least consider the possibility that some appealing alternatives exist.

Take into consideration that when a child is in full-smile mode, the facial muscles are contracted, and the eyes become smaller, less open. Are there other alternatives that you haven't explored that could convey the personality of the child as well as, or better than, the full, cheesy grin? A child's face in repose is often the most revealing of the eyes and personality.

Don't be disappointed if a child you're photographing covers his eyes and shows his bashfulness, as in 7-6. The picture of this little boy turned out to be very charming and a true reflection of his personality at age 3.

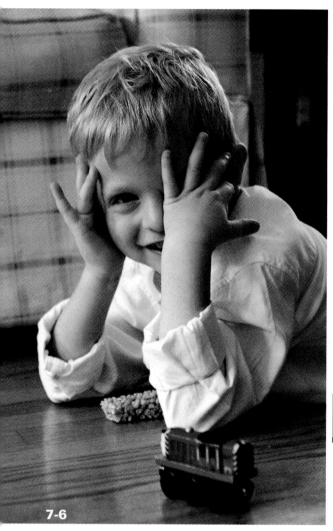

7-6

ABOUT THIS PHOTO *Getting down on the floor with a child is key to making him feel comfortable with you. Taken at ISO 640, f/4.0, and 1/60 second. ©Melanie Sikma / www.melaniesphotos.com*

The girl in 7-7 has a dreamy look in her eyes. The fact that she is looking right in to the photographer's eyes conveys a sense of trust and openness. Notice how her eyes are big and bright, and her facial expression is soft.

Most children eventually become comfortable with having their picture taken, as you can see in 7-8. This young boy has a gleam in his eyes because he was given time to get to know the photographer and to relax. A typical photography session can often take an hour or more to achieve photographs like these.

Toddlers can be a joy to work with, especially if you can distract their attention away from the camera. You can observe their quirky expressions and movements. The redhead in 7-9 is looking wistfully at the photographer. Notice that the image is cropped closely to emphasize his expression.

Don't be afraid to make the face and eyes the focal point of the image so that they take up most of the frame. Sometimes, beginning photographers believe that they need to include the entire body. That's not necessary. Getting up close and personal can result in images that are more visually interesting and intimate.

quote

"Children are natural Zen masters; their world is brand-new in each and every moment." ~John Bradshaw, author and philosopher

ABOUT THIS PHOTO *Dreamy eyes of a young girl in repose are captured in a romantic and vintage style. Taken at ISO 100, f/3.5, and 1/125 second. ©Abi Campbell / www.abicampbellphotography.com*

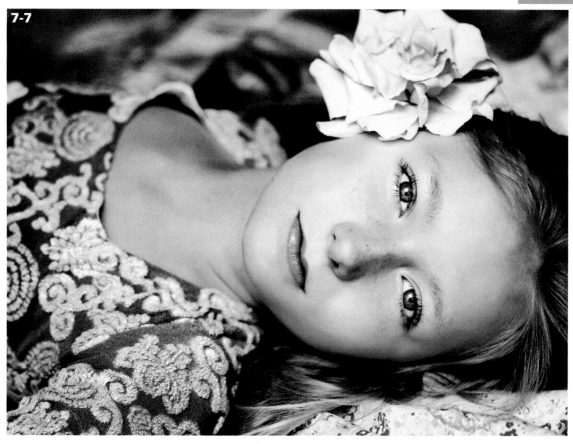

7-7

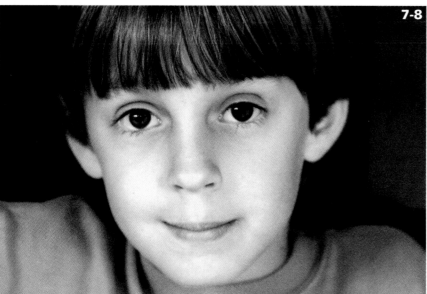

7-8

ABOUT THIS PHOTO
My nephew Benjamin exhibits a savvy yet elfish sweetness that beautifully reveals his nature. His dark and penetrating eyes convey openness and trust. Taken at ISO 800, f/5.6, and 1/50 second. ©Ginny Felch / www.photographing children.com

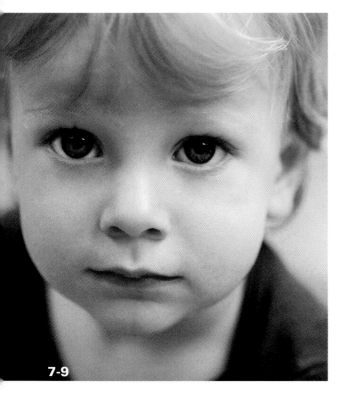

7-9

ABOUT THIS PHOTO *Could you look into these eyes and not feel a connection with this wide-eyed, penetrating expression? Well, I couldn't, but I'm his "Gammy!" Taken at ISO 400, f/3.2, and 1/200 second. ©Ginny Felch / www.photographingchildren.com*

When a child is gazing, observing, listening, or thinking, the eyes are generally wide open, and the face is soft and relaxed, as in 7-10 and 7-11. If you can encourage those moments while making a photograph, by all means do so.

After you go beyond the fear that you should be making the child smile or laugh, you might be pleasantly surprised by the character and soulfulness that comes forth in your imagery.

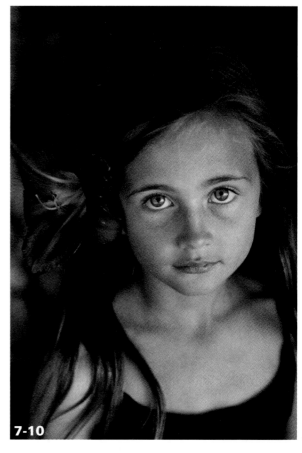

7-10

ABOUT THIS PHOTO *This reflective and musing expression really draws you into this portrait of the little girl in the garden. The circular line of her shirt frames her face delicately. Taken at ISO 320, f/5.6, and 1/125 second. ©Patrisha McLean / www.patrishamclean.com*

ABOUT THIS PHOTO *Perhaps his first experience with spaghetti evoked this perplexed little fella's expression. Taken at ISO 1000, f/3.5, and 1/250 second.* ©Jen Sherrick / www.jensherrickphotography.com

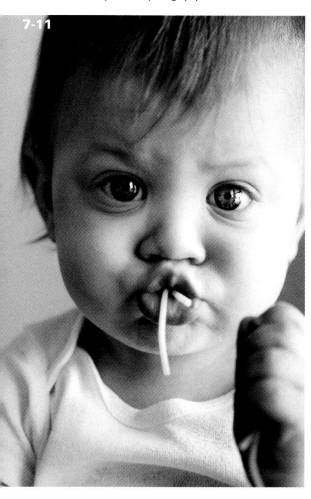

7-11

CAPTURING THE PERFECT SMILE

Smiles are okay, too, if they are not forced just for the photograph. Even if you choose to have children smile, try to find the moment in which the smiles are subtle or natural looking, as in 7-12.

Of course, a fine line exists between pensiveness and petulance, and you learn to discern the difference with experience. This difference often lies in what could be called "sweetness." When a child is looking at you, all it might take to evoke that sweetness is a little smile of your own or a subtle tilt of your head.

INVOLVING YOUR SUBJECTS WITH NATURE

When you are outside with a child, isn't it ironic to see what attracts her? You brought along the bubbles, balloons, and other entertainment only to find that she looks down, picks up an interesting rock or a broken shell, tosses it, smells or tastes it, and absorbs it in any way she can. You planned the trickery, and it didn't work!

In 7-13, a magical moment was created when this little girl discovered a beach treasure and became absorbed with it. Try to avoid reverting to "Put that down; it's dirty," or "Look at the red balloon." You might lose the chance to observe and capture a child full of wonder.

A child sees a blue bird, skips over to try to touch it, and then plops down in the tickly grass, getting grass stains on her clean shorts. That's when to click the shutter and thank your lucky stars for the gift of the expressiveness of childhood (if you can just get the mothers to play along).

tip

When photographing children in nature, please be wise, careful, and safe. Don't leave toddlers unsupervised and watch out for prickly or poisonous plants, snakes, and other intruders. Work with an assistant if you want to be extra cautious.

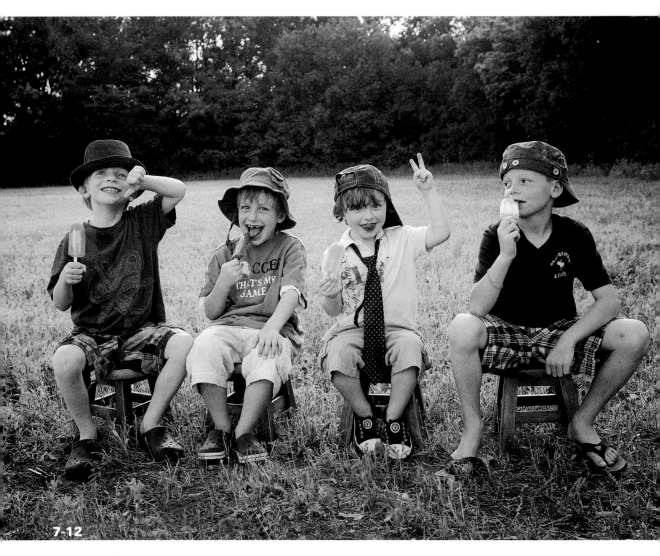

7-12

ABOUT THIS PHOTO *The photographer has evidently set things up for a hot afternoon play fest, and that is exactly what we see here. The boys are unabashedly and naturally going for the fun! Taken at ISO 640, f/6.3, and 1/250 second. ©Mary Schannen / www.melangephoto.com*

Are you getting it? Don't fight the child's natural instinct for wonder and play; join in — even anticipate and encourage it. What is more interesting in your photograph, a red balloon or a seashell? I make this point here and repeat it many times: Plan it, find the light, be prepared, and then let go. Let go and enjoy the spontaneity and remarkable whimsy of the child.

When you are at the beach or the park, find a location where the light is compelling and settle into the spot with your subject, as in 7-14, where the light is hitting the side of the child's face while she entertains herself with a dandelion.

ABOUT THIS PHOTO

A quiet and involved moment at the beach reminiscent of a vintage illustration was beautifully composed by the photographer. Florabella Vintage action, Summer II was used creatively in post-processing. (See Chapter 11 for more ideas.) Taken at ISO 200, f/2.0, and 1/3200 second. ©Valeria Spring / www.theredballoon photography.com

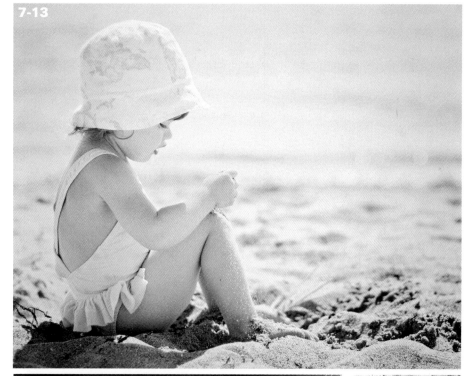

7-13

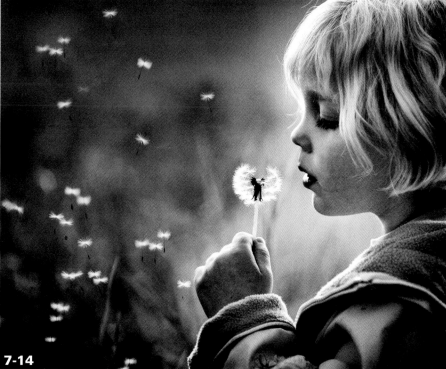

7-14

ABOUT THIS PHOTO

The photographer caught this child in the moment, as she was blowing on dandelion seeds, intentionally taking advantage of the late afternoon angle of the sun for stunning rim light. Taken at ISO 320, f/3.2, and 1/125 second. ©Michelle Walker / www.walkerportraits.com

Find a comfortable place to sit down on the grass, on a rock, or stump. Try to keep your voice at a whisper. "Shhh, listen! Tell me what you hear." The child will quiet down, perhaps widen his eyes, maybe look a bit to the side with his eyes, and begin to listen.

Wherever you are, there will always be something to listen to. It might be the bird chirping, the branches scratching together, a truck honking, or a dog barking. In that very brief moment when the child makes the switch from being conscious of having his photograph taken to the quiet act of listening, you can capture some natural, candid, and expansive expressions.

In 7-15, the children are so engaged in nature or with each other that they are no longer self-conscious that their picture is being taken.

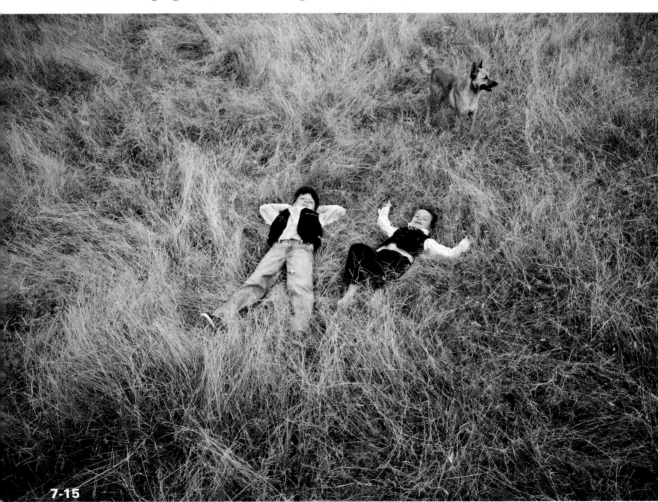

7-15

ABOUT THIS PHOTO *You can see a charming unity between these siblings lying down in a field. Even though the boys are centered, the dog's placement in the composition draws your eye to him. Taken at ISO 2000, f/5, and 1/640 second. ©Rachel Owens / www.rachelowensphotography.com*

"There is a garden in every childhood, an enchanted place where colors are softer, and the morning more fragrant than ever again." ~Elizabeth Lawrence

Trees, rocks, ponds, flowers, and so on are readily available props and backgrounds that abound in nature. Trees can be used to lean on, hide behind, and sit under. Their umbrella of branches and leaves can provide shade, cool air, and relief from the unappealing raccoon-eye look that strong overhead light can create.

Sometimes the environment itself can set a mood that can be captured without even showing the faces of your subjects, as in 7-16. You get the feeling of camaraderie and adventure from their body language and the magical mood from the setting. Notice the vibrant composition that frames the children.

When photographing on location, don't forget to get permission from the owners of private property before conducting your photo shoot.

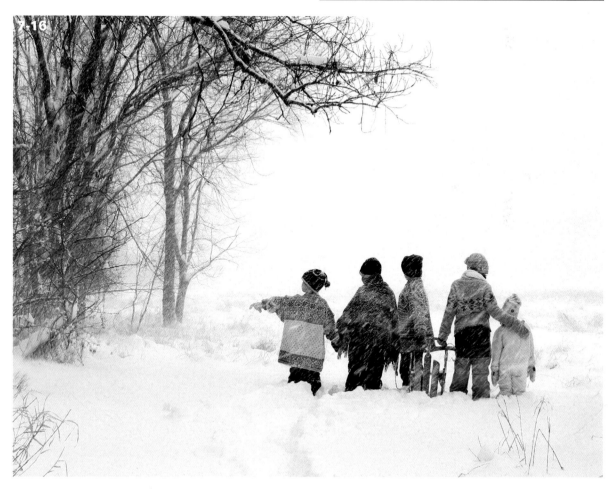

7-16

ABOUT THIS PHOTO *The enjoyment of a school snow day is revealed in this photograph. Notice the leading lines created by the edge of the forest. Taken at ISO 400, f/11, and 1/60 second.* ©Theresa Smerud / www.theresasmerud.com

Find a field, an expansive meadow, or shoreline, and ask the children to line up on a plane parallel to your camera view. Tell them you are going to walk away, and when you wave your hand, they can move toward you, but not to look at you or the camera. They can look at each other or at something in the distance and talk to each other or tell stories or secrets. After you wave your hand, you can start shooting away. You have set the scene and given them freedom within it.

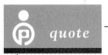

quote | "Give a little love to a child, and you will get a great deal back." ~John Ruskin

When they arrive by your side, ask them to turn around and go back to where they started. Follow them closely as well as from a distance, developing your photographic story as you go.

STUDYING BODY LANGUAGE, GESTURES, AND MOVEMENT

People watching with a keen eye should become your hobby as you seek to capture ever more interesting photos of children.

The images in 7-17 were taken as a result of intense people-watching. I began to take walks at the local beach in my town, during low tide on foggy days. Often these walks took place in the morning when the mist was lifting from the sand as the sun rose over the nearby mountain. It was so peaceful and quiet, and the few figures I saw really stood out as light silhouettes against the sand and shore. It became intriguing to observe the simplicity of the elements: the birds, footprints, dogs, and people. The low tide created vast smooth surfaces that offset the living and moving creatures.

I began to see the tide line as a music staff, and the people, birds, and dogs as notes of music for songs of life. Their gestures, as I stood far away with a telephoto lens, were spontaneous, often playful, and sometimes somber. After months of observing these intriguing scenes, my eye for children's portraits changed. This experience encouraged me to let go more, to try to control less, to appreciate the purity and uniqueness of the natural, human gesture. You can do a similar exercise in the surroundings where you live or on your next vacation.

This type of quiet observation improves your appreciation of, and ability to capture, more natural and sensitive portraits.

Of course, while the beach may be an ideal place for you or others to observe people, the financial district in the city, a sports field, a local park, a shopping mall, or even a farmers' market are also excellent venues.

If you are going to photograph children, watching their natural movements and spontaneous gestures can give you great insight and inspiration, as in 7-18, where the sprightly little toddler keeps her balance while walking on cobblestone, or 7-19, where the little girl digs her hands through the sand and low tide. Her reflection in the water and the line drawn to her hands creates a perfect composition. Becoming familiar with natural gestures might just make the difference between a static-looking pose and a genuine one.

ABOUT THIS PHOTO *This series of beach scenes reveals the grace of the natural movements and gestures of beach-goers ambling unaware of my camera. Taken at ISO 100, f/16, and 1/125 second. ©Ginny Felch / www. photographingchildren.com*

7-17

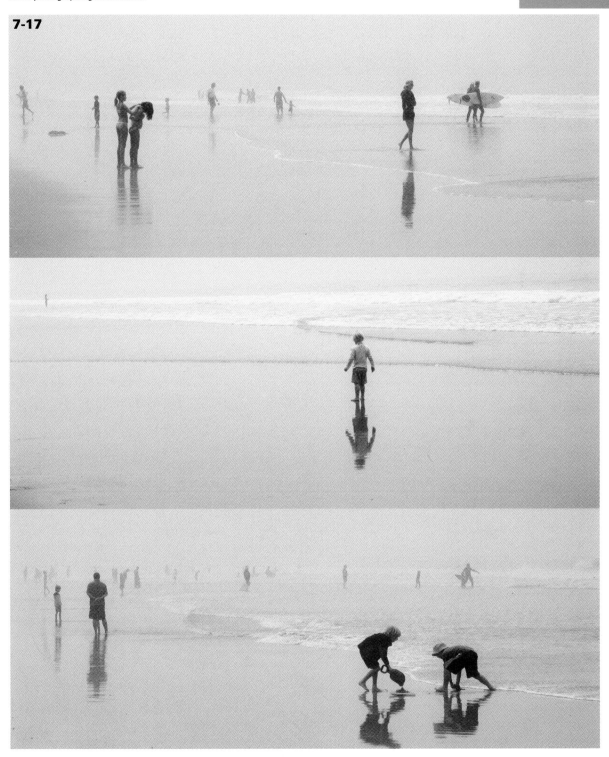

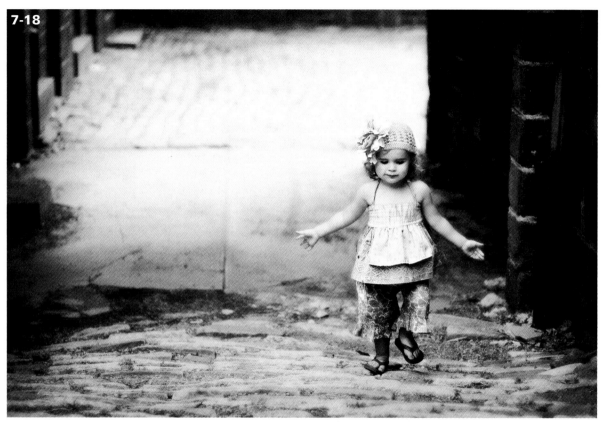

7-18

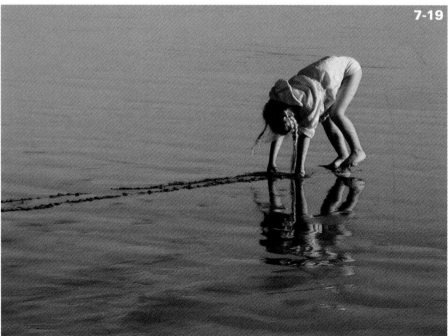

7-19

The boy in 7-20 is so absorbed in his play that he seems unaware of being photographed. If the photographer had asked him to pose or try to look natural, she would not have captured the easy gesture that you see in the image. Little boys and their toy boats are classic and captivating subjects.

x-ref Chapter 8 can help you understand the specific challenges and rewards when photographing each developmental stage of a child's life.

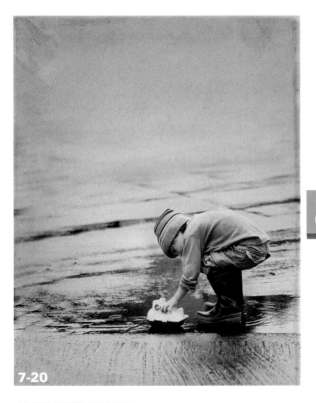

7-20

ABOUT THIS PHOTO *The little boy absorbed in directing his toy boat into a channel took no notice of the photographer. Embellished in post-production using Nik filters and Nichole Van textures. Taken at ISO 640, f/5.0, and 1/200 second. ©Mary Schannen / www.melangephoto.com*

TELLING A STORY WITH YOUR PHOTOGRAPHS

Creating intimacy in a child's photograph always captures the parents' heart. A portrait is a wonderful opportunity to allow unabashed cuddling, kissing, or otherwise relating to another person, pet, or toy. Adding a warm and inviting environment and soft lighting to a child's outward affection can enable you to create a photograph that is so much more than a snapshot.

As an exercise, the next time you are at a park or crowded shopping center, specifically watch children and parents relating. If you keep your eyes and heart open, you can see obvious and subtle exchanges between mother and child or father and child. Sometimes, it is a glance, a gentle pat, holding hands, or a quiet talk. Take a minute before you launch into your next photo shoot and observe how the children interact with their parents and use their natural body language and interactions to add life and spontaneity to your work.

tip While you supervise, let the children have a look at your camera and maybe even fire off a shot or two. They will be amazed at being allowed to play with an adult's "toy." They will want to make a lot of shots so you can use this as a reward for doing as you ask.

As you photograph children with parents or grandparents, you can invite a situation in which this kind of exchange might happen. It might take a little coaxing, such as "Can you snuggle a little closer?" You might suggest that a parent read to a child or vice versa. Dreamy looks out windows or into the sea give a sense of togetherness. A mother looking into her baby's eyes conveys intimacy.

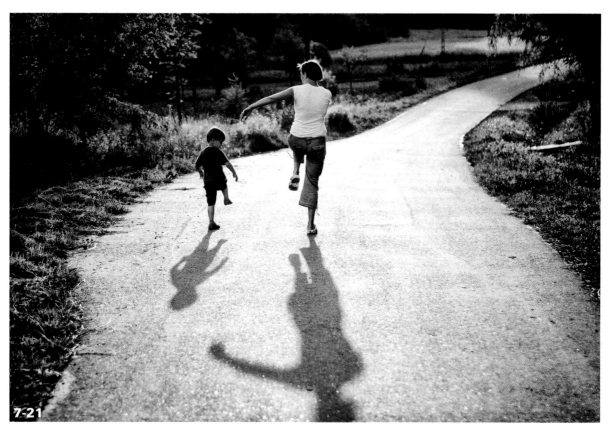
A mom skipping down a path with a child, even if you can't see the faces, tells a story about a relationship, as in 7-21. Don't underestimate the power of this kind of photograph. Faces only tell part of the story.

Involving a child with something or someone adored, or in play, often makes it easier to make a strong statement in a photograph. It is a great distraction to the child and often a great comfort. Consider some of these scenarios when taking photos of a child or children:

- Two sisters reading quietly on a couch

- A child playing a piano

- A toddler with her cuddly stuffed lamb

ABOUT THIS PHOTO *The photograph of a mom and her son as they skip together playfully was composed elegantly on the curve of the road. The shadows are as interesting to observe as the subjects. Taken at ISO 200, f/2.8, and 1/250 second.* ©*Aneta Ludwig / www.anetaludwig.com*

- A child and his dog or cat
- Children playing dress-up
- Sisters picking flowers together
- A father and children fishing
- A child looking at his reflection
- A child tossing stones into water

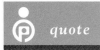 *quote*   "Everything is ceremony in the wild garden of childhood." ~Pablo Neruda

Sometimes, a poignant story about a child can also be told by photographing his essence or only part of him. For example, try photographing the following:

- Baby or toddler shoes that are well worn
- A small chair with a child's loved doll or stuffed animal
- A baby's feet peeking out from under the covers
- A baby's hands in the hands of a parent
- The back of a toddler holding on to Mom's skirt or Dad's pants
- A summer dress blowing in the wind or hanging on a door

What you are going for here is a feeling, a mood, an expression. All of these elements take your photograph one step closer to becoming a dynamic and beautiful portrait.

THE PSYCHOLOGY OF PHOTOGRAPHING CHILDREN

Unless you are someone whom children are attracted to immediately and unconditionally, you might at some time need a few tricks of the trade. Arriving as a stranger, carrying a strange black object (the camera), you could indeed be frightening for a younger child. Many children, however, by the age of four or five are ready and waiting with a generous smile pasted on their face the moment they realize you are there to make a photograph.

Most photographers prefer to photograph without gimmicks, tricks, or toys, but even without them, psychology is always in use. Try to beckon your innermost child to relate to the child or children before you. Take into consideration that they have been put up to this by parents, and may have been told to behave, not to make their usual faces, and so on. This suggests to them that this is going to be drudgery at best, so send the message to them that this will be fun, perhaps interesting, and over with quickly. Tell them that you don't need for them, or even want them, to smile like they do for a school photograph. If they are old enough (over two), immediately involve them with the camera to see whether you can strike up an interest.

Can you whistle like a bird or grunt like a pig? Talking like Donald Duck is a definite plus in the business of child photography. Silly noises are helpful in getting the attention of your subject and often result in some very interesting and silly expressions. Disagreeable or frustrated young children (especially those younger than three-years-old) sometimes require toys or gimmicks to distract or please them. Even crying children can sometimes be cheered up with a simple toy. Child photographers are often great connoisseurs of toys! If you want to engage a child in a photo session, try packing a few items like these: quacking ducks, barking dogs, oinking pigs, harmonicas, whistles, clickers, castanets, balloons, or bubbles.

My very favorite is Obie, also known as Bug Out Bob — the rubber doll shown in 7-22. When you squeeze him, the ears, eyes, nose, and mouth pop out. I use Obie sometimes to transfer any negativity

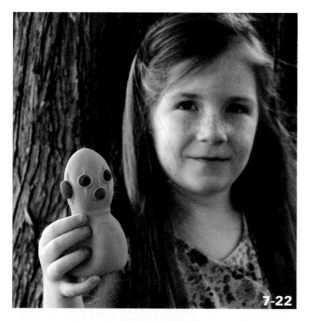

7-22

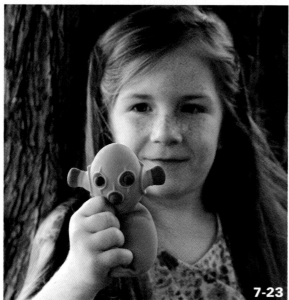

7-23

ABOUT THESE PHOTOS *Daisy demonstrates how Obie works. The ears, eyes, nose, and mouth pop out to the delight of children when I squeeze him. Naughty Obie! Taken at ISO 640, f/5.0, and 1/200 second.* ©Ginny Felch / www.photographingchildren.com

from the child to the puppet. For example, if the child exhibits "attitude" (negativity, petulance, or scowling), out comes Obie to take over that sentiment! It never fails.

Another good time to get out the "sure thing" toy is the end of a session when the children are finished, but you are not! In order to engage children, ask them questions such as:

- What is your favorite flavor of ice cream?
- Do you like pizza?
- Do you ever misbehave?
- Does your sister have a boyfriend?

These questions are sure to evoke unique expressions and distract the children from the camera.

Children are the least-inhibited humans on the planet. Take advantage of this unselfconscious time in their lives to capture their wonder and innocence. Avoid the temptation to make a photo shoot more complicated than it has to be. Forget the props and extraneous camera equipment and just spend some time getting to know your little subjects.

Talk to them and find out what they like. Put the camera down for a minute and listen to them. Let them look over your equipment and explain what you are going to do. Once they are more familiar with you and know that you are truly interested in them, getting honest expressions is easy.

Assignment

Tell a Story

Take a photo that captures a child's image — with a sibling or parent or not — telling a story. You can use a prop if you want, but be careful not to be too cutesy or have the subject(s) too posed. That is the challenge. It might literally be posed, but it should look natural to the viewer. Practice some of the approaches you have learned in terms of involving yourself with the child in order to evoke a sense of comfort and flow. This should reflect back into your image.

Here the assignment was completed with this photograph of a "special ritual the siblings have of placing their foreheads together. It is easy to see the trust and adoration between the two, especially from the younger one with his expressive eyes." This photograph won first prize on my Facebook Photographing Children contest, and Shari won a full edition of Adobe Photoshop. Taken at ISO 1000, f/4.5, and 1/80 second.

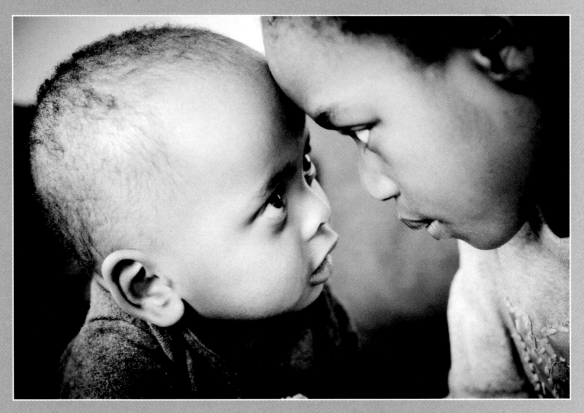

©Shari Yasseri

 Remember to visit www.pwsbooks.com after you complete this assignment and share your favorite photo! It's a community of enthusiastic photographers and a great place to view what other readers have created. You can also post comments, read encouraging suggestions, and get feedback.

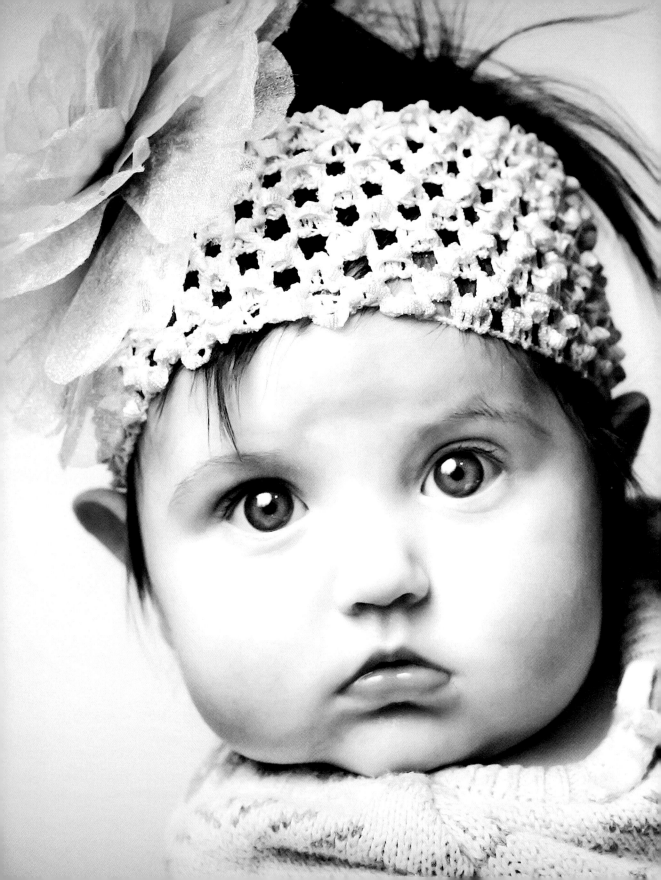

AGES, STAGES, AND GROUPS

©Cheryl Baase

Although it can be helpful to speak of children in terms of ages and stages, it is vital to keep in mind that every child is unique and individual. Your intuition is your best guide as to how to handle different ages and stages. Paying attention to the child's unique presence teaches you a great deal about how you might react and connect with him, in order to capture more of his true personality in a photograph.

If you are a parent, you will likely want to document your child's life to preserve your own memories of his or her birth and childhood. By capturing these photos you are literally illustrating a life story. How many times has a son or daughter asked, "What was I like when I was little?" Posed portraits from a photo studio or a school yearbook never tell the whole story. It's the pictures of children laughing or sleeping as babies, skiing down a hill for the first time, running in circles, reading quietly as a teenager, or a million other images that record a history of childhood that tell the real story. This chapter is a guide to each developmental stage of a child's life, addressing the challenges and rewards of photographing each stage with tips to help you along the way. The ideas covered in this chapter are meant to serve as guidelines developed from experience, rather than hard-and-fast rules. Your own experience with children is your best advisor.

NEWBORNS

Photographing newborns is not for the faint of heart. It takes a great deal of patience, but it is rewarding for many reasons. Who can deny the miracle of a newborn baby? Perhaps at no other time in a child's life do stunning changes take place on almost an hourly basis. This stage of development is endlessly fascinating to the parents as they watch each captivating gesture and expression to figure out what part of their baby looks like Mom or Dad.

To capture a photo of a newborn looking like a newborn (wrinkly skin, furry ears, and all), try to photograph the baby in the first couple of weeks of life. At this stage the babies are still very flexible and can be "folded" over into the fetal position and, for example, easily placed into Mom's hands, as in 8-1. In many instances, very young babies haven't yet developed the baby acne so their skin is more clear, which results in less retouching after the photo session.

tip For optimum results when photographing a newborn, keep the room a bit warmer than usual. This keeps the baby comfortable even when undressed for the naked-baby shots.

CHALLENGES

Newborns seem to arrive prewired to sense tension in a room. If mom is stressed about the photo shoot and tension is high, most often the baby can sense it and becomes very fussy. Calm moms make for calm babies so spend a minute soothing the mother's concerns about the photo session. Let her know that she can stop and comfort or feed the baby at any time.

Newborn's sessions are almost always a hurry-up-and-wait proposition. The baby nods off for half a second and you make a few photographs before the baby's eyes open and he or she starts to scream. You might be surprised to know that many of the seemingly serene infants in these photos were hysterical mere moments before their photograph was taken. Go ahead and take a few photographs of the crying, fussy, or yawning baby, as in 8-2; this is certainly a big part of a developing infant.

tip Because newborns are often reddish or slightly jaundiced, it can be more flattering to convert the images to black and white for a more timeless look.

ABOUT THIS PHOTO
The sleeping and smiling baby is folded and placed into the mother's hands. This can only be done with a very new newborn. Taken at ISO 1600, f/4.0, and 1/400 second. ©Theresa Smerud / www.theresasmerud.com

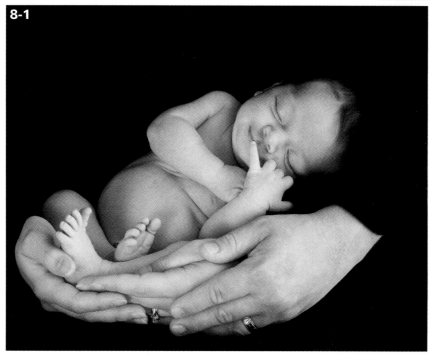

ABOUT THIS PHOTO
Great big, expressive yawns from a tiny newborn are great fun to capture spontaneously. Taken at ISO 800, f/2.8, and 1/60 second. ©Zofia Waig / www.zofiaphoto.com

8-2

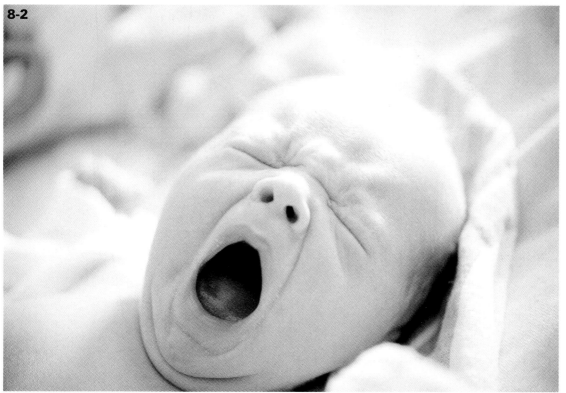

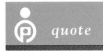
Don't photograph a naked baby on any surface that isn't washable. Backgrounds, furniture, parents, and photographers can and will be wet on or drooled upon by the little bundle of joy, so plan accordingly. You may want to have on hand a stash of inexpensive solid color (white is always great) blankets to wrap or lay the baby on.

Very young newborns have not developed the ability to focus their eyes yet, so it is easy to get an image of a very cross-eyed baby. If a baby is getting the cross-eyed look, you may want to turn the baby's head into a different position or just wait a minute for a more pleasing expression.

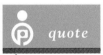
REWARDS

The soft cheeks, wrinkly skin, and tightly curled fists of a newborn are unmistakable. Capturing this stage is well worth the effort, and there are many photographers who specialize in newborn photography. Newborns can't talk back or run away. They are so flexible you can curl them up and let them sleep while you shoot away. Take the time to get the baby to sleep. Ask the mother to feed the baby just before she comes to the photo session so the baby arrives full and ready to nap. Wrapping an infant snugly in a blanket so that the arms and legs are tight against the body (also called swaddling) is an almost-guaranteed sleeping pill for infants. There are many resources on the Internet for handmade designs, such as Natalija Brunner's creations (www.daidalorange.com).

Rock the tightly swaddled baby until he or she is fast asleep (this usually takes about 15 minutes, so you have to be patient). When the infant is finally sleeping, you can move around freely, placing props, blankets, and even the baby, or babies, in just the right places, as in 8-3. There is nothing more universally appealing than the sight of a sleeping baby.

Newborns tend to be very floppy, so use the parents as a prop to hold the baby in their arms or even lay the baby over their shoulders, as shown in 8-4. This type of posing offers great opportunities for photographers and parents to come up with very unique, creative, and touching images.

BABIES

The first year of life presents one milestone after another. As babies grow older and can recognize and respond to people around them, their range of expressions and gestures increases, giving the children's photographer much more to work with. Darling expressions can be evoked by the simplest click of your tongue or breath on their cheeks. It seems like their smiles come unwarranted at this point because they have learned that smiling pleases the people around them.

THREE TO SIX MONTHS

Before they are able to walk, you can photograph babies in the three-to-six month age range sitting in a chair, lying on the grass, or holding themselves up by a table or wall. At this time, the mother, a babysitter, or older sibling can be a great asset to you as an assistant, just to watch carefully and make sure that the baby is safe at all times. It is important that you are comfortable with your camera and its settings so you can spend your time fully focused on the baby and her expressions rather than fiddling with your camera.

8-3

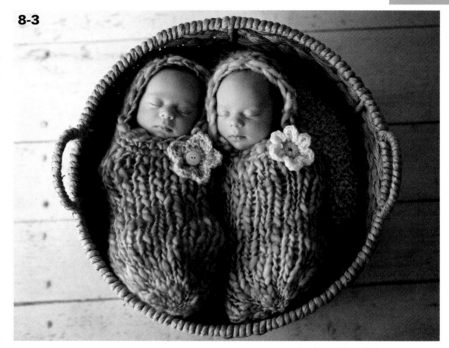

ABOUT THIS PHOTO
Newborn twins swaddled in hand-crocheted pods in a basket make a delightful portrait for posterity. Taken at ISO 200, f/2.8, and 1/200 second. ©Sara Kovacs / www.babybeanportraits.com

ABOUT THIS PHOTO
This very tender and beautiful portrait of a father supporting his newborn child was made by placing the baby by his shoulder after sleep set in. Taken at ISO 200, f/3.5, and 1/500 second. ©Sara Kovacs / www.babybeanportraits.com

8-4

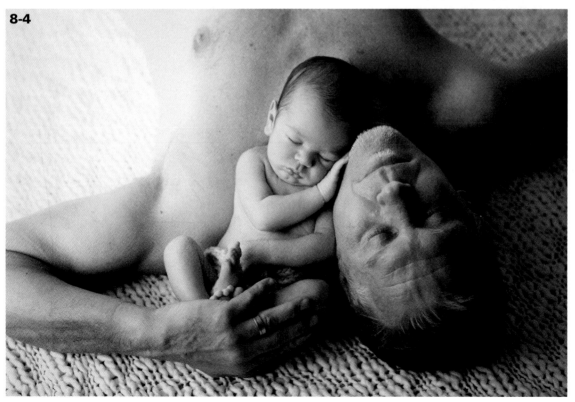

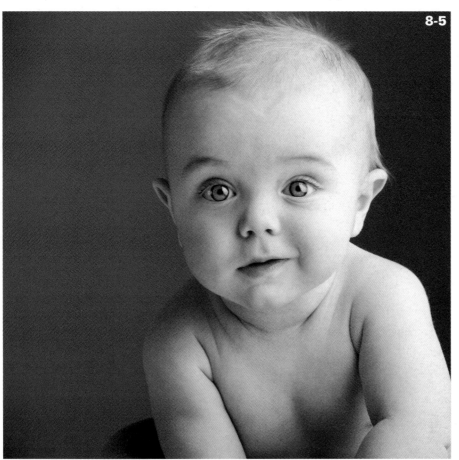

quote

"If a child is to keep his inborn sense of wonder, he needs the companionship of at least one adult who can share it, rediscovering with him the joy, excitement, and mystery of the world we live in." ~Rachel Carson

Between three and four months, wonderful and unique expressions can be elicited by parents, so it pays off to always have a camera nearby. Be sure to get down to the baby's level to seize the moment (see 8-5).

SIX TO TWELVE MONTHS

Between six and nine months, a baby is usually able to sit up, but isn't yet crawling — ideal for a photo opportunity. Babies often lean to one side or another like they are going to crawl, giving you ample opportunities for capturing their chubbiness. They imitate the faces you make at them and are able to hold on to a toy. Remember, everything goes into their mouth at this stage so be careful what you leave within their reach. Perch them on a table, a chair, or even in a favorite basket for a more creative twist on the typical baby portrait, as in 8-6.

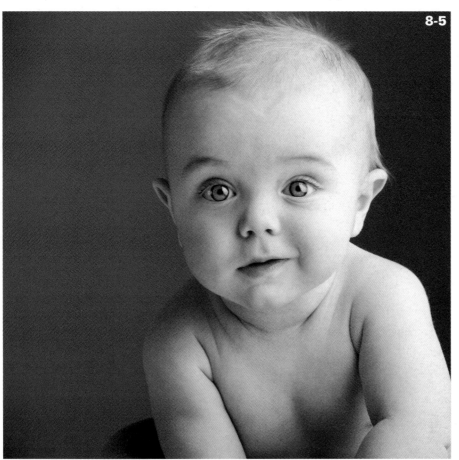

8-5

ABOUT THIS PHOTO
Be ready to capture those unique and amusing expressions that babies come up with spontaneously. Taken at ISO 200, f/9.0, and 1/250 second. ©Allison Tyler Jones / www.atjphoto.com

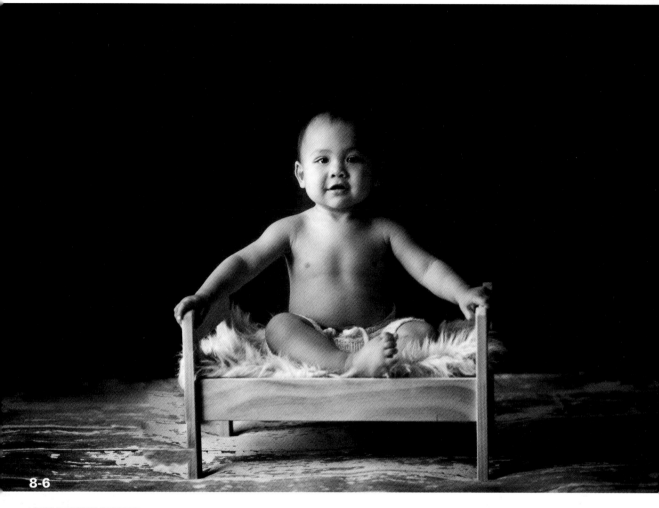

8-6

ABOUT THIS PHOTO *This little boy holds such a profound presence and confidence for his age. The soft window light gives the portrait dimension and mood, while highlighting his soft skin. Taken at ISO 200, f/1.4, and 1/200 second. ©Sara Kovacs / www.babybeanportraits.com*

Between nine and ten months, many babies begin crawling and might even be able to stand next to a chair while holding on. Make sure that any chair or prop you use to photograph a baby on is sturdy and won't tip over onto them. If the baby isn't steady, have Mom or an assistant stand just out of camera view to prevent any mishaps.

Most babies start walking at about the one-year mark, and this is a common milestone for parents to chronicle with a portrait. It is a perfect time to capture those first tentative steps when they walk, using their arms to give them balance, as in 8-7.

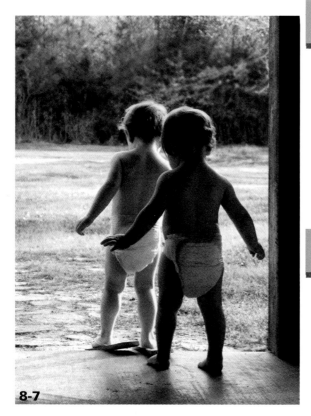

8-7

ABOUT THIS PHOTO *A photographer and the grandmother of these two girls captured the wobbling youngsters as they exited the house. The lines of the doorway frames them well, and the silhouetting light separates them from the background. Taken at ISO 1250, f/9.0, and 1/200 second. ©Elizabeth Sanford / www.momentsbyliz.com*

TODDLERS

Toddlerhood is defined by activity and movement. Toddlers are usually very responsive to toys and to your words and expressions. These little ones need to be in an environment where they have freedom to move and explore in complete safety. Their walking skills usually progress quickly from being a little clumsy to ambling at the speed of lightning.

note The latest generation of children has started to pose much earlier because parents and others constantly peer at them through cameras and cell phones, starting at the very moment of birth. This makes it a bit more challenging at times to elicit a natural expression, even from a toddler.

The toddler stage is characterized by a lot of growth and change, mood swings, and some negativity. Toddlers are long on will and short on skill. This is why they are often frustrated and misbehave.

quote "A three-year-old child is a being who gets almost as much fun out of a fifty-six dollar set of swings as it does out of finding a small green worm." ~Bill Vaughan

When working with toddlers, assess whether an assistant or parent present is an asset or liability. The parent in 8-8 was an asset. This photo turned out beautifully because she was holding and interacting with her child, so that the baby felt secure and comfortable.

A relaxed parent usually creates an atmosphere for a relaxed child, and the opposite is almost always true. If you have a parent who is overly coaching the child, you may want to kindly suggest that the child might perform better if she stepped back for a moment. This takes courage but is often worth it in the end.

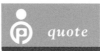

quote "A mother understands what a child does not say." ~Susan Sarandon

ABOUT THIS PHOTO Bright complementary colors and a contrast of uptown and rural make this photograph of a fashionable mother and child very contemporary. The mom's arms and legs provide a very safe and dynamic frame for the baby. Taken at ISO 200, f/2.5, and 1/800 second. ©Melanie Johnson / www.melaniejohnsonphotography.com

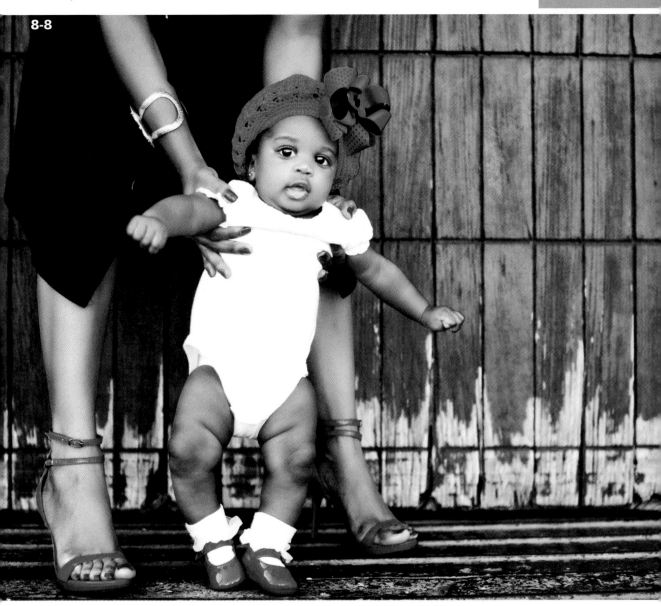

8-8

Activities such as peek-a-boo and blowing kisses are likely to induce charming reactions. Whistles, bells, and squeaky toys are likely get an expressive response. Some photographers like to make noises like dogs barking and cats meowing for a reaction. You might be better at pig noises or talking like Donald Duck.

Toddlers are distractible, so be armed with many entertaining and spontaneous diversions. Being a children's photographer requires that you learn to be comfortable being silly and uninhibited.

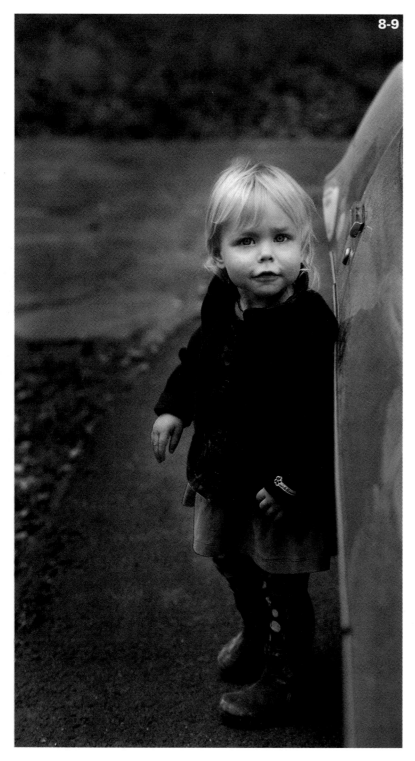

8-9

ABOUT THIS PHOTO *The color and reflection on the car gave me a frame, and the car itself offered support when photographing this toddler dressed for a country excursion. Taken at ISO 200, f/3.5, and 1/320 second. ©Ginny Felch / www.photographingchildren.com*

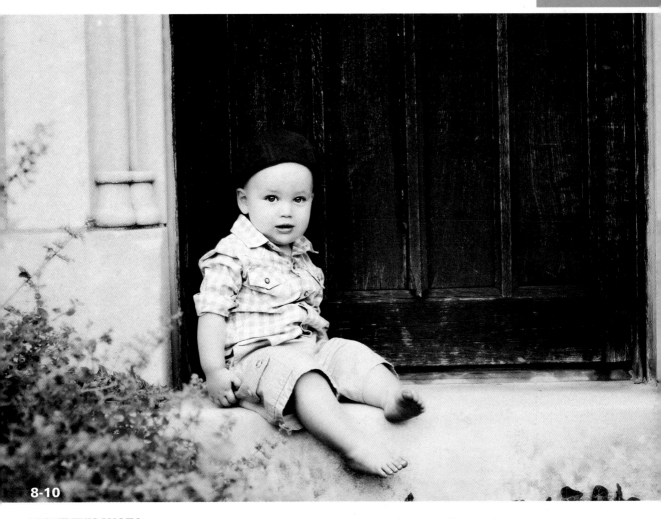

8-10

ABOUT THIS PHOTO *The step served as a useful perch to add support and structure for the baby. The stone door frame also provided a dynamic background and L-composition to enhance the photograph. Taken at ISO 400, f/2.8, and 1/200 second. ©Jen Carver / www.jencarverphotography.com*

Asking a child to stand near a strong vertical structure, as in 8-9, or propping a child on a door, as in 8-10, frames the child and provides a perch — someplace that is just off the ground that makes him or her hesitant to jump down and run around, allowing you a fleeting few seconds to get the shot. Other good perches are benches and tables. Always make sure there is an adult next to the child, just out of camera range, to catch the child if he or she should decide to make a jump for it.

Give toddlers something to become involved with while photographing them. The portraits in 8-11, 8-12, and 8-13 show different tactics taken with toddlers during a photography session. Props such as ledges, chairs, and beds work well if the toddler is willing and able to sit still. If not, offering them flowers or crayons or something to keep their hands busy can keep their attention for a few minutes. Of course, if you are a parent at home with your children, these things happen quite naturally, and then all you need to do is capture them!

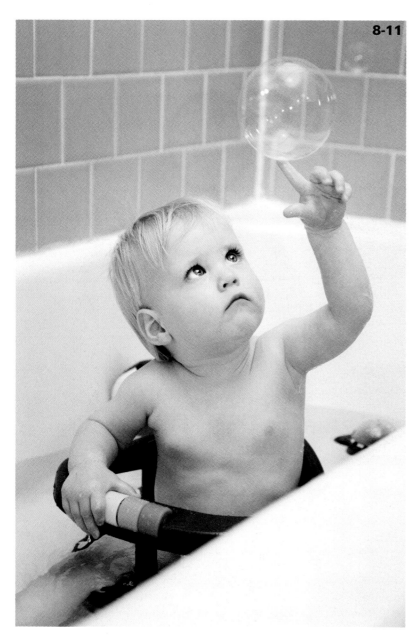

8-11

PRESCHOOLERS

Every child photographer has a favorite age. For many, preschoolers present the best of all worlds. Preschool children are communicative, responsive, spontaneous, playful, silly, talkative, and generally charming.

Many preschoolers are trusting, engaging, and fun to be with. Children who are three to about four-and-a-half years old stand out because they are still babies in all the best ways. They haven't usually lost their chubby baby cheeks, as in 8-14, nor given up their unself-conscious and innocent expressions.

ABOUT THIS PHOTO *A little girl's preoccupation with a small flower offered the photographer a still moment with this toddler. The tussled hair and soft coloring add to the mood. Taken at ISO 200, f/2.8, and 1/125 second. ©Lori Nordstrom / www.nordstromphoto.com*

8-12

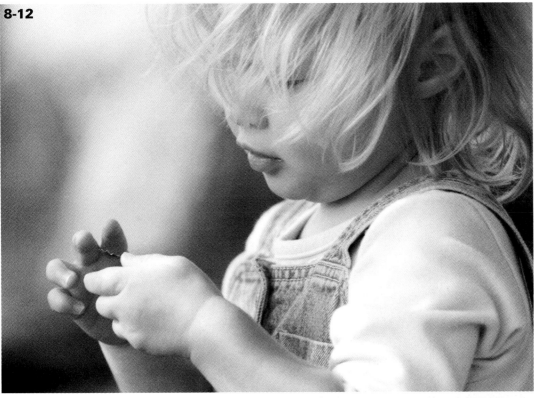

ABOUT THIS PHOTO
Involving a friendly family pet offers humor and tenderness. The dog here seems to be intent on supporting the baby on the bed, while the photographer takes advantage of exquisite window light. Taken at ISO 500, f/3.5, and 1/125 second. ©Elizabeth Sanford / www.momentsbyliz.com

8-13

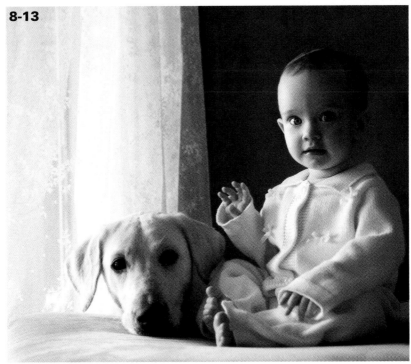

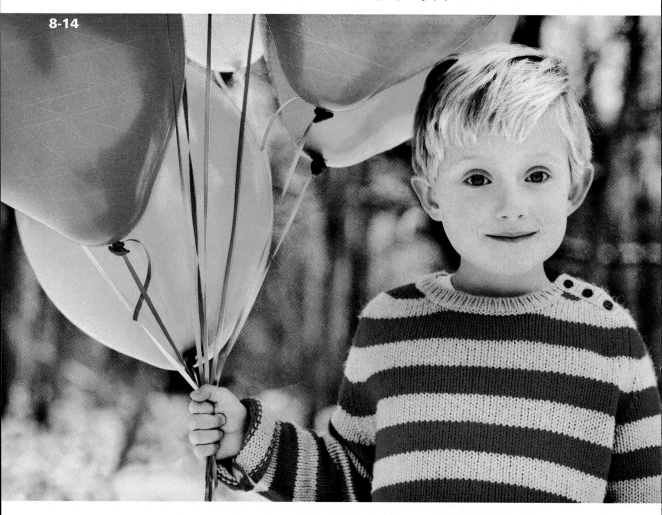

8-14

You can entice a three-year-old to stay put for a few minutes as you engage him or her in conversation. This is one of the times to ask quietly "Shhh! What do you hear? Do you hear the birds? Can you hear the truck?" The expressions that come forth are looks of inquisitiveness, engagement, preoccupation, and delight. Your reactions can elicit further responses as well.

Stuffed animals, shells, flowers, pets, and little trucks can be great props and also encourage more natural body language, as in 8-15 and 8-16. However, you usually don't have to worry too much about a child at that age over-posing, because he is usually not that self-conscious yet.

Capturing quiet activities such as reading, daydreaming, or snuggling with a pet can also lead to compelling images.

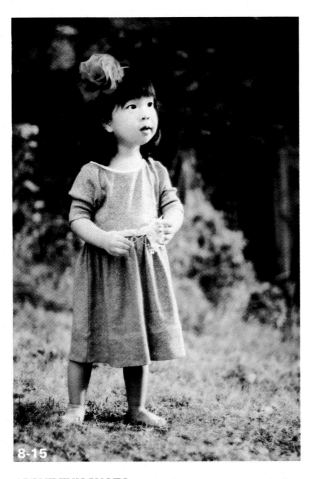

8-15

ABOUT THIS PHOTO *A sense of wonder and moment of reflection can be captured more easily when a toddler is distracted by nature. Taken at ISO 400, f/1.4, and 1/2500 second. ©Jen Carver / www.jencarverphotography.com*

SCHOOL-AGE CHILDREN

As children grow up and start school they are exposed to more social interaction and, as a result, become more self-conscious. There is something about five- and six-year-olds that makes them ever-ready to pose with the big, cheesy grin with no provocation. You need to really listen and learn about these children, so that you can engage them in conversation or activity that distracts them from themselves.

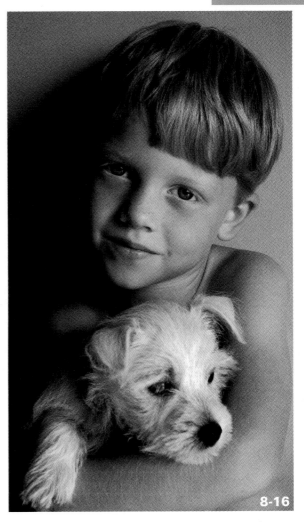

8-16

ABOUT THIS PHOTO *A puppy can certainly divert a child's attention from the business at hand, fortunately. His affection comes through both in expression and gesture. Taken at ISO 200, f/6.3, and 1/160 second. ©Heather Jacks / www.heatherjacksphotography.com*

They are on to the say-cheese tricks of the trade and consider it cooperative to smile broadly no matter what (well trained by some school photographers and well-meaning parents). It then becomes your challenge to distract them from that, as in 8-17 and 8-18, where the family dogs were the perfect solution. One way to do this is to

ABOUT THIS PHOTO *Nothing warms the hearts of children more than their dog, and this image shows a natural and tender moment proving just that. Taken at ISO 100, f/5.0, and 1/200 second. ©Angela Hibbert / www.angelahibbertphotography.com*

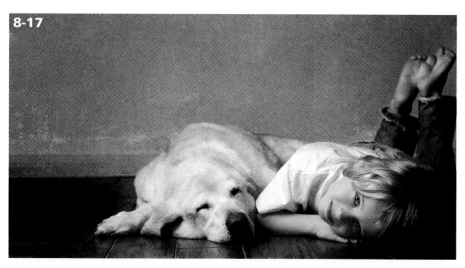

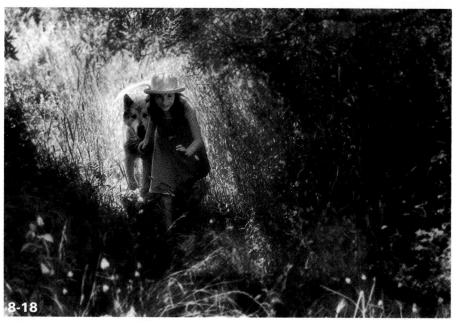

ABOUT THIS PHOTO *Our venture through the woods with her dog gives Daisy the kind of joy that shows in her body language and relaxed, ebullient gesture. The shallow depth of field was created in post-processing using blurring selectively. Taken at ISO 640, f/6.3, and 1/500 second. ©Ginny Felch / www.photographingchildren.com*

take a photograph of the cheesy grin and let children see the image. Then tell them that they don't have to do a big smile; they can do a quiet smile and ask them to do it. Take the shot and show them again. Eliciting their help can make your job much easier.

As they get older, children have developed interests and passions that you can find out about in a sincere conversation.

Most of the difficulties that arise with overly cheesy kids are when parents are present. Children know their parents' buttons and push every one of them if they can. It is natural for parents to want their kids to look good, to not make those funny faces that Uncle Harry makes, to sit up straight, and so on. The tension this can add is palpable. Diffuse the situation by letting the parents know ahead of time what you expect from the photo session; that you don't expect the kids to be perfect and that, while you are photographing them, you are in charge.

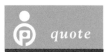

quote

"A sister is a little bit of childhood that can never be lost." ~Marion C. Garretty

Children of just about any age tire of the whole process, no matter how interesting you make it, within a relatively short period of time. Take advantage of these precious moments and work as quickly as you can. Depending on the age of the children, this magical time can last from 10 minutes to 45 minutes at the most. Let this be a warning, particularly if you are being hired to get the job done.

TWEENS AND TEENS

Adolescents, also known as tweens and teens, at their best, can be respectful and involved and, at their worst, sulky and disinterested. They are least likely to buy in to any hype and appreciate a more straightforward approach. Many teens want to look cool, and it will behoove you to figure out what cool is for them. Their parents might differ in their opinions, however. It is up to you as a photographer to make it work.

In some way, you must invite teens into the process, whether it is subtle or direct. Involving them in the photography discussion is a good possibility, giving them the respect they would like to have and making them feel they have a choice in the matter.

GET TO KNOW YOUR KIDS AGAIN Sometimes, taking photographs of other people's children is easier than taking photographs of your own. In fact, almost always. But maybe that's because it is easier to get frustrated with your own kids when you are trying to get them to cooperate for photos. While you might wheedle and cajole your neighbor's kids into doing what you want, you expect your own to hurry up and get with it! Try to step back and pretend like you're getting to know your kids for the first time. The results may be photographs that are timeless in quality.

Some of the most beautiful and profound images can come from a quiet photography session with an adolescent child whose trust you have earned. Notice the eyes and the serious facial expressions of the young man in 8-19 and the girls in 8-20. Some day, they will look back on this photograph and probably remember how they felt at that age and, maybe, what they were thinking at the time the images were captured.

In the meantime, you will have captured very meaningful portraits. These photos portray children on the cusp; they are still children, but there is an older, wiser look in their eyes.

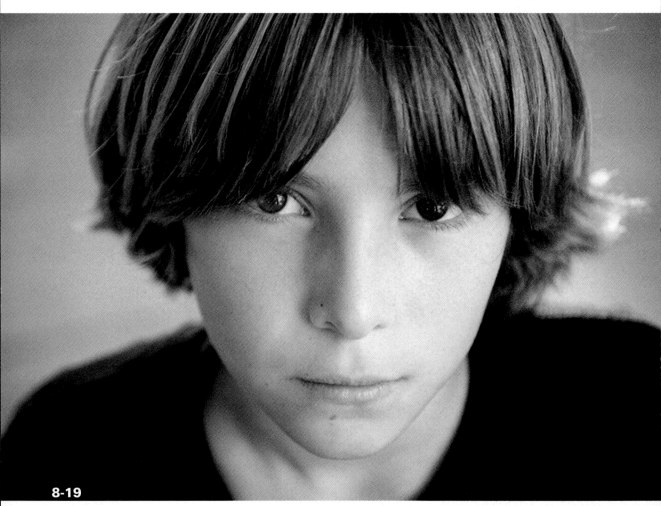

8-19

ABOUT THIS PHOTO *This is a direct, captivating close-up of an adolescent boy that makes you want to look deeply into his eyes. Taken at ISO 100, f/2.8, and 1/250 second. ©Matthew Reoch / www.mattreoch.com*

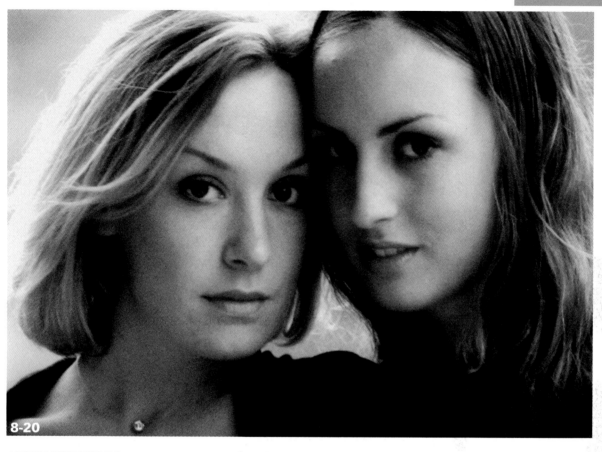

8-20

ABOUT THIS PHOTO *This glamorous shot of two teenage sisters is bold yet soft, just as the girls are. Taken at ISO 400, f/4, and 1/125 second. ©Ginny Felch / www.photographingchildren.com*

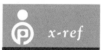 quote | "Family faces are magic mirrors. Looking at people who belong to us, we see the past, present, and future." ~Gail Lumet Buckley

x-ref | For tips on how to change the look of your photographs after they have been captured, turn to Chapter 10.

When I arrived to photograph these young teenaged sisters in their home, they were scurrying around, trying new makeup, fixing their hair, and excitedly throwing around clothing.

Had I been in a hurry to get this done, I would have been frustrated, because I thought they would be ready when I arrived.

Instead, I decided to reawaken the teenager in myself and jump right into the preparations and excitement. The drama and playfulness added great energy to the day, and by the time they were photographed, as shown in 8-20, I had earned their trust and respect. We had great fun as well!

The theme here is that all human beings want to be respected and honored. When children are little, you might be able to get away with tricks and treats for a while, but basically, you really need to relate authentically to your subjects in order to produce natural and illustrative photographs.

Often photos taken of tweens and teens commemorate a milestone — graduations, first dances, rites of passage, and so on, as in the photograph in 8-21. The clothing choice, setting, and lighting make it a timeless portrait.

If you are photographing two or more pre-teens together, as in 8-22 and 8-23, the mood will probably be quite different (more energetic and fun) than when you're photographing them by themselves. Adolescence can be an awkward time for children, so the more fun you can elicit, the more expressive and contemporary your images will turn out.

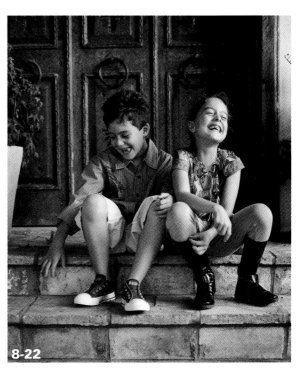

ABOUT THIS PHOTO *Two casual and engaged siblings in a doorway entrance are being really silly and having fun, something that certainly can't be forced at these ages! Taken at ISO 200, f/2.8, and 1/100 second. ©Allison Tyler Jones / www.atjphoto.com*

ABOUT THIS PHOTO *My son, Zach after sixth-grade graduation, looked so mellow and laid back at the beach in his new clothes. The bright, clean background and the L-shape of the window of our beach house framed him beautifully. Taken at ISO 200, f/5.6, and 1/125 second. ©Ginny Felch / www.photographingchildren.com*

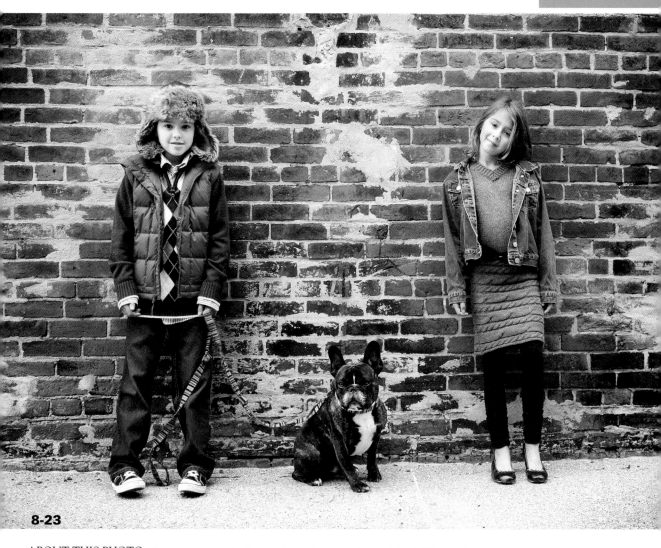

8-23

ABOUT THIS PHOTO *Allowing or encouraging teens or tweens to wear their own style of clothes feeds in to their security. This urban background and the inclusion of their dog contribute to the contemporary style. Taken at ISO 400, f/4.0, and 1/160 second. ©Jen Sherrick Photography / www.jensherrickphotography.com*

TEEN BOYS

Teen boys can be challenging to photograph. They usually have two modes: smiley or tough, with no in-between. They usually have to be bribed by a parent to get their photograph taken in the first place so your job is to make it as painless as possible for them. It's helpful to fire off a few shots, even if you know they aren't exactly what you are looking for, and give him a few, "That's great, looking good" comments to put him at ease. If he feels successful early on, he'll relax more quickly. The smiles come more easily and you get a natural expression, as shown in 8-24.

8-24

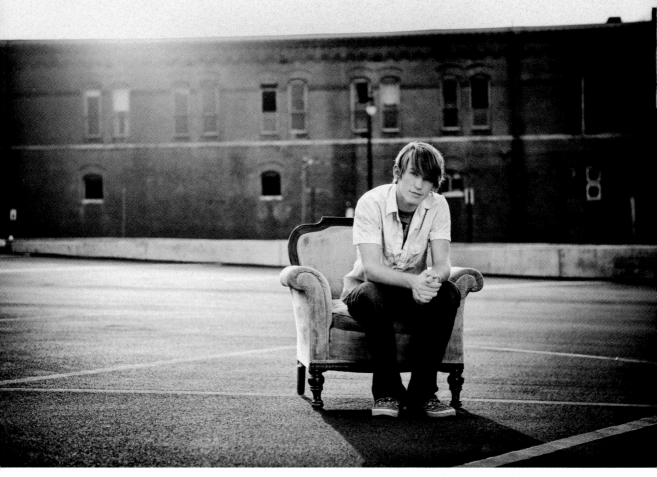

TEEN GIRLS

While teen boys are reluctant to be photographed, most teen girls are ready to be the next supermodel. They love to change outfits, try different poses, and will do just about anything you suggest to get the shot. Show them some of the shots you are taking as you go along to show them what is working and what isn't. Complimenting her on how she looks and how she's doing will keep confidence high and the energy flowing, as in 8-25.

PARENT AND CHILD

When you photograph families, spend some time photographing individual relationships within the family — that is, siblings, father/son, mother/daughter, and so on. This is extremely rewarding because there is usually special bonding and tenderness that comes to the surface when you are sensitive and encouraging.

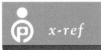

x-ref | For more on using leading lines like diagonals in your photography, see Chapter 5.

Sometimes an initial awkwardness disappears when you say something like, "Okay, guys, I want to see some serious snuggling!" The barriers come down, and you start to see some genuine connection going on before your eyes. It's almost as though they are waiting for your permission. That is when your heart beats fast and you are able to capture moments that will be treasured for generations.

When life gets frenetic and stressful, and the world news is depressing, fragile and profound moments, such as the one shown in 8-26, are very uplifting.

quote | "Call it a clan, call it a network, call it a tribe, call it a family. Whatever you call it, whoever you are, you need one." ~Jane Howard

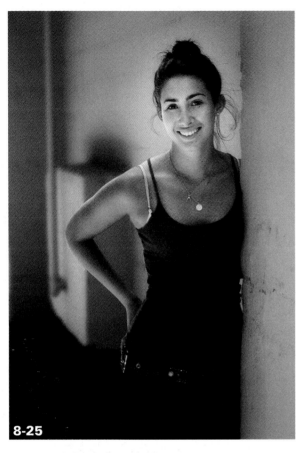

8-25

ABOUT THIS PHOTO *This teenage girl was already confident, but even so I gave her positive feedback during the session, evoking a natural and beautiful expression. Taken at ISO 200, f/6.3, and 1/60 second. ©Ginny Felch / www.photographingchildren.com*

GROUPING FAMILIES

As you photograph children's relationships with parents and siblings, keep in mind that the opportunities to tell a story in your images are waiting for you at every turn. The story can be about connection, either with each other, their environment, or activities.

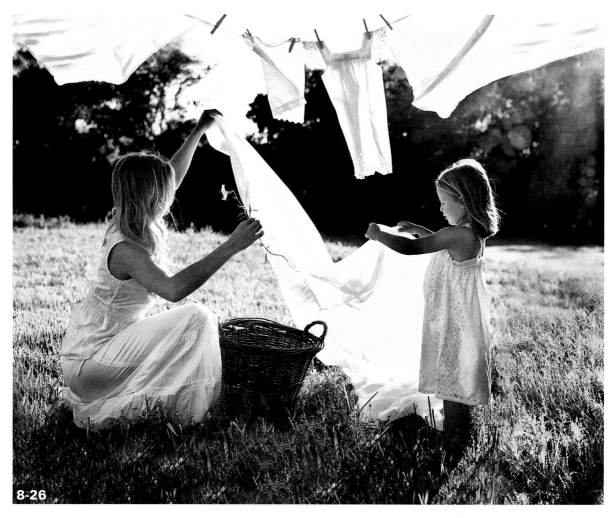

ABOUT THIS PHOTO *Evoking memories and nostalgia, the photographer set up a motherly scene, using late afternoon back lighting to make the sheets glow and give haloes to the subjects. The composition and gestures enhance the sense of connection. Taken at ISO 200, f/5.0, and 1/400 second. ©Mary Shannen / www.melangephoto.com*

Don't rule out dads in terms of eliciting emotional connection. For example, in 8-27 the photographer captured Dad in a seriously tender snuggle, and the blissful feelings of this special moment. The father was not afraid to show his emotions, and that was captured forever.

If you want to evoke a connection between people, you must relate to it yourself and let it mirror back ... from your eyes, via your heart, and back out through the lens!

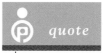 *quote*

"The family is one of nature's masterpieces." ~George Santayana, photographer

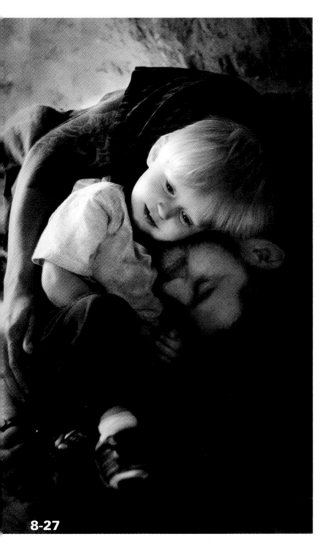

8-27

ABOUT THIS PHOTO *Playtime can be an opportune moment for some extra snuggles, as seen in this peaceful and tender image of a father and his young son. The father's arms provide a circular composition that wraps up the story. Taken at ISO 400, f/2.2, and 1/100. ©Rachel Owens / www.rachelowensphotography.com*

Another dad and his daughter roughhouse in 8-28, this simple studio portrait of a connection worth capturing. Placing them in the studio where the background is simple and the light is predetermined offers a freedom for expression and spontaneity.

Move in close for a tight shot of a mother and child, as in 8-29. The expressions here say it all.

SIBLINGS

If it is energy you are seeking when working with children, siblings generate it in abundance. It seems that their personalities bounce off of one another, which can be fun to witness and capture.

Sibling relationships are primal and authentic, for better or worse. If there is tension, and there usually is, it shows. If you can be there to provide some incentive for fun, competition, or yes, even physical connection, your images will shine.

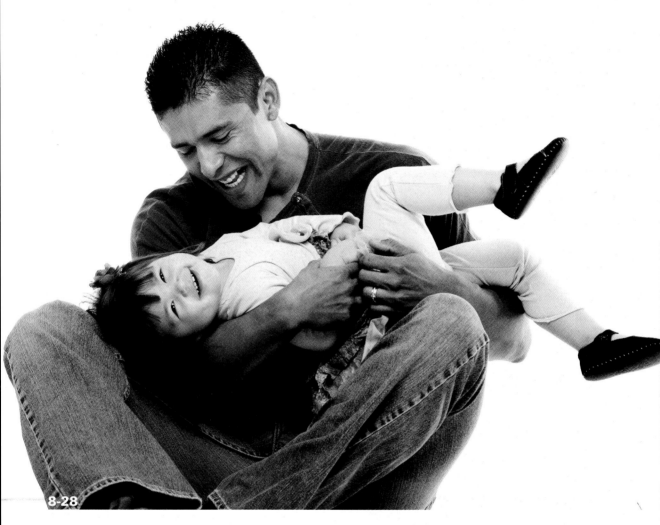

8-28

ABOUT THIS PHOTO *A contemporary studio portrait of a father and his wiggly toddler in a silly moment is amusing and tender all at the same time. Taken at ISO 200, f/10, and 1/200 second. ©Allison Tyler Jones / www.atjphoto.com*

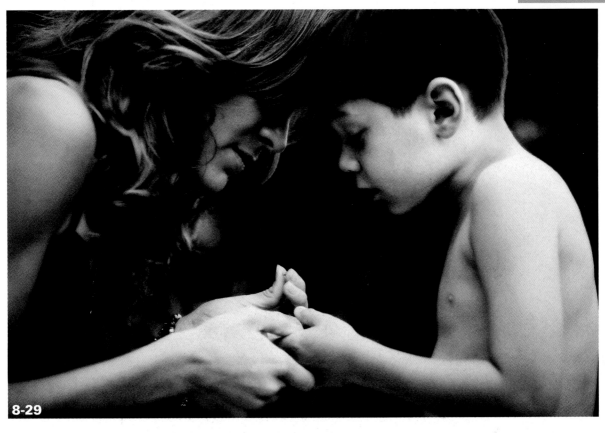

8-29

ABOUT THIS PHOTO *The love and connection is obvious between this young boy and his attentive mother. Moving in close puts the focus on the relationship. Taken at ISO 400, f/2.8, and 1/250 second. ©Marianne Drenthe / www.marmaladephotography.com*

Often the relationship reveals itself immediately without anything but your observation. It might not show through in conversation, but perhaps in body language, as in 8-30. Be on the lookout.

Don't enter into the session with preconceived notions and stereotypes such as boys will be boys or girls will be girls. Stay open to the possibility that your expectations can be blown right out of the water. Don't miss out on opportunities to surprise yourself and entertain the eye of the viewer.

Photographing siblings is a great opportunity to make a storytelling photograph, while the children are interacting with each other or the environment. Try to have them engaged in the same thing, even if it is the photographer, so that there is a semblance of unity, as in 8-31 and 8-32.

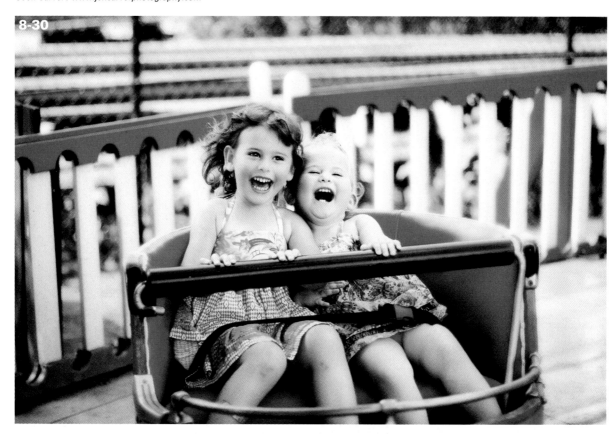

8-30

You can photograph siblings telling secrets, exploring nature as in 8-33, playing together as in 8-34, sharing pets, and so on. Always be prepared for spontaneous eruptions that can occur, no matter what you plan — some might work well for your photograph. A fit of laughter or surprise can tell a lot about siblings together and make a memorable photograph. Don't feel as though you must direct everything; let them discover some of these on their own.

Endless stories can be told in photographing siblings; you are limited only by your imagination!

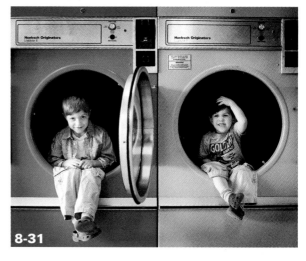

8-31

ABOUT THIS PHOTO

These teens are close enough in age that they have a tender relationship, and I brought them together in front of a modern painting in their home as a warm and textured background. I like the familiarity of the background for future referral and nostalgia.
Available window light helped create the soft, warm skin tones. Taken at ISO 1600, f/4.5, and 1/60 second. Ginny Felch / www.photographingchildren. com

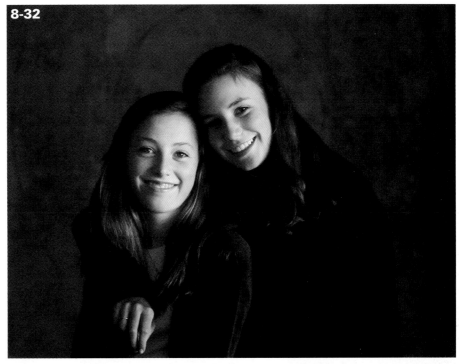

8-32

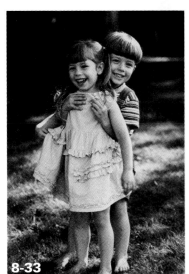

8-33

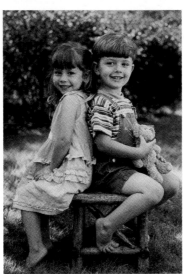

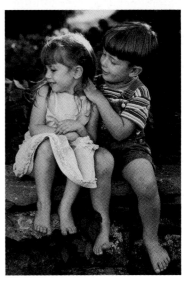

ABOUT THESE PHOTOS *This classic and enchanting series of siblings reveals many facets of their personalities and relationship. The dappled light of the garden and the classic outfits create illustrative portraits. Taken at ISO 320, f/5.6, and 1/125 second. ©Patrisha McLean / www.patrishamclean.com*

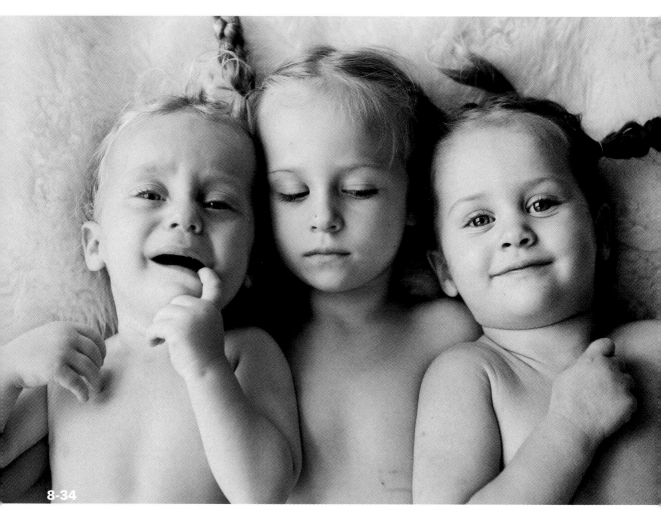

8-34

ABOUT THIS PHOTO *Two sisters and their baby brother playing on the bed created an opportunity for the mom to capture an intimate and expressive moment for her memories. The high-key approach emphasized the lovely skin tones. Taken at ISO 400, f/4.0, and 1/50 second.* ©Natalija Brunner / www.daidalorange.com

FAMILIES

Photographing families can be as complicated and unique as each individual member. It takes a bit of patience and a lot of psychology, but if you try to make it fun, you'll have a better chance of success.

Depending on the number of family members, it can be difficult to find a location that accommodates everyone graciously. It is also difficult to avoid the cliché of just having family members sit or stand and smile for the camera. The challenge becomes how to photograph a family creatively.

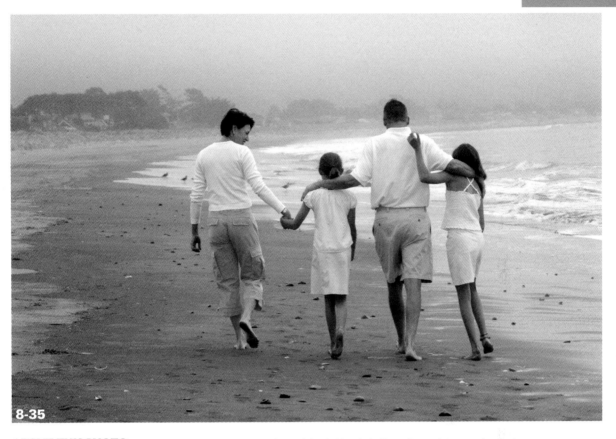

8-35

ABOUT THIS PHOTO *The color harmony between the setting and the clothing tie it all together, and the curved path of the shoreline leads you forward. Taken at ISO 400, f/8.0, and 1/125 second. ©Ginny Felch / www.photographingchildren.com*

If you have the luxury of knowing the family or of spending some time with them before the portrait, you are at an advantage. If they have particular interests, such as fishing, picnicking, walking on the beach, and so on, you can plan accordingly. Also, you can learn a little about the personalities, relationships, and so on.

It's a good idea to take different kinds of photographs during the session so that the family has some choices. If you are going to photograph

family members in a straightforward way (facing you, smiling, and so on), you might also encourage them to interact with one another.

Most families today prefer a family portrait that is more than just a visual representation of the family together. They want a family portrait that tells a story about their relationship with each other. For 8-35, a portrait of a mom and dad and their two daughters, I encouraged them to walk along

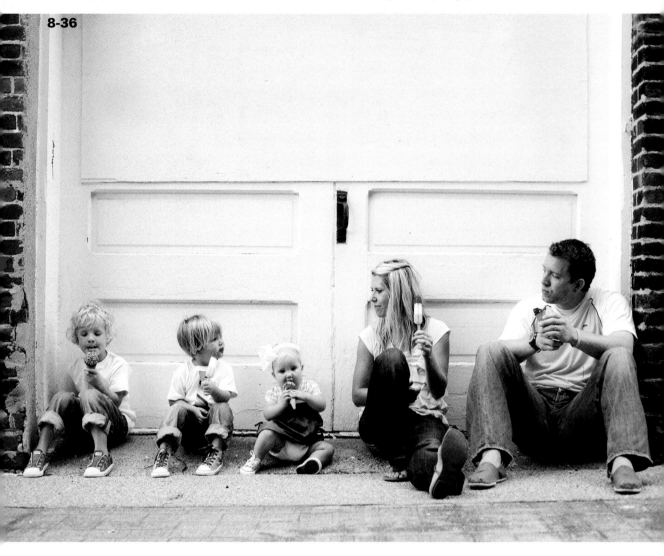

8-36

the tide line. I asked them to line up parallel to each other so that they would all be in focus. Then I told them to try to forget about me as they interacted with each other.

Once the family started walking, I ran up the beach, and using a telephoto lens, followed them coming and going. The result is a photograph with a feeling of lightness and the elegance of a dance. These were not awkward, preadolescent girls, but if they had been, it still would have worked very well.

Modern families are less likely to want their photographs to be serious or posed; they often opt for more natural and candid images. That was the concept by the photographer of the family shown in 8-36 with three small children. The popsicles provided a perfect distraction to keep everyone in one place for a few minutes!

ABOUT THIS PHOTO *As a family poses on a quilt outdoors on the grass, the creative and agile photographer figured out a way to photograph from above, eliciting spontaneous behavior and expressions. Taken at ISO 640, f/3.2, and 1/400 second. ©Jen Sherrick / www.jensherrickphotography.com*

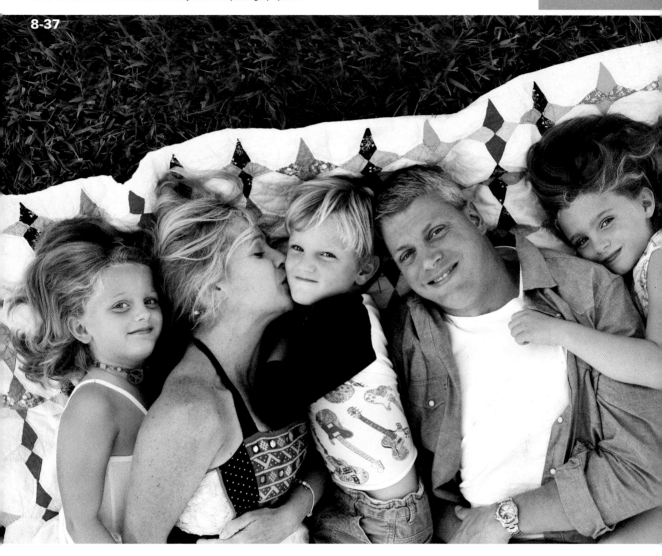

8-37

This kind of photograph forces you to move out of a comfort zone if you are used to posing families. However, if you roll with it and join in on the fun and energy, you can be successful.

As more and more photographers enter the hobby, clever ideas abound, such as approaching the family from an unusual angle, as in 8-37. Can you imagine trying to be too serious in that environment?

Photographing families outdoors or in their homes lends itself to informality automatically, as opposed to photographing in a more-structured studio environment. It also enables you to be more creative as you find new places in which to work. An outdoor location gives you more room to roam when photographing larger family groups, as in 8-38.

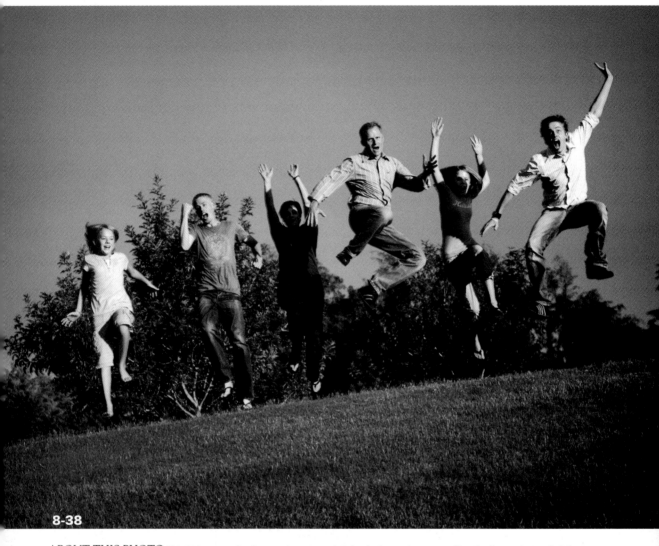

8-38

ABOUT THIS PHOTO *This high-energy family portrait captures their fun-loving, active nature. Shooting in a park near their home allowed for a lot of room for running and jumping. Taken at ISO 100, f/2.8, and 1/800 second. ©Allison Tyler Jones / www.atjphoto.com*

Assignment

Families and Siblings

Take a photo of a family or siblings together. How are you grouping them to tell a story? Is the photo candid or posed? You can utilize some of the other elements you have learned — for example, composition and lighting — so that you have a stronger image. However, if you have to compromise, do it with light and composition. What is important here is to unite the subjects in one way or another, making a strong statement about the relationship.

In this photograph of a family, the goal was to capture a feeling, something more than just their likenesses. Babies of this age and stage are most often in the arms of their parents, and this image chronicles a very special time in a contemporary style. The beautiful, soft window lighting added to the tender mood. Taken at ISO 200, f/5, and 1/250 second.

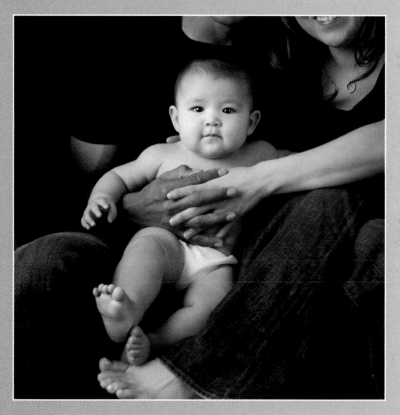

©Allison Tyler Jones / www.atjphoto.com

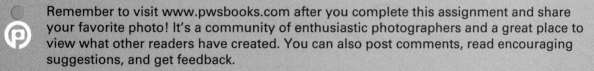

Remember to visit www.pwsbooks.com after you complete this assignment and share your favorite photo! It's a community of enthusiastic photographers and a great place to view what other readers have created. You can also post comments, read encouraging suggestions, and get feedback.

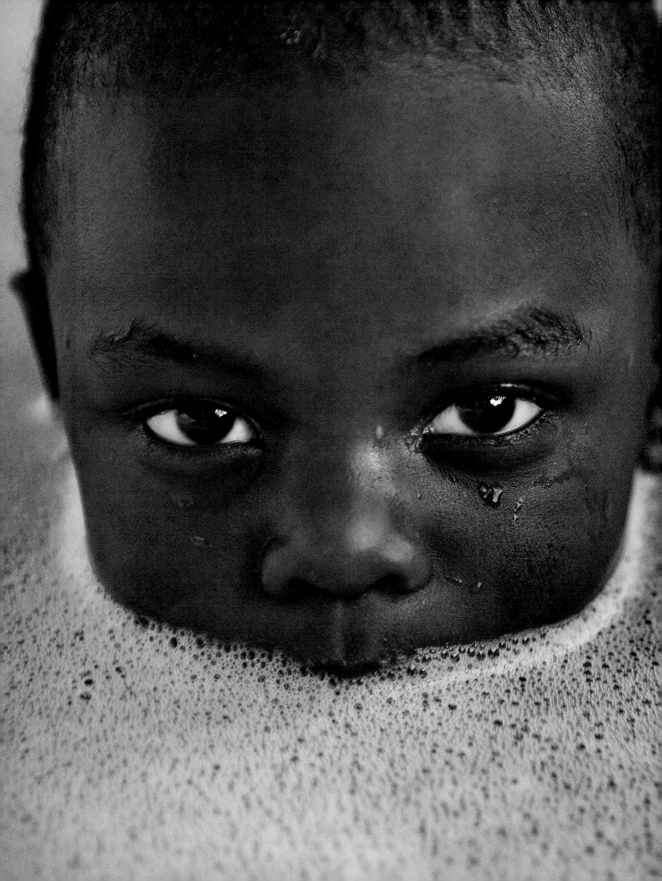

EQUIPMENT FOR THE CHILDREN'S PHOTOGRAPHER

©Barbara Peacock / www.barbarapeacock.com

Although the emphasis throughout this book has been that equipment and technology are secondary to making your images of children, it is helpful to have a starting point when purchasing expensive equipment. There are so many equipment options available: where do you start? The choices and preferences are personal and change a bit from photographer to photographer. Making your own decisions depends on your needs, your level of experience, your budget, and even your brand preferences.

CONSIDERING A CAMERA UPGRADE

Consider that updates, upgrades, and new products hit the market on a daily basis. What is perfectly suited for you today could change on a moment's notice. If you are in the market for some new equipment or are just interested in learning what's out there, do your research first. Here are a few websites that might aid you in your camera and post-production research:

www.imaging-resource.com/TIPS/CHOOSE/ CHOOSE.HTM

www.cnet.com

www.dpreview.com

www.photo.net/equipment/digital/choosing2/

www.tamron-usa.com/lenses/fundamentals.asp

www.canon.com

www.nikon.com

You save time and money by deciding ahead of time what you really need in the near future. The best advice is to start with what you have. Learn whatever camera you have inside out and backward and forward and only upgrade when you

x-ref — Chapter 2 covers more advanced camera settings and photography concepts, such as aperture, ISO, and depth of field.

know what you need to move on. Technology moves very fast, so don't leap before you know what you need or you'll find yourself with old technology that you still don't know how to use. Most beginners start with a simple point-and-shoot camera and use its automatic settings. However, inexpensive SLR cameras with zoom lenses are also an option. If you need to advance to a camera that gives you more control over your settings (as covered in Chapter 2) ask yourself the following questions:

- Do you have the time and motivation to learn new things?

- What will you be comfortable using for the challenge of photographing children?

- Do you need a camera that enables you to choose your depth of field, either by modes such as Portrait, Landscape, and so on, or by Aperture Priority (Av) mode? Does your existing camera offer that now?

- What size prints do you want to make? Are you ready to progress to a camera that produces higher-quality, larger-image files? This is going to be determined by the number of megapixels the camera offers. If you eventually want to print a high-quality 8-x-10-inch print, you need to buy a camera with at least 5 megapixels. If you are making photographs for e-mail or the web, you don't need to worry about having a lot of megapixels. Megapixel is the measurement of resolution: the larger the number, the greater the resolution or quality of the photograph produced.

■ Do you want to be burdened with a lot of equipment when you are photographing children? Usually, you must make a trade-off here. Point-and-shoot cameras are light and lend themselves to spontaneous moments.

■ Would you like to use interchangeable lenses? In that case, you need an SLR camera. Are you intimidated by all the bells and whistles, or can you simplify your approach? Can your budget afford a selection of lenses?

■ Is video capability important to you? Many consumer-level cameras can capture both still and video beautifully.

■ How much can you afford to spend? More expensive doesn't always mean better. The best camera for you is the one that meets your needs without having more features than you'll use.

When you are ready to purchase equipment and have narrowed your search, here are a few items to consider:

■ **Ergonomics.** When you hold the camera in your hands, does it fit your hands well? Can you find the basic settings without having to get out the manual?

■ **Reviews.** Check the reviews and get opinions from photographers whose work you admire. Find out what they are using. You may be surprised that it's not as flashy as you thought.

■ **Future upgrades.** If you upgrade your camera, can your computer equipment handle the change too? With digital photography, the camera and lenses are only half of the equation. You may need to upgrade your computer and software as well, as discussed in Chapter 10.

■ **Rent before you buy.** Renting equipment for a weekend before you decide to buy can save you money and buyer's remorse. Often, you don't realize how heavy the lens/camera is or that it might not give you the effect you are looking for. Rent equipment first and check out the options. If you are near a large city, you will have more local rental resources. Some great online resources for lens rentals are: www.lens rentals.com or www.borrowlenses.com.

Once you have purchased your camera, read your manual. You can also try to find online classes or instructions for your particular camera. Some people don't find camera manuals very captivating, so seek out any and all ways to learn all you need to use your camera to its fullest capacity.

USING INTERCHANGEABLE LENSES

When it comes to photography, the look or quality of your image is strongly influenced by the lenses you use. Lenses are your most important investment. You would be smart to buy a less-expensive camera and put your money into good lenses that can grow with you. The price of lenses is directly related to their speed and quality. Today's manufacturers produce lenses of exceptional quality and sharpness.

FAST LENSES

Aperture, or the lens opening, can only open as wide as the maximum aperture for that particular lens. Lenses with very large maximum apertures (that is, f/1.2, f/1.4, f/2.8) are considered *fast lenses* because, at their widest settings, they let in two, three, even four times more light than a lens

x-ref

In Chapter 2, I introduced the concept of aperture.

x-ref

In Chapter 2, depth of field was discussed at length. As I stated there,
"*Depth of field* is the field or area in the photograph that
is in focus. A photograph where just the family is in
focus but everything else in the foreground and background is out of focus would have a narrow or shallow
depth of field."

with a maximum aperture of f/3.5, f/4.0, or f/5.6,
for example. These wider apertures let in so much
more light than their slower counterparts that it
takes less time for an image to record on your digital sensor, allowing you to work at faster shutter
speeds. Many of the photographs in this book
were taken with faster lenses. For example, if you
look at the technical information under each
photo, you can see that many of the images were
captured with apertures of f/2.8.

LENS FOCAL LENGTHS

You will notice that the focal lengths in Table
9-1 are listed individually. If you own a zoom
lens, your lens length will likely encompass
several of these focal length ranges (such as
12-24mm or 70-200mm). Breaking them down
individually gives you more information as to
which focal length is used for certain types of
photography.

Table 9-1

Lens Types

Common Focal Lengths	Type of Lens	Uses
12mm	Wide Angle	Good for large groups
14mm	Wide Angle	
18mm	Wide Angle	
24mm	Wide Angle	
35mm	Wide Angle	
50mm	Standard Lens	Similar to what the eye sees
85mm	Telephoto	I use this for portraits
105mm	Telephoto	Often considered ideal for portrait close-ups
200mm	Telephoto	Good for blurring out backgrounds or for getting in close to the action

PRIME LENSES

Prime lenses are fixed focal length lenses. That means, instead of zooming from 12-24mm or 70-200mm, theses lenses are fixed at 50mm, 85mm, and so on. In the case of prime lenses, you are the zoom. High-quality prime lenses are often significantly more expensive than zoom lenses. They are often overlooked by beginning photographers for several reasons, including the following:

■ New photographers usually have a zoom lens that came with their camera when they bought it.

■ No one bothered to tell the newbie just what a great investment quality prime lenses are.

Photographers who are purists use only prime lenses for their speed, quality, and sharpness. The photograph in 9-1 was taken with a 50mm prime lens.

You can pick up prime lenses new or used online and in your local camera store or, better yet, rent one from your local camera store or online (www.borrowlenses.com) for the weekend and see if it's a good fit for you.

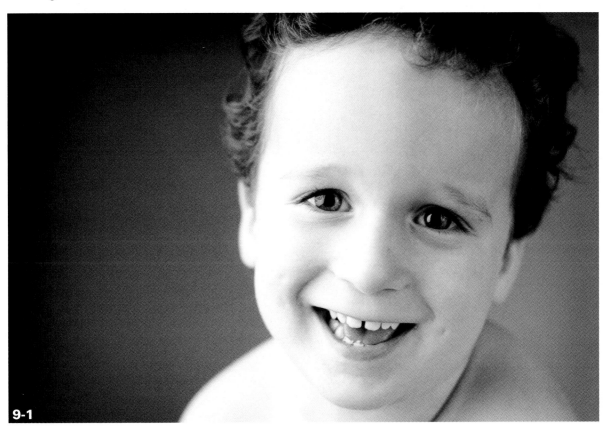

9-1

ABOUT THIS PHOTO *This photo was taken using a 50mm prime lens. Prime lenses are prized for their speed, sharpness, and quality. Taken at ISO 100, f/2.8, and 1/250 second. ©Allison Tyler Jones / www.atjphoto.com*

tip If you are unsure about a new equipment purchase, rent it first. Many camera stores rent equipment for a few days or over a weekend so you can get some hands-on experience with the object of your desire. Some stores may apply the rental fee to the purchase of the new item.

ZOOM LENSES

Zoom lenses provide several focal lengths in a single lens. You might be familiar with them already if your point-and-shoot camera is equipped with one. This is the most common type of lens in use today. If you look at your zoom lens, you will notice that there are two numbers denoting the focal length (such as 18-70mm or 35-135mm); this means that your lens will provide focal lengths from the smallest to the largest number. Zoom lenses are perfect for photographing children because they allow you to constantly change your focal length without actually switching out lenses or walking closer to the subject.

The images in 9-2 and 9-3 were taken with a zoom lens, illustrating the advantage of being able to capture images from a wide angle as well as a close-up without having to switch lenses.

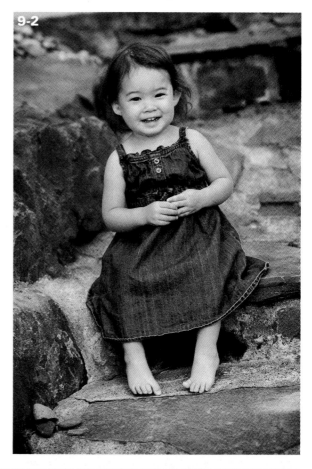

9-2

HOW CAN YOU DETERMINE THE MAXIMUM APERTURE OF YOUR LENS?

Look on your lens (sometimes around the end of the lens barrel and sometimes on the front element of your lens) for a number that starts with "1:" (for example, 1:2.8). These numbers indicate the largest or maximum aperture for this lens is f/2.8. Your lens might have more than one number (for example, 1:3.5-5.6). A number like this can be found on a zoom lens. Having two numbers means your aperture gets smaller as you zoom your lens in. So, when you shoot photos and your lens is pulled back, your maximum aperture is f/3.5, but when you zoom all the way in to pull your subject in closer, your maximum aperture is f/5.6 (hence the term variable aperture lenses). There are also zoom lenses with apertures that remain constant as you zoom in and out.

ABOUT THIS PHOTO *This photo was taken using the same 70-200mm zoom lens as in 9-2, but this time the lens was zoomed in to approximately 200mm. Taken at ISO 100, f/2.8, and 1/125 second. ©Allison Tyler Jones / www.atjphoto.com*

9-3

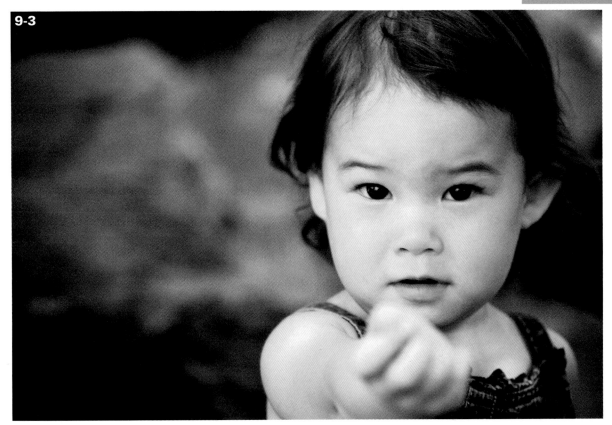

The five photographs shown in 9-4 through 9-8 are of Obie, a toy you met in Chapter 7. These images were shot with the photographer standing in exactly the same place while using a zoom lens at different focal lengths. Use these as a guide to see the effects that various focal lengths can create in image width and depth of field.

A 300mm lens, used for 9-4, is considered a telephoto lens, which magnifies objects that are very far away. These lenses can be quite expensive, especially if you buy one that is fast. You could pay around $1,500 or more. A 300mm lens is great for taking shots of children at the beach or sporting events when they are far enough away that you want to hone in on them more closely.

A 200mm focal length is achieved using a 75-300mm telephoto lens, as in 9-5. The 200mm doesn't bring Obie as close as the 300mm, but it is a good choice for some portraits when you're taking a picture of a child in the distance.

A 135mm focal length is also achieved using a 28-135mm telephoto lens, as in 9-6. It still allows a longer focal length than a wide-angle lens, but has a narrower area that it will capture. I recommend it for portraits and great candid shots as long as your subject isn't too far away.

A 50mm focal length is achieved using the same 28-135mm zoom lens, as in 9-7. This wider-angle perspective is great if you are taking family or sibling portraits because it allows you to get in closer and eliminates more of the background.

ABOUT THESE PHOTOS *9-4 was taken with a 75-300mm lens at ISO 400, f/5.6, and 1/160 second. 9-5 was taken with a 75-300mm lens set at 200mm at ISO 400, f/5.6, and 1/200 second. 9-6 was taken with a 28-135mm lens set at 135mm at ISO 400, f/5.6, and 1/250 second. 9-7 was also taken with a 28-135mm lens, this time set to 50mm, at ISO 400, f/5.6, and 1/250 second. 9-8 was taken with a 28-135mm lens set to 28mm at ISO 400, f/5.6, and 1/400 second. ©Ginny Felch / www.photographingchildren.com*

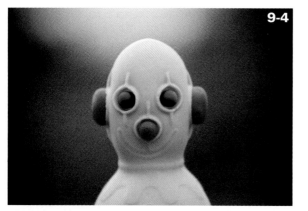

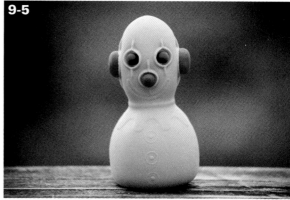

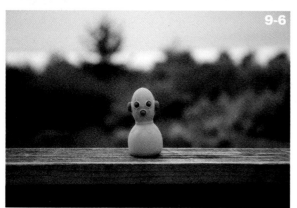

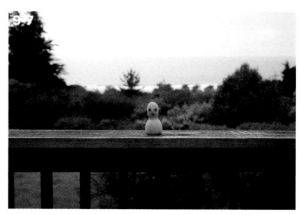

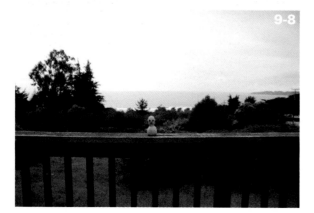

because it can distort your image, making whatever is closer to the lens appear larger (like noses).

LOOKING INSIDE YOUR CAMERA BAG

Most professional photographers learn very quickly to streamline their equipment to the bare essentials so that they aren't hauling tons of equipment to every session. Being loaded down with too much equipment can affect your spontaneity. If you carry your camera by its strap over your shoulder, try carrying a Shootsac over the other shoulder to hold your lenses and cards (www.shootsac.com). This gives you a great deal of freedom and flexibility.

A 28mm focal length, used for 9-8, is a standard wide-angle lens. This is a good focal length for group pictures, but not for close-up portraits

Consolidate your equipment so that everything fits into one bag. The contents of my camera bag is shown in 9-9. Take a peek into a working photographer's bag.

To be a successful children's photographer, you need some non-camera-specific equipment with you at all times. This equipment is entirely optional and depends on how much you want to carry and how you interact with your subjects. Here's a list of the items in my bag:

■ Spray bottle of water (for bad hair days)

■ Small brush (for bad hair days)

■ Small bottle of hair spray (for hair emergencies, with parent's permission)

■ Duct tape (for clothing emergencies)

■ Child's toy or comfort item such as a small, stuffed animal

■ A few small noisemakers like a kazoo (to distract restless subjects)

Your camera bag also should include the following pieces of camera equipment:

■ Extra memory cards, preferably 1 to 8 GB

■ Your favorite lens (mine is 85mm)

You can also pack some optional items in your bag or in a separate bag that you keep in your car:

■ A backup camera (I use a Canon 5D as a backup to my Canon Mark II 5D)

■ Additional lenses (I also use my 70-200mm 1:2.8 zoom lens)

■ Two extra batteries, charged

Always double-check that you have packed those extra batteries and media cards before you leave the house or studio for a photo shoot. These are two items that you can't make an image without, no matter how fancy your camera is! Of course, be sure your camera default is set so that you can't press the shutter button if a memory card is not in the camera.

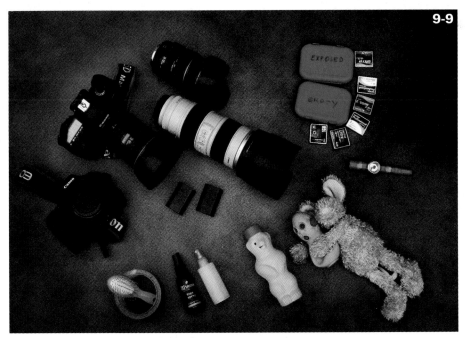

9-9

ABOUT THIS PHOTO
Here is a photograph of the equipment and other goodies that I always keep in my carrying case or in my car. Taken at ISO 80, f/3.7, and 1/200 second. ©Ginny Felch / www.photographingchildren.com

Assignment

Exploring the Limits of Your Zoom Lens

Take the time to shoot some reference images using your zoom lens. Photograph the same subject from the widest to the longest focal length your lens will accommodate and notice how the appearance of each image changes. Print the images and keep them for future reference to help you visualize what your lens is capable of.

This image was taken by zooming all the way in at 200mm on a 70-200mm lens. This allowed the photographer to be on dry land and still capture the boy in the middle of a very large pool during his swimming lesson. You can see that the depth of field is very short (shallow) with just his goggles being in sharp focus, which enhances the mood as he breaks through the surface of the water. Taken at ISO 200, f/2.8, and 1/1000 second.

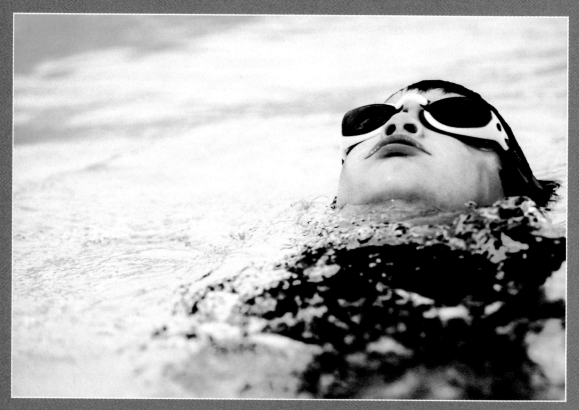

©Allison Tyler Jones / www.atjphoto.com

 Remember to visit www.pwsbooks.com after you complete this assignment and share your favorite photo! It's a community of enthusiastic photographers and a great place to view what other readers have created. You can also post comments, read encouraging suggestions, and get feedback.

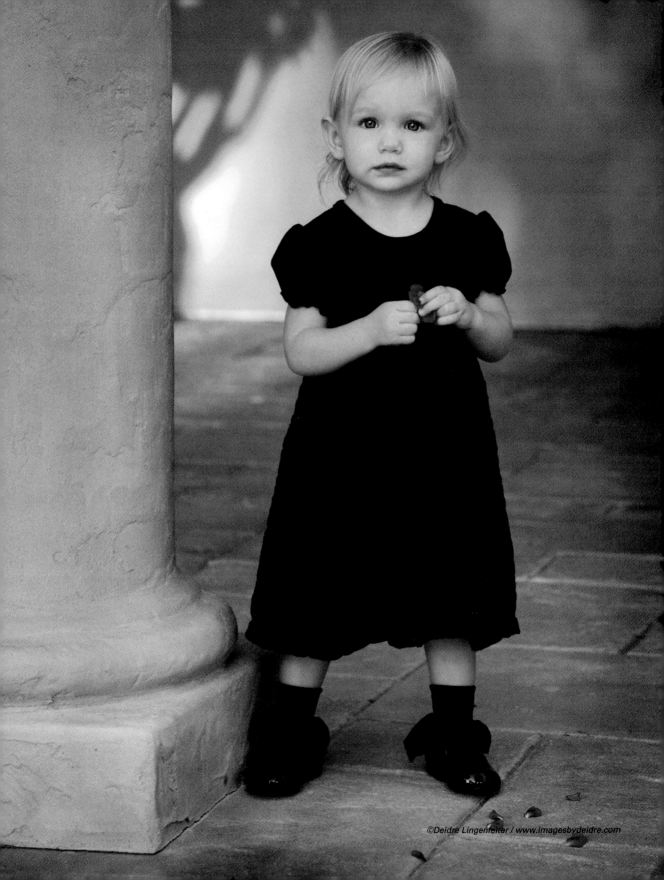

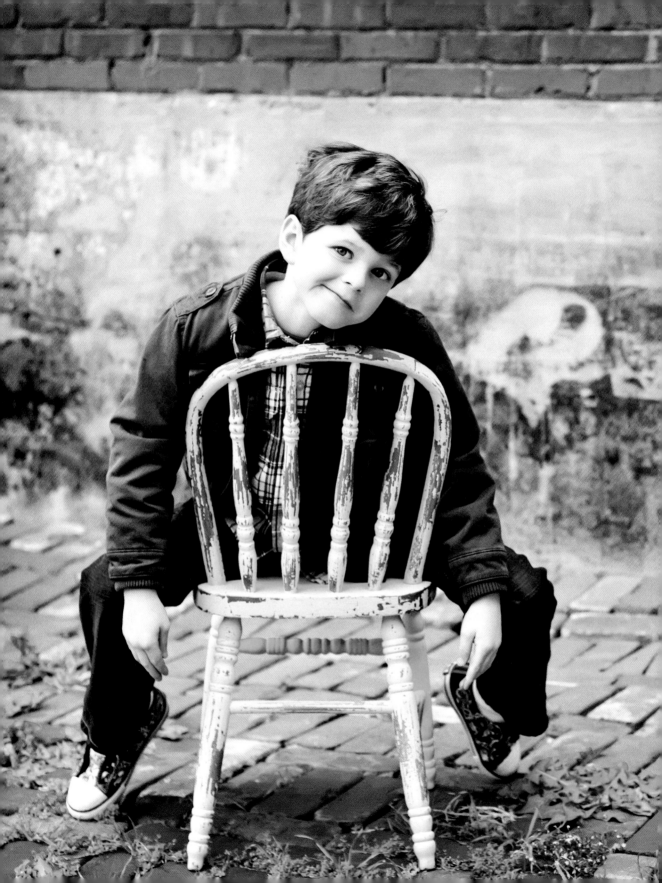

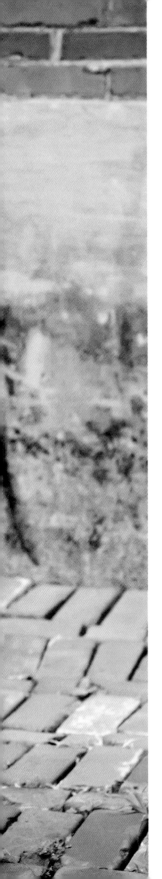

POST-PRODUCTION AND PRESENTATION

©Melanie Johnson / www.melaniejohnsonphotography.com

Capturing the image with your camera has always been just the first step in creating a final image. In the film days, the darkroom became the next step in manipulating an image. Today, your darkroom is digital, and there are more possibilities than ever before.

This chapter encourages you to learn the basics of a digital darkroom and then experiment and play with your images. It's like doodling: The more you play, the more you see what you can do with your images, which enables you to find styles that appeal to you.

ESTABLISHING YOUR WORKFLOW

Post-production is the term photographers use to indicate everything that happens after the image is captured. That includes loading your images from your media card to your computer and working in an image-editing program, all the way to the final printed image hanging on your wall. There are a lot of steps to get you from here to there, and each photographer has his or her own unique way of working, which is called workflow. Workflow is defined by Wikipedia.com as a reliably repeatable pattern of activity.

A good, consistent workflow is critical for digital photographers. Digital files can be easily deleted, corrupted, or just plain lost, so establishing an easy-to-follow workflow for your images is critical. It allows you to:

- Consistently back up and archive your images

- Organize your images so you can find them quickly

- Preserve an untouched set of images so that you aren't working on your originals

- Virtually eliminate the chance of lost or deleted images

tip If you are planning to use photo labs or do book publishing, it's wise to invest in monitor calibration software, such as X-Rite or Spyder. This can assure WYSIWYG or *what you see is what you get*. You can save yourself angst and frustration by completing this easy process a couple of times a month. Many labs offer free test prints to confirm that your monitor is properly calibrated before you invest in your prints.

Even if you are "just a snapshooter" you have probably already accumulated a fair number of images on your computer. Can you find the image you need quickly? If not, set up a workflow that works for you. The following is a basic workflow that you can follow as you get started. Once you expand your skills and understand all the components of the workflow, you can begin to adjust it to fit your specific needs.

1. **Transfer your images.** Download your images from the media card as soon as possible after capturing the images to avoid accidentally formatting or overwriting the card. Create a folder on your computer desktop using a name or numbering system that makes sense to you (the important thing is to keep the naming consistent).

2. **Back up your files.** Back up the folder by dragging it to an external hard drive (recommended but optional) or burn a disc with the renamed images, label it ORIGINALS, and name it using your chosen naming/numbering system. Put this disc in a safe place (a fireproof safe or safe deposit box are good options). Another convenient option is to store your photo files in *cloud storage* online at sites such as Dropbox, Box, Sky and SugarSync. Some are free, but most charge per gigabyte. The obvious advantage to this type of storage is that is is accessible from any computer anywhere.

3. **Retouch, crop, and enhance images as necessary in your chosen image-editing software.** You now have at least one (hopefully two) backups on disc of your original out-of-camera images. That disc with your original images on it is just like your negatives with a film camera and should be treated as carefully. You should complete all the previous steps before you do any enhancements to any images. Now you can play all you want with the images in the folder on your computer desktop because you know that your originals are safe and untouched.

4. **Back up your edited images.** When you finish retouching and enhancing your images, back up those enhanced images to your external hard drive or burn another disc. This time you can label the disc FINAL PROOFS and reference your original number/naming system.

5. **Output your finished images to a lab or printer.** Output your final proofs to your favorite lab or your printer if you are printing your own images.

Ultimately, the key to a good workflow is consistency. If you unload, save, and file your images the same way every single time, you will have no trouble locating an image when you need it.

GETTING STARTED WITH IMAGE EDITING

Not long ago, when choosing imaging software, you would have been limited to Photoshop and Photoshop Elements, but now many entry-level programs are available, and some are free. For example, Gimp and Photoscape are available as a free download. If you work on a Mac, iPhoto is a very easy-to-use image manager. Lightroom has risen to the top of the line of image-editing soft-

 tip

For $99 a year, you can join the National Association of Photoshop Professionals (NAPP) and receive its publications. This membership allows you to enter the website (www.photoshopuser.com) and learning centers to receive discounts and other perks. NAPP sponsors training workshops which are relatively economical and extremely thorough.

ware and is particularly helpful if you have hundreds of files to organize and edit at the same time. Additionally, many online vendors sell *presets* that allow you to create styles at the mere click of a button.

Image-editing software enables you to manage your photographs in the following ways:

- Batch-rename files (for example, change from IMG_0932_2.jpg to grace_2007.jpg)
- Organize and rate
- Crop and rotate
- Brighten, darken, increase, or decrease contrast
- Color correct
- Add filters, such as sharpening or blurring, adding noise and grain, and so on
- Correct red-eye
- Convert color to black and white or even sepia tone

If you are seriously entering the world of digital imaging, don't spend a lot of time on entry-level programs — Adobe's Photoshop Elements, Photoshop, and Lightroom, and Apple Aperture are industry standards for image-editing software.

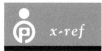 *x-ref*

You might as well spend your valuable time learning Photoshop Elements (PSE). I recommend finding a good, entry-level book on PSE such as *Photoshop Elements 9 For Dummies* (from Wiley).

Some excellent resources for learning include the following:

www.photoworkshop.com

www.kelbytraining.com

www.lynda.com

www.photoshopelementsuser.com/learningcenter

www.jkost.com

www.photoshopdiva.com

Photoshop Elements has many great, high-end features, and once you get comfortable with it, you should find it intuitive and easy to use. It also lays the groundwork for eventually stepping up to the full version of Photoshop. The commands and working space are identical between the two, with Photoshop providing more options and control.

IMAGE-EDITING WORKFLOW

Many budding photographers start image editing with Photoshop Elements, but even if you use different image-editing software, you can still follow the basics presented here. Setting up a consistent order of working in image-editing software allows you to work more quickly and achieve more consistent results. The following order is a generally accepted workflow for enhancing your images. The basic idea is to work from large changes to small changes in a logical order.

1. **Make tonal adjustments.** It's best to make any exposure adjustments (a little bit lighter, little bit darker) as your first step. This includes any Levels or Curves adjustments that affect the overall lightness, darkness, or contrast of the image.

2. **Make color corrections.** Adjusting your white balance before you take the photo means much less work at this stage. Check Chapter 4 for white balance details. However, you might have an image that has a strange color cast, such as too blue or too orange that needs adjusting. Do color corrections after tonal corrections.

note   Photoshop Elements is a great tool, but it's important to remember that properly exposed images usually need very little done to them in post-production. Make it your goal to improve your technique on the front end or at the capture stage of photography rather than relying on an image-editing software fix later.

USING CAMERA RAW Many cameras offer the option of shooting RAW images as well as JPEGs. If you have the opportunity, you are better off using the RAW option for several reasons: The file you will obtain will allow you to perform non-destructive editing — nothing you do to it in post-production will alter or diminish the pixels; Photoshop Elements and all the state of the art post-production software perform RAW conversion to read and manipulate RAW image files; and you can then save those changed files as JPEGs, TIFFs, and so on. But the original RAW file remains the same complete, high-quality, original capture. Another advantage is that if you make a huge error in exposure or white balance, you can easily fix it in the RAW software. The disadvantages are that RAW files are huge and require a lot of storage space; if you are shooting rapid-fire shots, the camera can process many more JPEG images in a burst than RAW files.

3. **Retouch as needed.** Only after you have corrected the exposure and color should you begin other adjustments or enhancements to the image. This means that all the adjustments that affect the entire image have been made and now you are working on refining the details.

4. **Make any image enhancements.** These include conversions to black and white or actions that give a different look to your image such as a super-saturated colors or high-contrast treatments.

5. **Back up your files.** After you finish fixing and retouching your image, back up the file that has been worked on, and save a copy for cropping and or sizing.

6. **Crop and size your images.** Working with a copy of your final file, crop to the size you want your final image to be. Because a digital file doesn't fit into the standard 8 × 10, 5 × 7 crops you are used to seeing, you will need to size your image before uploading to a lab to ensure that the crop is how you want it to be. If you don't resize/crop your image, the lab may do it for you and your final print might be different than what you originally envisioned.

BASIC RETOUCHING

Portrait photographers most often use retouching techniques to eliminate blemishes and wrinkles in their subjects and eliminate distractions in the background. Fortunately, kids don't have wrinkles, so most retouching involved in children's portraits is limited to removing any marks on the face, such as scratches; disguising a runny nose; or removing blemishes.

Here are the most commonly used techniques when retouching a portrait of a child:

■ Removing a blemish such as a scratch, pimple, or mark on a face or body

■ Whitening the teeth

■ Enhancing the eyes

■ Eliminating distractions in the background

USING LAYERS

If your chosen image-editing software has layers or something similar, you are in luck! One of the best things about Photoshop Elements is that it allows you to work in layers; one use for layers is to create a quick copy of your image so you can manipulate it. If you mess it up, you can throw it away.

If it's just right, you can save the image and you're done. Before you try any of the following fixes, press Ctrl+J/⌘+J to create a duplicate layer of your image (this preserves your original working image without changes). Then try the following fixes. When you have your top layer the way you like it, you can flatten the image (merge the layers), which allows you to save the image as a smaller file that it would be with several layers.

REMOVING BLEMISHES AND SMOOTHING SKIN

The easiest way to remove a minor blemish or to smooth out the texture in your subject's skin is to use the Clone tool set at 30-percent opacity so that it just smooths out the texture of the skin rather than drastically altering its appearance. Ideally you don't want an image to appear to be altered, so it is important to develop a soft touch.

The Clone Tool allows you to clone copies of a portion of the image and apply that copy somewhere else in the image. This comes in handy when there are areas you would like to cover up or delete altogether.

Most children have beautiful skin, but when you are photographing adolescents, this is a great trick for smoothing out the occasional blemish. Select from unblemished skin close by the area you want to fix and brush over the area that needs to be fixed, and the blemish will slowly disappear. This is also a good fix for dark lines under the eyes, as in the before and after photos in 10-1 and 10-2.

The key to all retouching is to keep it subtle because you don't want your subjects to look like plastic dolls. A little image editing goes a long way.

EYE AND TEETH ENHANCEMENTS

A quick fix for whitening the whites of the eyes and whitening the teeth is to set your Dodge tool at 20-percent opacity and carefully brush over the teeth and whites of the eyes until they are how you like them. Setting the tool at 20 percent allows you to lighten the teeth and the whites of the eyes without making them appear as though they are glowing.

You can also use the Dodge tool to put a little sparkle into the irises of the eyes, but be careful that you don't overdo it and make your subject look like an alien child! You can see the results of

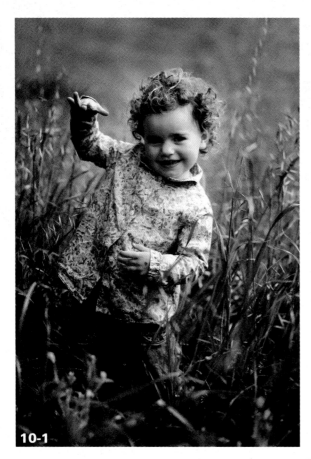

10-1

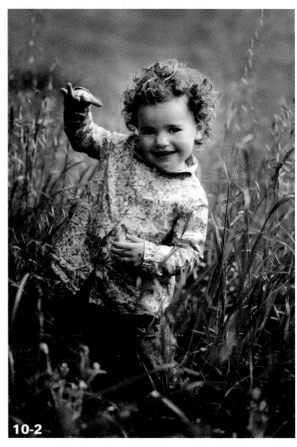

10-2

ABOUT THIS PHOTO *Notice the dark circles under the girl's eyes. Taken at ISO 500, f/3.5, and 1/2500 second. ©Ginny Felch / www.photographingchildren.com*

ABOUT THIS PHOTO *After using the Clone tool set at 30-percent opacity and selecting form the lighter skin on the cheeks, the dark circles have been eliminated. Taken at ISO 500, f/3.5, and 1/2500 second. ©Ginny Felch / www.photographingchildren.com*

both the Clone tool and the Dodge tool on this before image of a little girl (10-3) and the after image (10-4). The teeth were slightly whitened. The whites of her eyes were lightened, the edges of the iris darkened and the pupils darkened to give them more sparkle.

CLONING OUT DISTRACTIONS IN THE BACKGROUND

Sometimes, no matter how hard you try, a distracting element makes its way into the background of your image. In this case (10-5), it was

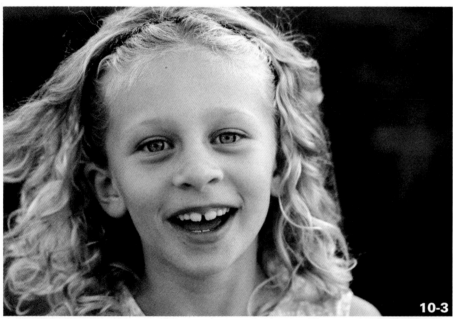

10-3

ABOUT THIS PHOTO
A before photo of a girl before using the Dodge tool to brighten her eyes and the Clone tool to remove the blemish on her face. Taken at ISO 400, f/4.0, and 1/640 second. ©Ginny Felch / www. photographingchildren.com

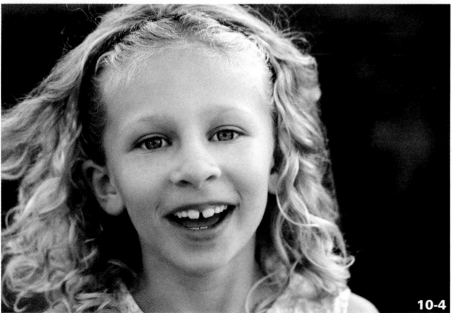

10-4

ABOUT THIS PHOTO
The results after using the Dodge tool at 30-percent opacity to lighten the whites of her eyes and lighten her iris, with a slight darkening on the edge. Taken at ISO 400, f/4.0, and 1/640 second. ©Ginny Felch / www.photographingchildren. com

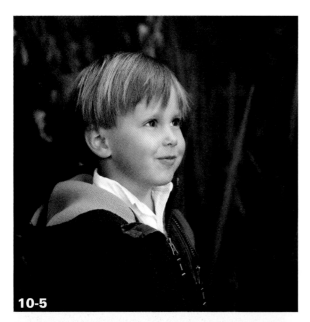

10-5

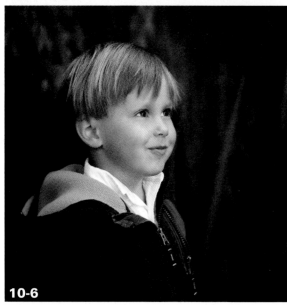

10-6

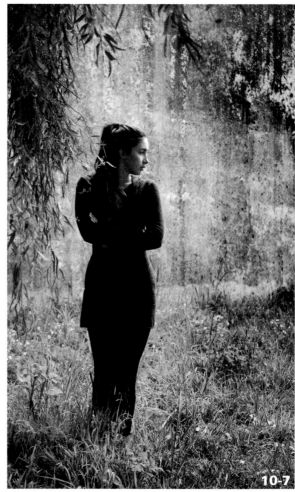

10-7

x-ref   Please refer to Chapter 5 if you need
help with the finer points of composition. If you want to spend more time behind your
camera and less time behind your computer fixing
images, improve your technique in composition.

ABOUT THESE PHOTOS *I felt that the purple flowers in this cropping of the before photograph were distracting from the boy's smooth face, so I cloned them out. After further observation, I decided to select some of the background and blur it so that it gave the effect of greater depth of field. Taken at ISO 400, f/3.2, and 1/250 second. ©Ginny Felch / www.photographingchildren.com*

the purple flower and highlights on the plants. I used the Clone tool and a blurring filter to eliminate the distractions in 10-6.

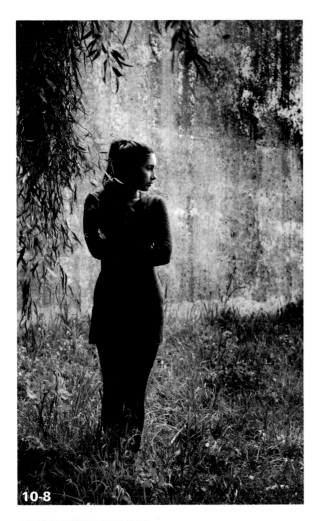

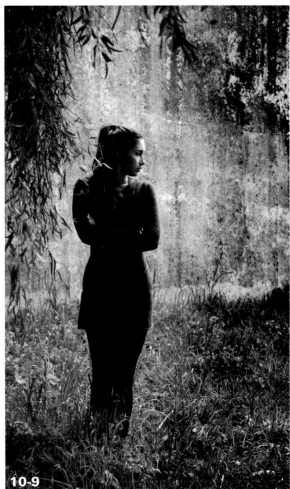

ABOUT THESE PHOTOS *This senior portrait was photographed on an overcast day in San Francisco, creating a subtly colored photograph (10-7). 10-8 shows the same photograph reworked in Photoshop Elements; I followed the easy directions in one of the software's tutorials to remove color to create a black-and-white photo. 10-9 shows the same photograph reworked in Photoshop Elements to create a sepia image by adjusting the color. Taken at ISO 500, f/4.0, and 1/500 second. ©Ginny Felch / www.photographingchildren.com*

CHANGING COLORS FOR IMPACT

Many photographers exercise their artistic license by altering their original captures to enhance or refine their story or style. With the advent of digital photography, the toolbox is much bigger, and the possibilities are infinite.

BLACK-AND-WHITE CONVERSIONS

Converting an image from color to black and white is probably the most common form of color manipulation you can use, and even the most basic image-editing software can handle this job fairly well. If you are just starting out, you may want to purchase ready-made actions, plug-ins, or presets for Photoshop Elements, Photoshop, and

Lightroom that automate these steps for you, allowing you to manipulate your images quickly and easily.

ACTIONS AND PLUG-INS

Plug-ins and actions enable you to tone your color prints (10-7) in just about any direction you want once you convert them to black and white: for example, black and white (10-8), sepia (10-9), and brown tones. You can make your own actions, but if you are just starting out, it is easiest to just download them from the Internet. There are many free actions available on sites such as www.atncentral.com, or you can purchase actions from manufacturers such as Nik Software and Kevin Kubota. If you are using Photoshop Elements, make sure the actions you download are compatible with the Elements software. Many of them are only available for Photoshop and Lightroom.

CROPPING TIPS

If you are absolutely certain of your framing and composition, go for it and press the shutter button. Otherwise, it is advisable to leave a little room around the image as you have composed it before you press the shutter button so that you can refine the cropping at a later date, especially if you are planning to print them at the standard photo sizes (4×6, 5×7, and so on).

FAVORITE PLUG-INS You might not be ready to tackle some of these products now, but later on when your skills advance, you may want to try some of my favorite Photoshop plug-ins. I use them to enhance my images in a very natural way. This list steers away from filters and tools that distort things too drastically.

- **Nik Color Efex Pro.** Nik Color Efex Pro includes a myriad of different artistic filters, including Classical Soft Focus and Brilliance and Warmth. The use of these two filters together, modified to your taste, works really well to help make a digital image look more like a film image. Use them subtly, and you should find that they just decrease the sometimes harsh look of digital compared with film.

- **Nik Sharpener Pro.** This filter is used for sharpening images or parts of images as you see fit. There are varying degrees of sharpening available, and it is extremely user friendly.

- **Alien Skin Software's Exposure.** This is a wonderful and useful filter system for those of you who want to replicate the qualities of certain vintage films. The software also enables you to see your image in various tones (selenium and sepia) as well as with grain or softening. Both color and black-and-white options are available. After your photograph is shown on the screen, you can simply scroll through the choices and see the changes as you go.

- **Flaming Pear Software's Melancholytron.** This plug-in provides extra mood when you want to go a bit beyond the ordinary.

- **Kitestrings Publishing's On the Edge Photographic Edges.** There are a stunning set of edges that are simple to use and artful. For more information about this software, visit www.kitestringspublishing.com.

ABOUT THIS PHOTO *The cropped photograph is imposed on top of the entire original capture. You can see that cropping can change the story told by the image by either including or leaving out elements. Taken at ISO 400, f/8.0, and 1/250 second. ©Ginny Felch / www.photographingchildren.com*

10-10

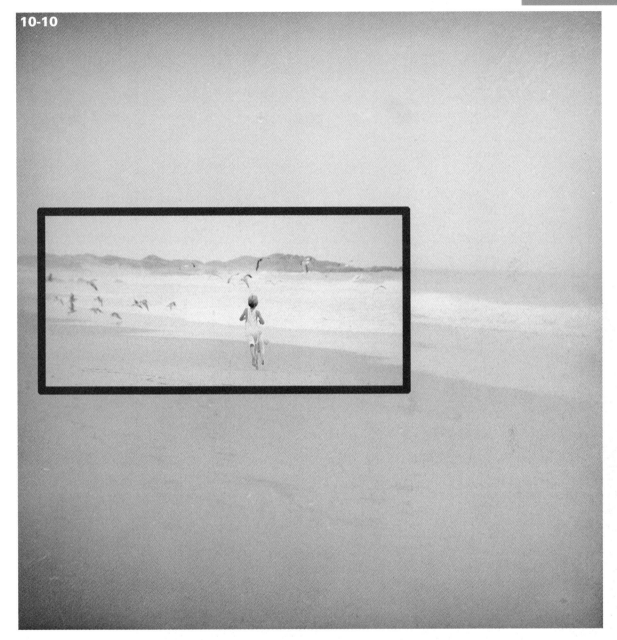

How you crop a photograph after you take it is as important as the original composition and final presentation of your image. After the photograph is made, you have a chance in post-production with imaging software to pay close and final attention to your cropping. Look at the example in 10-10. You can clearly see that cropping this image makes a huge difference in the impact it has.

When trying to decide on a crop after the photo has been taken, such as the one in 10-11, keep the following guidelines in mind:

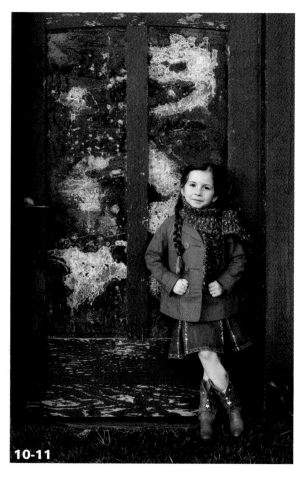

10-11

ABOUT THIS PHOTO *This is the full image taken of Daisy. Taken at ISO 1600, f/4.0, and 1/320 second. ©Ginny Felch / www.photographingchildren.com*

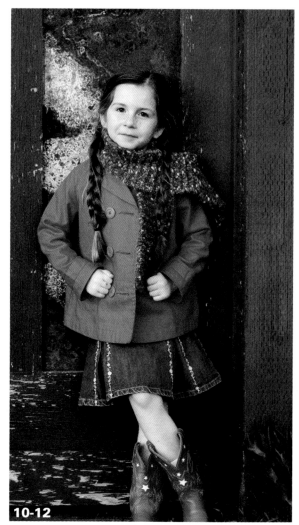

10-12

ABOUT THIS PHOTO *Uh oh, no feet, no photo!*

- **Never crop off the hands or feet, as in 10-12.** This cropping error is often referred to as amputation. Either crop close to the head and shoulders, or move out and crop below the hands, as in 10-13; or back off completely and include the whole body.

- **Don't automatically place the subject in the center of the photograph.** Refer to general composition guidelines in Chapter 5, such as the Rule of Thirds. You may choose to center your subject, but look at other possibilities first.

x-ref In Chapter 11, you can find more ways to enhance your images creatively using textures and actions, as well as a list of resources.

- **Leave plenty of growing room around the child, particularly above the head.** It is comforting visually to create a sense of space, as in 10-14. This also applies if the child is

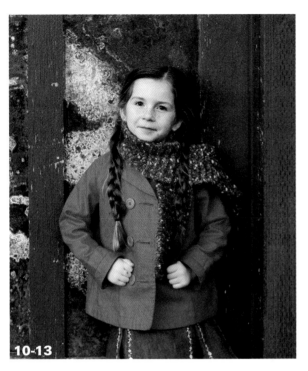

10-13

ABOUT THIS PHOTO *Successfully cropping an image to 3/4 length requires you to leave in the hands and to crop at mid-thigh rather than chopping your subject off at joints, such as the knees, hips, and so on.*

moving: Leave space in the direction he is going or came from, which also helps to keep the subject off center.

■ **If a horizon line is visible, be sure it is straight.** You can do this in a variety of ways in post-production if you didn't get it just right when taking the photo.

■ **If you weren't able to eliminate all back-ground distractions when composing, try to remove them with careful cropping afterward.**

■ **If the children are looking away from the camera presenting a profile, crop leaving more space in front of their line of vision.** This gives the impression there is space before them, creating a sense of openness.

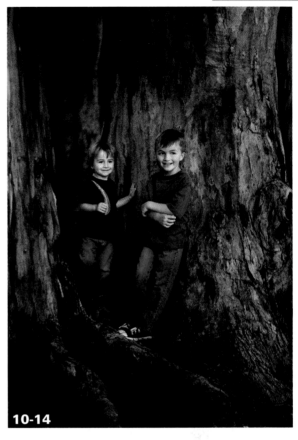

10-14

ABOUT THIS PHOTO *I wanted to focus on the perspective of the small children in the giant eucalyptus tree, so I placed them on the huge roots, stepped back, and created this image. Taken at ISO 400, f/5.6, and 1/250 second. ©Ginny Felch / www.photographingchildren.com*

PRESENTATION GALLERY

Capturing your image digitally gives you so many more options when it comes to printing your photos. Not only can you create different crops from the same image and change color to black and white for printing, but you can also create online galleries at websites such as www.snapfish.com and www.shutterfly.com.

Additionally, many of these websites have products you can purchase to place your images on to give as gifts, such as mouse pads, note cards, calendars, and so on.

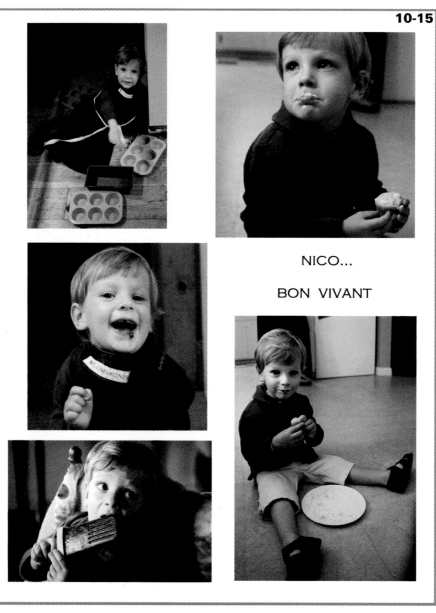

NICO...

BON VIVANT

Many photographers present their work, and network on their blogs, on Facebook, and Flickr. You
can join the Facebook Group, Photographing
Children (based on this book) to share your
images and ask for advice.

STORYBOARDS

Once you learn your way around Photoshop
Elements (or another chosen image-editing program), you know how to retouch, enhance, and
crop your images. You can then create your own
custom storyboards that will add a graphic

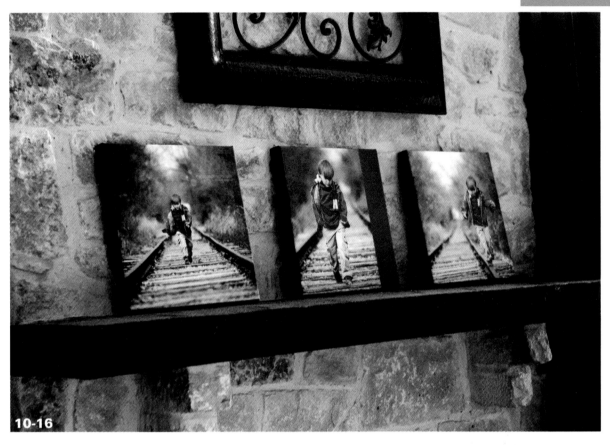

10-16

ABOUT THIS PHOTO *Photographer Mary Schannen decided to create a tryptic of her son's photographs printed on stretched canvas. The impact is tasteful and entertaining. ©Mary Schannen / www.melangephoto.com*

element to your work. Storyboards use multiple images from a photo shoot to tell a larger story than a single image can.

Start with a blank document in Photoshop Elements, sizing the document to the desired size of your finished storyboard. Next, open several different images that you would like to use for your storyboard project. Using the Move tool, just drag and drop each image onto your original blank document. Press Ctrl+T/⌘+T to transform each image and size it to the desired size on your document. Creating storyboards can be addictive, and you can use them in many different ways.

For example, the image in 10-15 could be used as a large wall print, as the cover of a Christmas card, or for the cover of your very own coffee-table book, as mentioned later in this chapter.

GALLERY-WRAPPED CANVAS PRINTS

A gallery-wrapped canvas print is an image that is printed on heavy artist's canvas and then stretched on stretcher bars with the image wrapping around the sides of the stretcher bars. Available through your local photo lab as well as many online outlets, gallery-wrapped canvases

ABOUT THIS PHOTO *I created a small portfolio for shops by uploading my images to www.mypublisher.com. It also manufactures coffee table books. Photos and book ©Ginny Felch / www.photographingchildren.com*

10-17

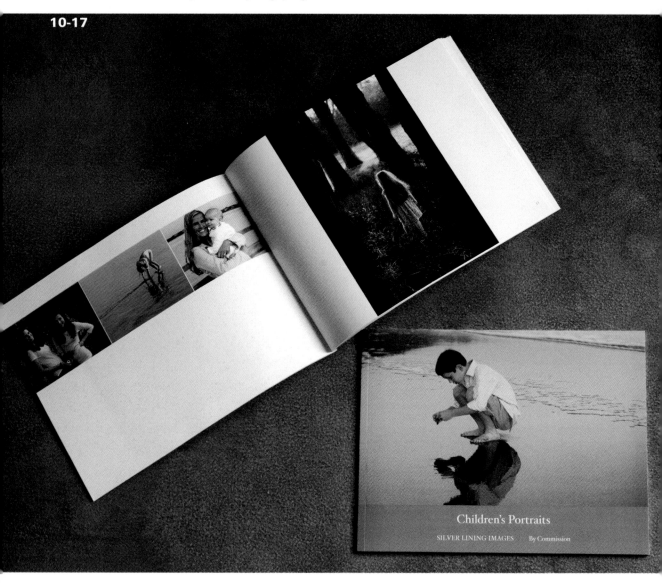

are a bold, contemporary statement and so fun to do with children's portraits, as in 10-16. If you are planning to print a very large image, you will want to first check with your lab to make sure the file you have has a high enough resolution (size) to enlarge it to your specifications. Bay Photo (www.bayphoto.com) and other companies produce very high-quality canvasses.

COFFEE TABLE DIGITAL BOOKS

It doesn't cost thousands of dollars anymore to have your very own coffee-table book printed full of your own images, as in 10-17. Check your local photo lab as well as online companies such as www.mypublisher.com for hard- and softcover books that you can customize using the layout templates, fonts, and wording they offer.

The options for outputting your digital images are endless. Working with your photographs in a book format can really help you learn to edit and create beautiful portfolios.

TABLETS AND CELL PHONE GALLERIES

A very convenient way to present your photographs and galleries in person is to upload them to your tablet and cell phone galleries, as in 10-18. The portability enables great opportunities to show off your favorites to friends and co-workers, or even clients. The quality is excellent, and you can add or change galleries whenever you wish.

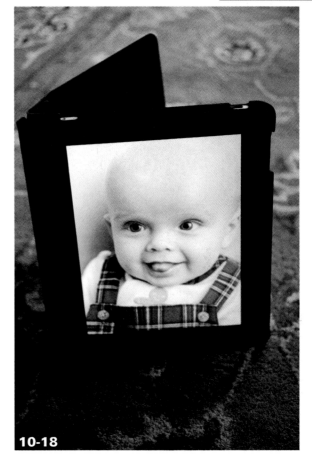

10-18

ABOUT THIS PHOTO *I use my iPad to display my photographs to friends, family, and clients. ©Ginny Felch / www.photographingchildren.com*

Assignment

Cropping for Impact

Create a photograph keeping in mind the cropping guidelines discussed in this chapter. Find an image that you like but could possibly be made better by creatively cropping it. Crop it three to four different ways and note how the impact of the image is changed for the better or worse.

My assignment photograph demonstrates three of the cropping tips. I chose to leave the little girl small in the photograph relative to the environment, and there is extra space before her as she skips down the stairs. This cropping gives the perspective of a little girl in a bigger environment, and you can see some of the foreground toward which she moves. If it had been cropped differently, to eliminate the stairs, for example, the girl might look as though she were flying. I also moved around so that the stairs formed a strong diagonal leading to the child. Taken at ISO 400, f/6.3, and1/200 second.

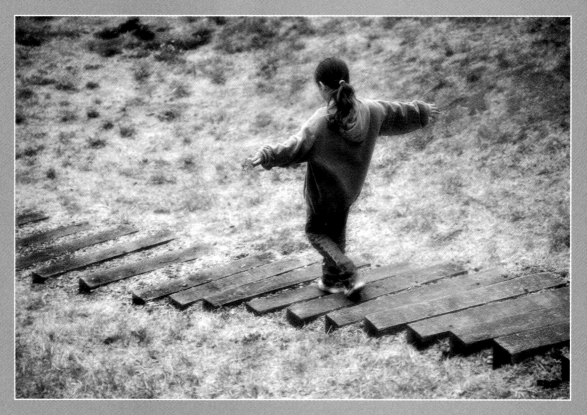

©Ginny Felch / www.photographingchildren.com

 Remember to visit www.pwsbooks.com after you complete this assignment and share your favorite photo! It's a community of enthusiastic photographers and a great place to view what other readers have created. You can also post comments, read encouraging suggestions, and get feedback.

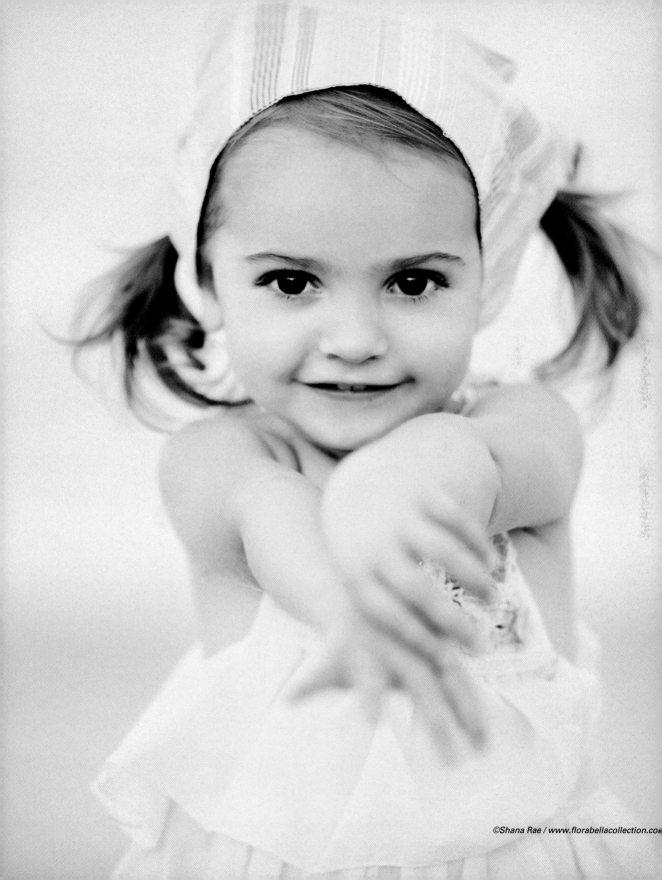

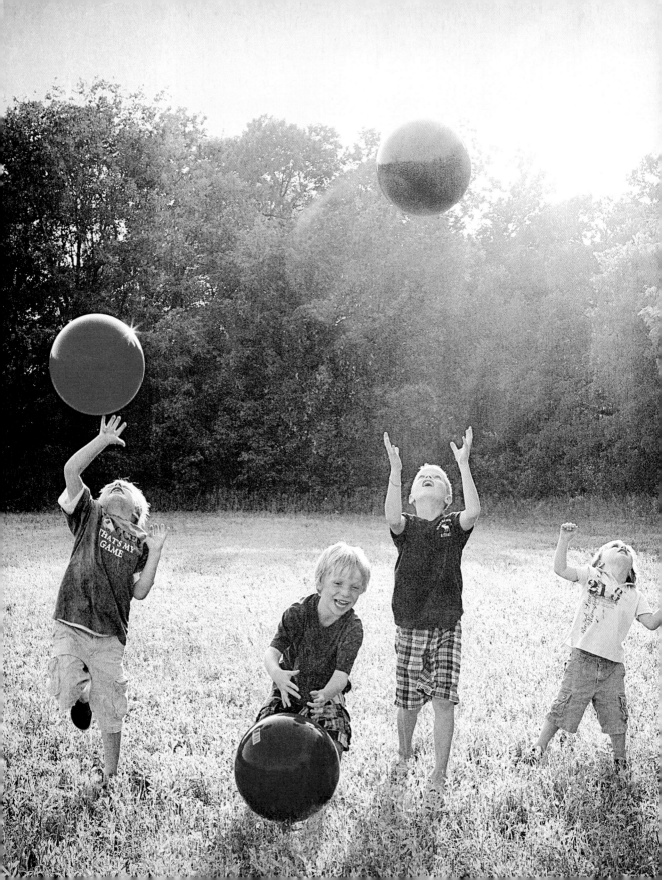

©Mary Schannen / www.melangephoto.com

Since the earliest days of photography, artists have been altering the *straight out of camera* image by etching, layering, or sandwiching negatives or steeping the final prints in countless chemicals. Just as with painters, the simple representation is often not enough to satisfy creative hunger.

So far in this book, you have learned to produce a more vibrant photograph by learning to see brilliant and defining light, to compose elements of the photograph, and to evoke captivating expressions.

This bonus chapter explores how some contemporary photography artists use their more advanced digital skills, along with the products of creative online entrepreneurs, to enhance their original images, as in 11-1 and 11-2. Hopefully you will find it inspiring enough to take some of your images into post-processing software and play away.

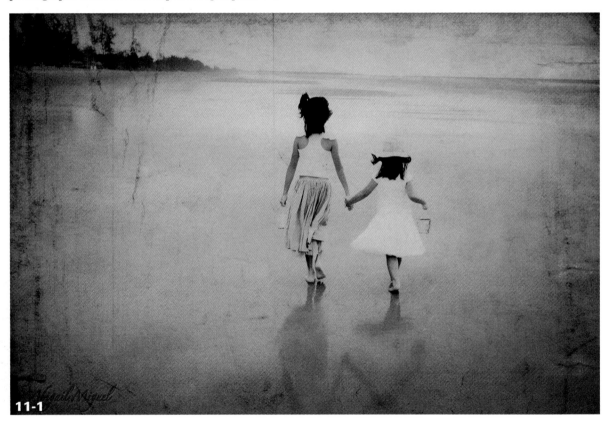

11-1

ABOUT THIS PHOTO *The stunning golden look of this photograph was created by merging a photograph of two girls on a very smooth beach with two Florabella textures (Moulon Rouge and Vintage Screen). The result is completely unique and has received a great deal of attention on the Internet. Taken at ISO 320, f/3.2, and 1/125 second. ©Abigail Roma Miguel / www.fourangelsphotography.blogspot.com*

When you are very skilled with Photoshop, the tools are so complete and vast that you can intricately create any look or correction you wish, However, many of the online vendors who are very popular with the mamarazzi set have cut to the chase and enabled photographers to arrive at enhanced and embellished images with the fairly simple use of actions, presets (Lightroom), and texture files.

Some of the possibilities include:

Added sky

Brightened eyes

Brighter skin tones

Color pop

Color shifts

Moody textures; for example, 11-1 and 11-3

Painterly look

Sepia toning

Sun flare

Vintage look; for example, 11-1

note

To clarify, Photoshop Elements (PSE) is Adobe's entry-level software and is reasonably priced so it is accessible to most beginners. Adobe Photoshop is a more advanced, state-of-the-art software, priced for professionals and devotees who desire detailed and specific editing (it is six times the cost of PSE). The learning curve is steep if you want to take advantage of all its features. Adobe Lightroom (twice the cost of PSE) is a great choice for photographers who process thousands of images (wedding photographers) and photographers who wish to enhance and embellish their photographs at the push of a button. The current versions of PSE, Photoshop, and Lightroom handle RAW files or JPEGs. Some photographers use the combination of Lightroom and Photoshop.

In this chapter, you will see examples of a few artists and how they work in post-production. Again, while most photographers who eventually decide to enhance their photographs choose Adobe Photoshop and Lightroom, some demonstrations here utilize the entry software Adobe Photoshop Elements (PSE). It is reasonably priced, accessible to most budgets, and friendly to beginners.

Once you master PSE, you will easily be able to transition into more sophisticated, state-of-the-art software and have a better understanding of why you might need it.

WHAT IS AN ACTION? According to Nichole Van, "An action is a like a small program that replicates a series of steps in Adobe PSE and Photoshop. Actions allow you to adjust selective parts of an image and ensure that each specific part of a photo looks correct. Actions give you complete, tight control over the final outcome." You can create your own actions, but some photographers prefer to purchase them from vendors (see the list of vendors at the end of the chapter).

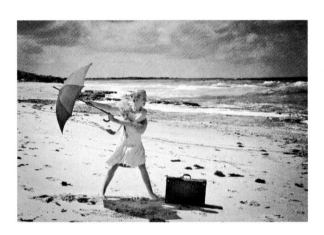
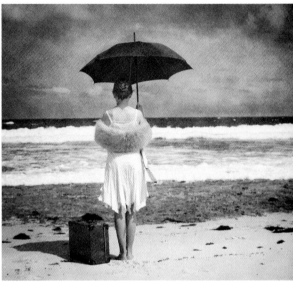

11-2

ABOUT THIS PHOTO *This award-winning triptych is an innovative treatment of three photographs put together for a vintage look, inspired by artist Jack Vettriono. In Lightroom, the photographer used the Yesteryear preset and Nichole Van's Powder Texture. Left to right: Taken at ISO 400, f/4.5, and 1/8000 second; taken at ISO 400, f/4, and 1/8000; taken at ISO 400, f/16, 1/640 second. ©Liz Ansley / http://web.me.com/lizansley*

CHOOSING A PHOTOGRAPH TO ENHANCE

While you can certainly begin with any photograph that you wish, the following suggestions will most likely produce the best results.

■ **Start out with a photograph that has merit all by itself, as in 11-3.** Don't get into the habit of using these techniques thinking that you can start with an inferior photograph and magically turn it into an outstanding piece of art.

■ **You might want to start out with a photograph that is more pictorial in nature, as in 11-4, rather than one that is a close-cropped head and shoulder.** These techniques are meant to add a mood to an already evocative image that contains interesting backgrounds and full bodies.

Be very careful to avoid adding blotchy textures to skin tones unless you know you are taking the risk of having unsavory results, such as mottled-looking skin. Of course, you can learn to erase the texture from the skin, but do be conscious of the risk.

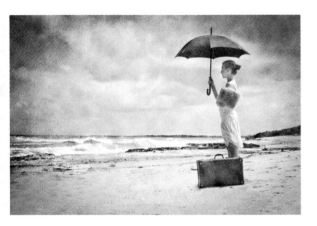

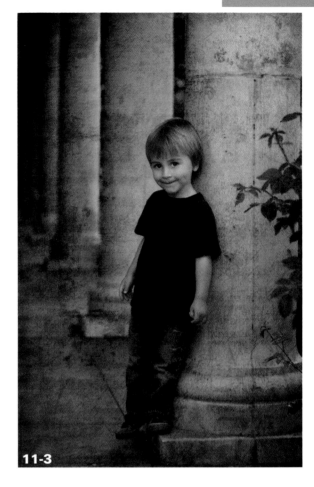

11-3

ABOUT THIS PHOTO *A contemporary play on a classic portrait of this boy was done by using an old architectural background using fun and casual clothing. The original capture was combined with my favorite textures in PSE after I did some basic editing in Photoshop. Taken at ISO 400, f/5.0, and 1/200 second. ©Ginny Felch / www.photographingchildren.com*

■ **If you think the photograph you have chosen needs adjustments, cropping, and/or re-sizing, make these changes before you begin your enhancement post-processing.** You will be able to do some adjustments later, but it is helpful to start out with what you think you will need.

Keep in mind that embellishing and enhancing your photographs can ultimately be extraordinarily creative; it is a process of discovery and intuitive response. Even if each artist starts with the same tools and the same photograph, the final product is as unique as an individual fingerprint, as in 11-5.

Only you will know when you have reached that "aha" moment, as in 11-6, when what you see before your eyes is utterly satisfying.

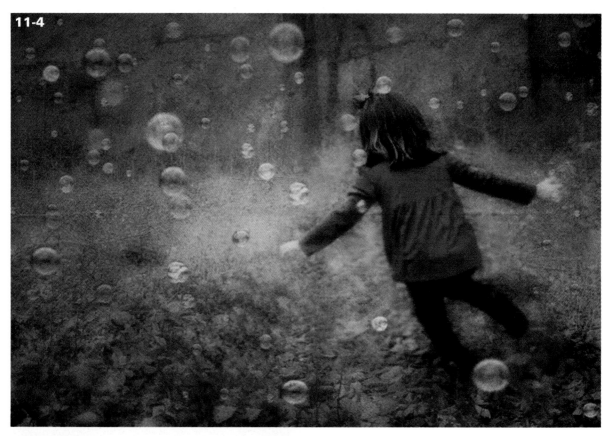

11-4

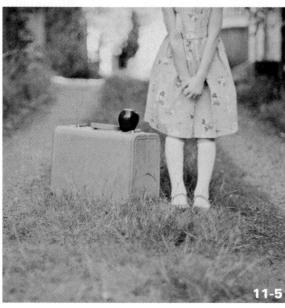

11-5

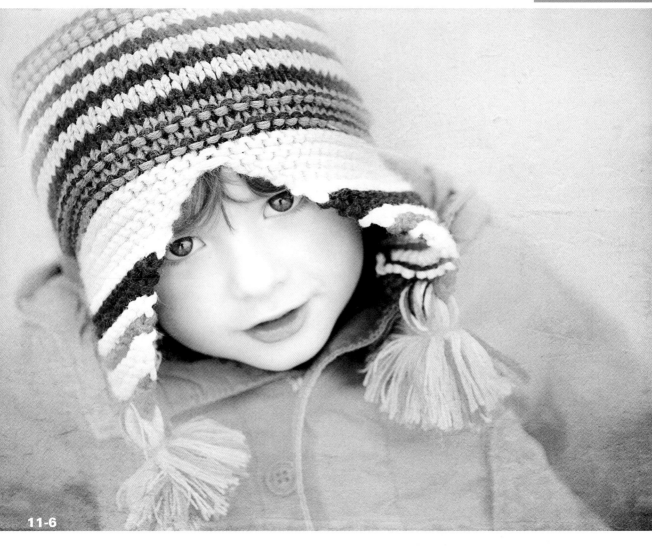

11-6

ABOUT THIS PHOTO *This charming little guy just sparkles in his knit hat. The production really makes the color and expression sing; the image was created using Jessica Drossin's Opening and MCP eye actions. Taken at ISO 200, f/2.8, and 1/160 second. ©Mary Schannen / www.melangephoto.com*

ENHANCING A PHOTOGRAPH WITH TEXTURE IN PSE

For this demonstration, my beach gesture study taken on a very foggy day is the *before* photograph. I felt this image reflected a quintessential story of typical, unselfconscious playtime at the shore.

Because it felt like a timeless image, I wanted to add more of a mood by adding one of my favorite textures. I collect textures on my camera and from vendors (see 11-7) everywhere I go, knowing that one of them could well provide the feeling I seek in my imagery.

To add a texture to your photograph, follow these steps:

11-7

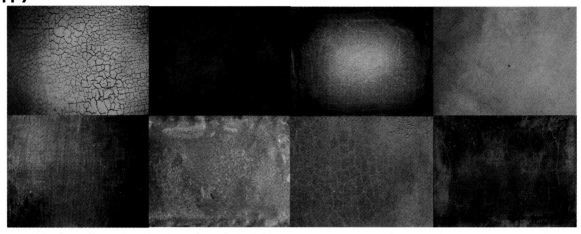

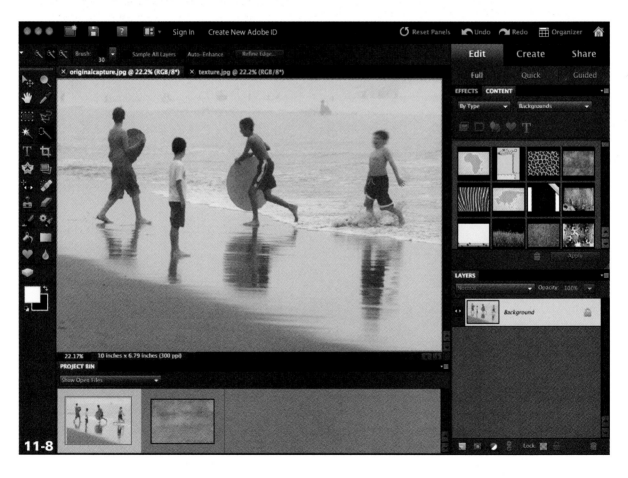

11-8

1. **Import the original photograph and the texture photograph into PSE by choosing File⇨Open (find in archives).** See 11-8.

2. **Highlight and double-click the *before* photograph.**

3. **Drag the texture photograph from the Project Bin up to the workspace.** Your original image will be obscured. See 11-9.

4. **The layers workspace is found in the lower right-hand corner.** Directly under Layers, you will see Normal. You can scroll down through each "blending mode" and see the results of the layering on the original photograph. You can also adjust the opacity in each mode.

You are seeking the "aha!" moment. I decided on the Multiply blending mode, using 100-percent opacity. See 11-10.

5. **In the upper right-hand corner, choose Edit⇨Guided for a full menu of editing possibilities.**

6. **Click Adjust Levels, then click the Create Levels Adjustment Layer, and then click OK.** See 11-11.

7. **Tweak the levels while watching the effect on the image and find your "aha" moment.**

8. **Once you are certain your photograph is satisfactory and final, flatten the layers to take up less room.** Then save the new version of your image.

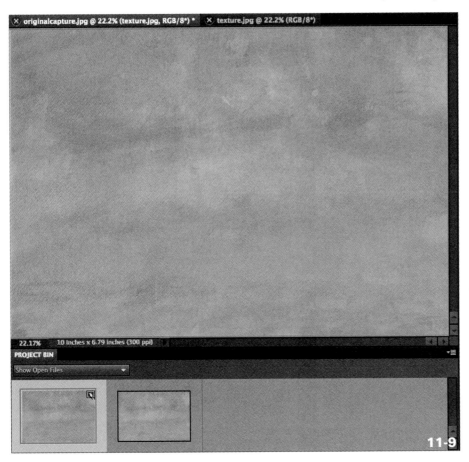

11-9

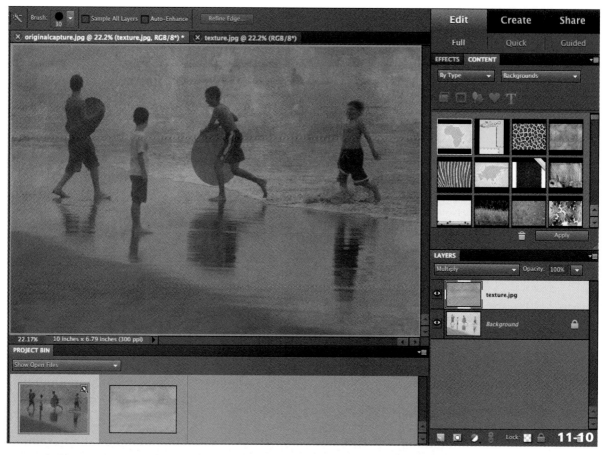

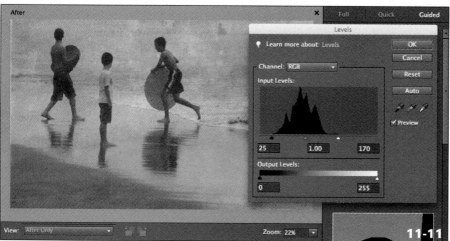

ABOUT THESE IMAGES
Figures 11-8 through 11-11 illustrate the process I used to add a texture to my original photograph. They correspond with the numbered steps as indicated. Original photograph was taken at ISO 200, f/4.0, and 1/125 second. ©Ginny Felch / www. photographingchildren.com

COLOR POP IN PSE BY MARY SCHANNEN

Mary Schannen of Melange Photo used this workflow to add a boost to the color in the photograph of her son. She is quite the post-production wizard, and was greatly inspired by the first edition of this book to move into photography. Her workflow is as follows:

1. **Import the original photograph and the texture photograph into PSE by choosing File⇨Open (find in archives).** Crop the photo. See 11-12.

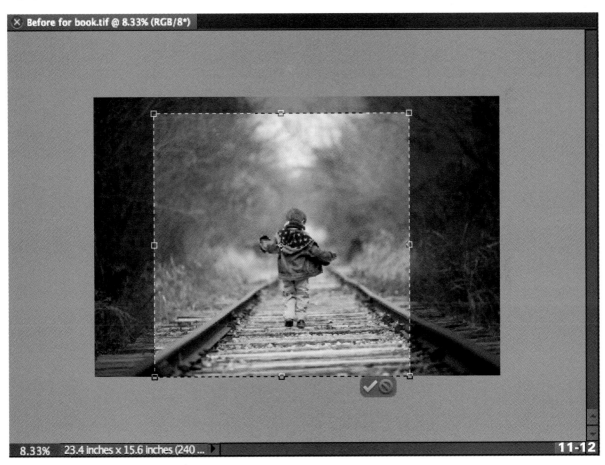

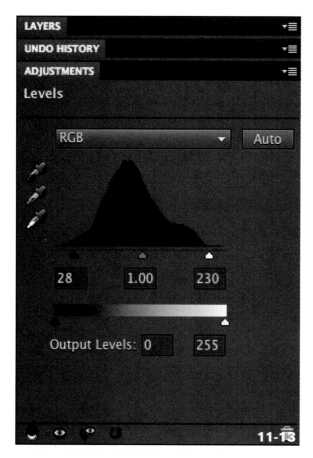

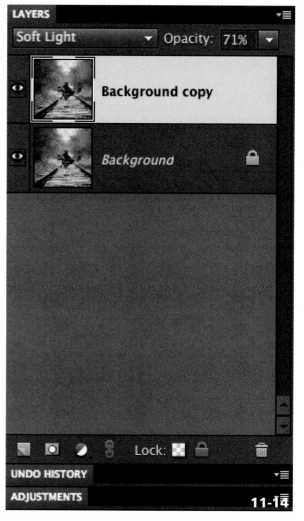

2. **Choose Layers⇨New adjustment layer⇨Levels.** Move the left slider toward the right slightly and the right slider toward the middle (see 11-13). This effect increases contrast slightly. Then choose Layer⇨Flatten from the upper menu.

3. **Choose Layer⇨Duplicate, and change the blending mode to Soft Light.** Change the opacity to 71 percent or to suit your taste. You can try the Overlay mode also. See 11-14.

11-15

4. **Select the eraser tool and brush over the hair to erase the effect there.** Make sure your soft-light layer is highlighted. Choose Layer⇨Flatten from upper menu.

5. **Choose Layer⇨Duplicate Layer from upper menu.** Then choose Filter⇨other⇨High Pass. Move the slider so just a slight line appears through the gray. The image on the screen will be gray with a slight outline of the elements in the photo. See 11-15.

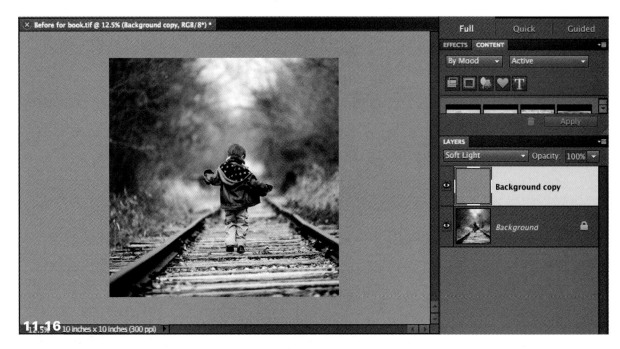

ABOUT THESE IMAGES *Figures 11-12 through 11-16 illustrate the process Mary used to enhance the color of the original photograph. They correspond with the numbered steps as indicated. Original photograph was taken at ISO 200, f2.8, and 1/1600 second. ©Mary Schannen / www.melangephoto.com*

6. **Change the mode to Soft Light (or overlay).** Lower opacity if it appears overly sharp. File⇨Flatten from the upper menu. File⇨ Save from upper menu, and you are done. See 11-16.

BLACK-AND-WHITE ACTION IN PSE BY SHANA RAE

Shana Rae is a photographer, artist, and entrepreneur who is very successful with her Florabella collection of actions and textures (see the resources at the end of this chapter). She used these steps to convert a stunning color photograph with her B/W Blush from Luxe II set of actions. They are installed already in PSE.

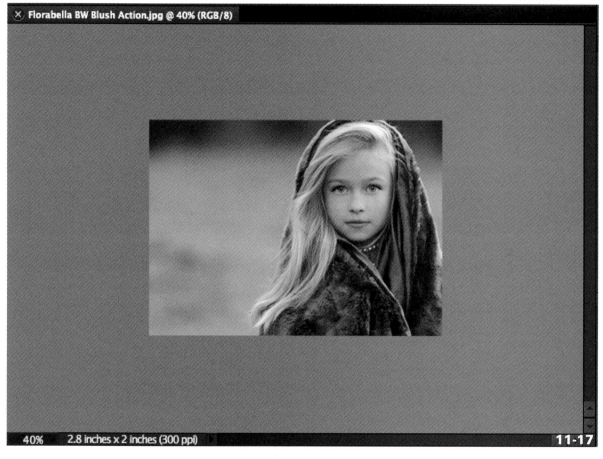

Florabella BW Blush Action.jpg @ 40% (RGB/8)

40%   2.8 inches x 2 inches (300 ppi)   11-17

1. **Import the original photograph into PSE from the Library.** See 11-17.

2. **Choose Edit⇨Guided Activities.**

3. **Choose Automated Actions⇨Action Player.** See 11-18.

4. **Select the action set Florabella Luxe II and then the action B/W Blush.** Click Play Action. See 11-19.

5. **Flatten layers if you wish (Layers⇨flatten), and save File⇨Save.** Voila – the final image! See 11-20.

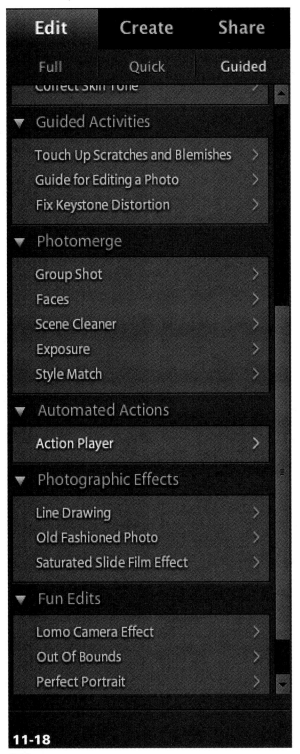

Edit | Create | Share

Full | Quick | **Guided**

Correct Skin Tone ›

▼ Guided Activities

Touch Up Scratches and Blemishes ›
Guide for Editing a Photo ›
Fix Keystone Distortion ›

▼ Photomerge

Group Shot ›
Faces ›
Scene Cleaner ›
Exposure ›
Style Match ›

▼ Automated Actions

Action Player ›

▼ Photographic Effects

Line Drawing ›
Old Fashioned Photo ›
Saturated Slide Film Effect ›

▼ Fun Edits

Lomo Camera Effect ›
Out Of Bounds ›
Perfect Portrait ›

11-18

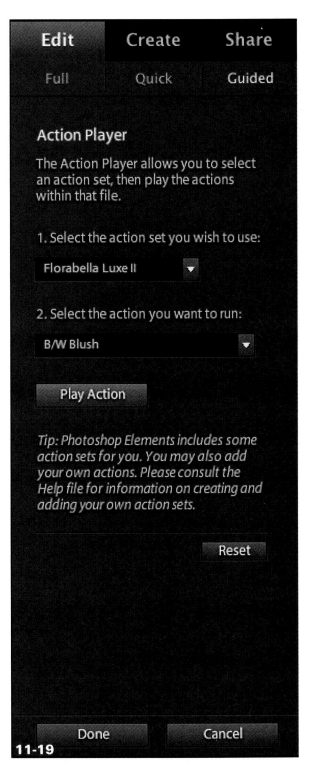

Edit | Create | Share

Full | Quick | **Guided**

Action Player

The Action Player allows you to select an action set, then play the actions within that file.

1. Select the action set you wish to use:

Florabella Luxe II ▼

2. Select the action you want to run:

B/W Blush ▼

Play Action

Tip: Photoshop Elements includes some action sets for you. You may also add your own actions. Please consult the Help file for information on creating and adding your own action sets.

Reset

Done | Cancel

11-19

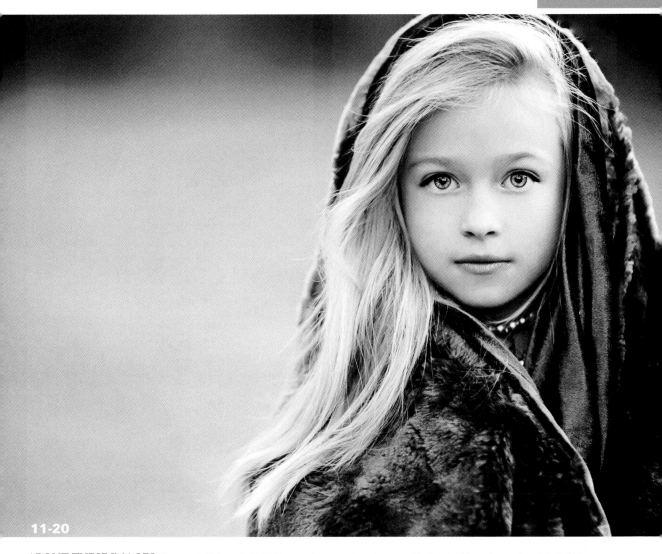

11-20

ABOUT THESE IMAGES *Figures 11-17 through 11-20 illustrate the process used to use a black-and-white action on the original photograph. They correspond with the numbered steps as indicated. Original photograph was taken at ISO 1600, f/1.6, and 1/160 second. ©Shana Rae / www.florabellacollection.com*

BRIGHTENING AND BALANCING SKIN TONES IN PSE BY ANNIE MANNING

A current trend is to increase the highlights in the skin tones to a point where there are almost no details. There are many ways of doing this, but artist, photographer, and vendor Annie Manning of Paint the Moon has developed an action that really makes it simple. Her workflow in PSE to develop the underexposed "before" capture to the refined and dazzling "after" image is as follows:

1. **Import the photo into PSE (see 11-21).**

2. **Chose Edit⇨Guided and scroll down to Action Player.** Scroll to find Banish the Cyan to get rid of some of the cyan cast.

3. **Choose Edit⇨Full to see layers, and adjust the new layer up to 70 percent.**

4. **Choose Edit⇨Guided, then choose Action Player.**

5. **Choose the PTM PPP Minute Makeover (All in One) action.** See 11-22. This all-in-one action can brighten, correct skin tone, warm/cool, retouch skin, eyes, teeth, and sharpen.

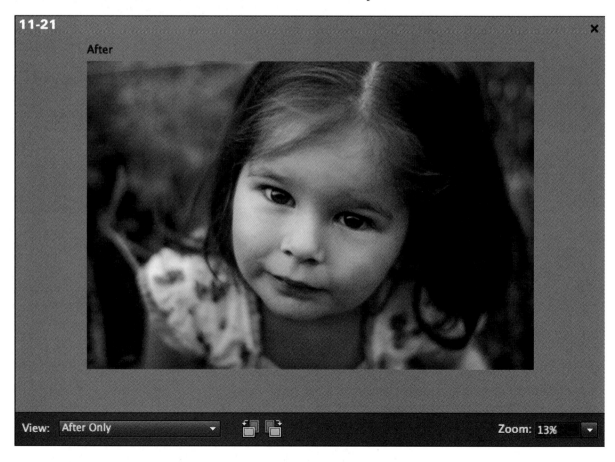

11-21

After

View: After Only   Zoom: 13%

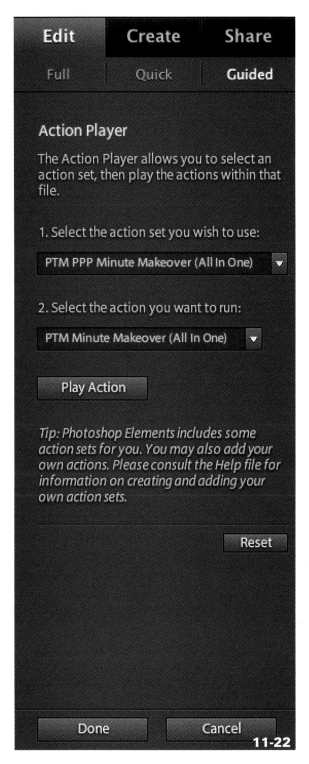

Action Player

The Action Player allows you to select an action set, then play the actions within that file.

1. Select the action set you wish to use:

PTM PPP Minute Makeover (All In One) ▼

2. Select the action you want to run:

PTM Minute Makeover (All In One) ▼

[Play Action]

Tip: Photoshop Elements includes some action sets for you. You may also add your own actions. Please consult the Help file for information on creating and adding your own action sets.

[Reset]

[Done]   [Cancel]

11-22

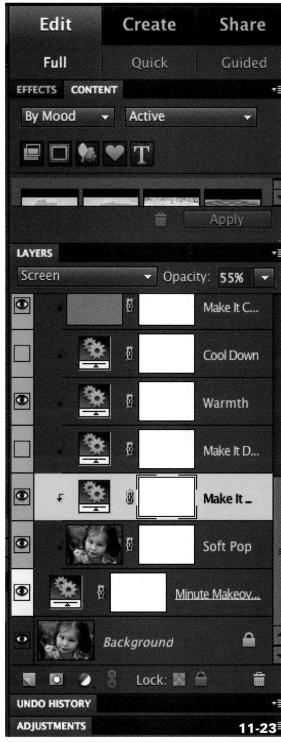

11-23

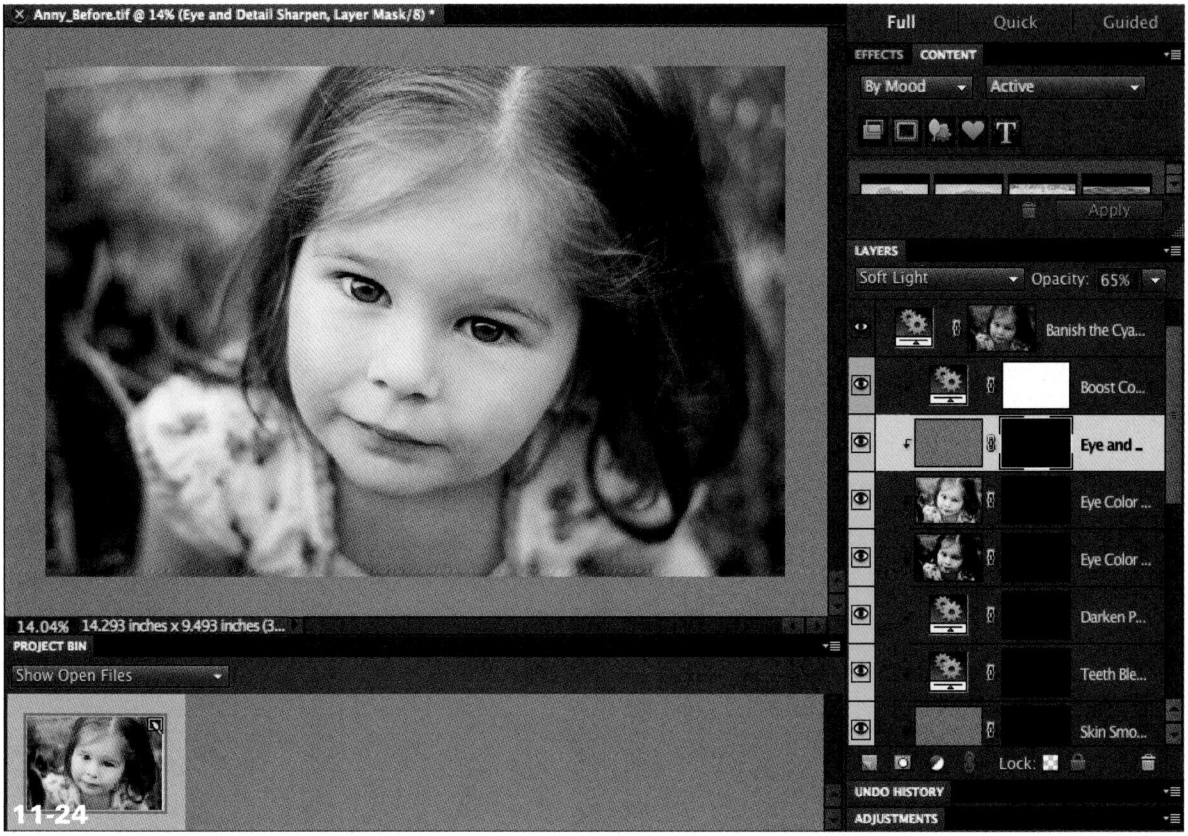
Anny_Before.tif @ 14% (Eye and Detail Sharpen, Layer Mask/8) *
Full
Quick
Guided
EFFECTS
CONTENT
By Mood
Active
Apply
LAYERS
Soft Light
Opacity: 65%
Banish the Cya...
Boost Co...
Eye and ...
Eye Color ...
Eye Color ...
Darken P...
Teeth Ble...
Skin Smo...
Lock:
14.04% 14.293 inches x 9.493 inches (3...
PROJECT BIN
Show Open Files
UNDO HISTORY
ADJUSTMENTS
11-24

6. **Choose Edit⇨Full to get back to your layers.** Click on the eye icons to choose various options such as Make It Crisp, Warmth, Make It Lighter, and Soft Pop. Adjust the opacity on the Warmth layer to 100 percent and the Make it Lighter layer to 55 percent. See 11-23.
7. **Brush over the subject's eyes using a soft white brush while in the Eye and Detail Sharpen layer.** See 11-24.
8. **Choose Edit⇨Guided, then Action Player, and run the Vintage Denim action.**
9. **Choose Edit⇨Full and lower the opacity of that layer to 40 percent.** Voila! See 11-25.

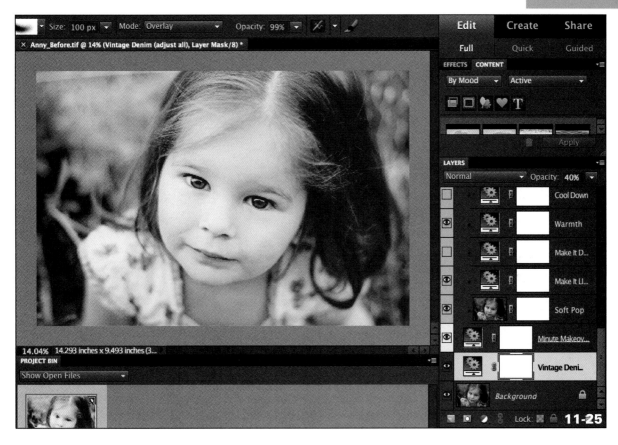

Size: 100 px | Mode: Overlay | Opacity: 99%

× Anny_Before.tif @ 14% (Vintage Denim (adjust all), Layer Mask/8) *

Edit | Create | Share

Full | Quick | Guided

EFFECTS | CONTENT

By Mood | Active

Apply

LAYERS

Normal | Opacity: 40%

Cool Down
Warmth
Make It D...
Make It Li...
Soft Pop
Minute Makeov...
Vintage Deni...
Background

14.04% 14.293 inches x 9.493 inches (3...

PROJECT BIN

Show Open Files

Lock: 11-25

ABOUT THESE IMAGES *Figures 11-21 through 11-25 illustrate the process Annie Manning used to brighten the skin tones on her original photograph. They correspond with the numbered steps as indicated. Original photograph was taken at ISO 250, f/1.8, and 1/500 second. ©Annie Manning / www.paintthemoon.net*

SUNFLARE LIGHTROOM WORKFLOW BY NICHOLE VAN

Nichole Van, photographer and teacher, uses her own set of Lightroom Presets to demonstrate her workflow. A preset is a file that contains settings that create an effect. Her presets were previously installed in Lightroom to add to the software's default presets.

Nichole talks about her concept: "I love how the prairie grass looks mid-summer, all shades of green and gold and cream. So I actually designed the child's dress to match the colors of the prairie: sage green and cream. From there, I just

wanted images of her in the scene, walking through the grass, lost in nature. I wanted her to be a part of it all and to blend with the scenery."

To emulate Nichole's sunflare, follow these steps:

1. **Import the original photograph into Adobe Lightroom from the Library Menu.** See 11-26.

2. **In the Develop menu, find the list of presets on the left side of the page. Apply the NV Vint Fresh preset from the BW and Vintage presets.** Reduce the Exposure slider to –0.75. Reduce the Blacks slider to 6. Adjust the Recovery slider to 50. See 11-27.

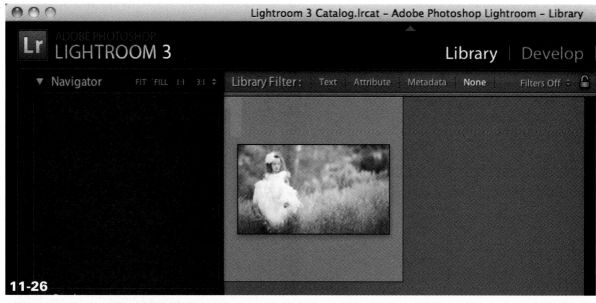

11-26

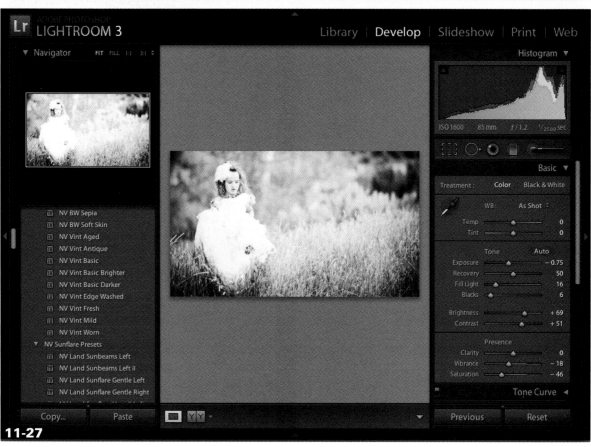

11-27

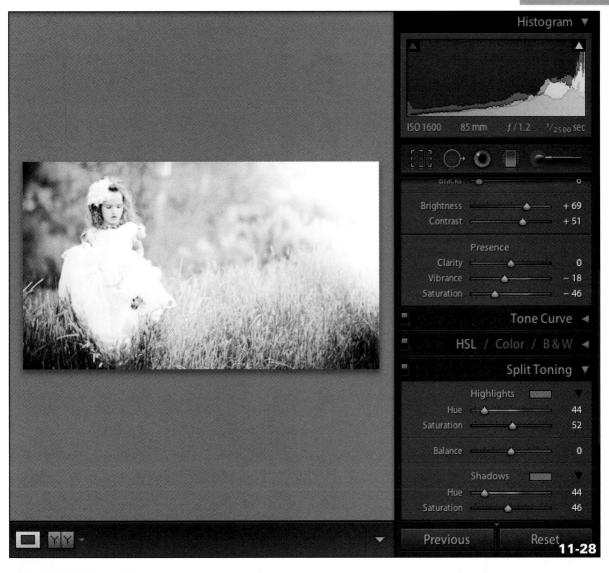

11-28

ABOUT THESE IMAGES *Figures 11-26 through 11-28 illustrate the process Nichole Van used to add a sunflare to her original photograph. They correspond with the numbered steps as indicated. Original photograph was taken at ISO 1600, f/1.2, and 1/2500 second. ©Nichole Van / www.nicholev.com.*

3. **Apply NV Land Sunflare II Right.** This last step is the trickiest because you're going to add a tone to the image.

4. **Use the gray vertical bar on the right to scroll down through the Treatment sidebar until you come to Split Toning.**

5. **Change the Highlights Hue to 44 and the Saturation to 52.**

6. **Change the Shadows Hue to 44 and the Saturation to 46.** See 11-28. And there you have your completed sunflare.

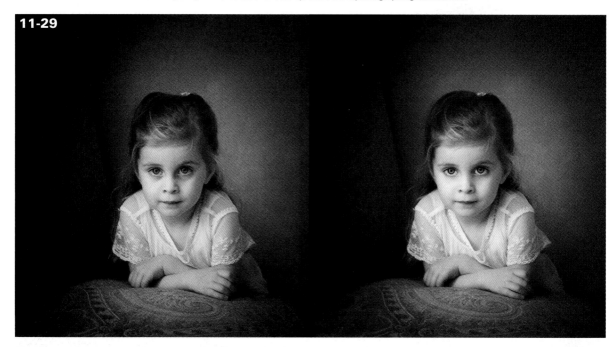

11-29

PHOTOSHOP AND LIGHTROOM POSSIBILITIES BY GINNY FELCH

As you can see by now, there is a myriad of possibilities, both very simple and very complicated, for photographic embellishment and enhancement in post-production software. Next, I thought it would be fun to show you some images that I have enjoyed in both Adobe Photoshop and Lightroom.

It's all about experimentation and play, going with your intuition, your muse, your conceptual ideas. The network of photographers, sharing and supporting one another, that has developed since the publication of my first book is dazzling and exciting. You can get information for free and you can pay for online classes, but you will never run out of tools for your creative toolbox.

Enjoy these renditions that have come out of some fairly extensive Photoshop editing (as in 11-29) as well as pre-loaded presets for Lightroom at the push of a button (as in 11-30). Then decide how you wish to go forward into Neverland. Remember: Always begin with a photograph with integrity!

RESOURCES

Below you will find the resources that I have gathered with the help of Mary Schannen, who is my inspiration for finding and using online boutique offerings.

TEXTURES

First are the textures, which are used to add via layers in post-production to create unique photographs.

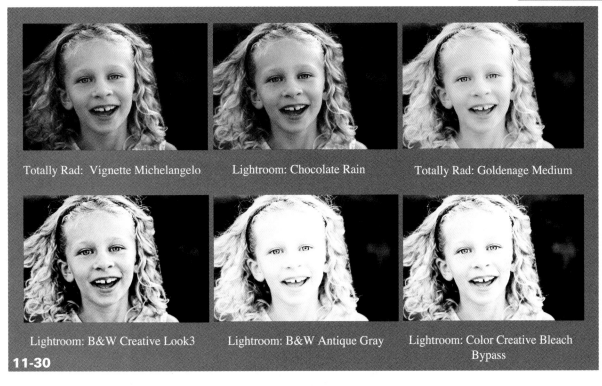

Totally Rad: Vignette Michelangelo

Lightroom: Chocolate Rain

Totally Rad: Goldenage Medium

Lightroom: B&W Creative Look3

Lightroom: B&W Antique Gray

Lightroom: Color Creative Bleach Bypass

11-30

ABOUT THIS PHOTO *By simply pushing a button in Lightroom, you can access a myriad of presets one by one and see which effect takes your breath away. Lightroom comes equipped with default presets (you can see them in the left-hand column of the Development menu), and you can also purchase others online. ©Ginny Felch / www.photographingchildren.com*

■ **Beth Armsheimer.** http://betharmsheimer textures.blogspot.com

■ **Digital Artistry.** http://sarahgardner photography.blogspot.com/p/new.html

■ **Flickr.** www.flickr.com; do a search for free textures and multiple people come up

■ **Flourish.** http://shop.nicholev.com

■ **Flora Bella.** www.florabellacollection.com

■ **Flypaper.** http://flypapertextures.blogspot. com

■ **From the Treetop.** http://fromthetreetop. com/blog/2010/10/introducing-ftt-vintage-textures-overlays-1-fine-art-photographer

■ **Inspired by Nadia.** http://inspiredbynadia. com/nadia-stalgic

■ **Jessica Drossin.** www.jessicadrossintextures. blogspot.com; see 11-31

■ **Kaleidoscope.** http://kaleidoscope.pattibrown photography.com

ACTIONS

The resources for actions I recommend are listed below.

■ **MCP.** www.mcpactions.com

■ **Flora Bella.** www.florabellacollection.com

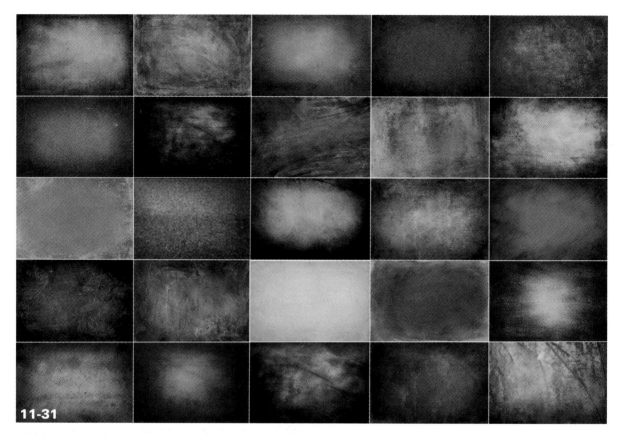

11-31

ABOUT THIS PHOTO *A gorgeous palate of colors and textures is an example of the products that Jessica Drossin has in her online shop.* www.jessicadrossinphotography.com/yhg

- **Child's Play.** http://childsplayactions.com
- **Journey.** www.fallintoblue.com/actions
- **Oh So Posh.** www.ohsoposhphotography.com/artstore
- **Bohemian Secret.** www.bohemiansecret.net
- **Lilyblue.** http://leahzawadzki.lilyblue.com/actions
- **Totally Rad.** www.gettotallyrad.com
- **Paint the Moon.** http://paintthemoon.net/blog

WORKSHOPS

The workshops listed here are some of the current popular and inspiring classes taught by talented and entrepreneurial photographers.

- **MCP.** www.mcpactions.com/workshops.html
- **Phaunt U.** www.photoshopnaked.com
- **Flourish.** http://shop.nicholev.com
- **Bloom.** www.everythingbloom.com
- **Online Natural Light Workshop.** http://the lightworkshop.wordpress.com
- **Crave Photography.** http://cravemy photography.com/blog/mentoring-4
- **Erin Cobb Clean Color.** http://erincobb.com/ ThePigBear/?page_id=3762
- **Fly: The Guide.** http://angiewarren.com/ mentoring
- **Captivate.** www.captivatephotogs.com/ ?page_id=15
- **503 Workshops.** www.503photography. com/#/workshop-home
- **Pinkletoes.** www.pinkletoes4photographers. com

EDUCATIONAL AND SOCIAL NETWORKING FORUMS

Forums and social networking are very commonly used by beginning and amateur photographers of children who wish to show their own work for critique and improvement. These are highly recommended:

- **Bloom.** http://thebloomforum.com
- **ilovephotography.com.** http://ilove photography.com/forums
- **Clickinmoms.** www.clickinmoms.com

GIVING BACK THROUGH CHARITIES

Many children's photographers love to use their blogs and networking to gather attention and support for their own charities. Here are some examples.

- **Now I Lay Me Down to Sleep.** www.nowilaymedowntosleep.org
- **Tiny Sparrow.** http://tinysparrowfoundation. org
- **Little Angels.** www.nordstromphoto.com/blog/ category/little_angels_by_lori_nordstrom

Assignment

Experiment with Textures

Start out by creating your own texture file by photographing something you feel will make an interesting image when coupled with a photograph you have in your archives. Be sure to have an intention of some kind, i.e., to make the photograph more painterly or moody. In the process, you may find that you might like to have a number of textures on hand to have the opportunity to play a bit.

Open both the original photograph and the texture file in to PSE or Photoshop in layers as seen in the demonstrations in this chapter. As you shift through the blending modes and opacity, you will most likely come up with something that you really like. You might even want to try using two layers! This is what I love about this creative process – everyone will arrive at a different place and thus have a unique photograph.

For this assignment, I found a 12-year-old print of my great-nephew. I photographed it with my camera first and opened the file in Photoshop. Then I opened up one of my own favorite textures and layered it with the original photograph. I finally arrived at what I had intended – a photograph that looks like an old tintype. Shown here are the original, the texture I used, and the final product.

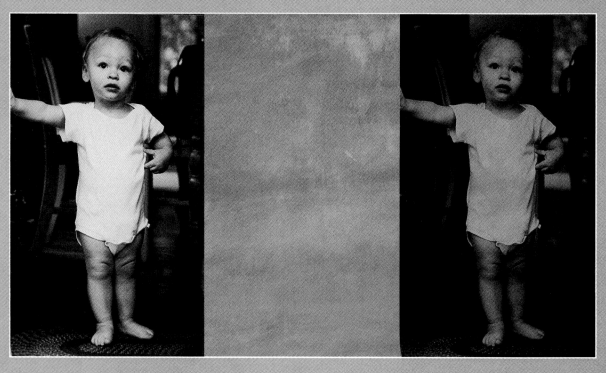

©Ginny Felch / www.photographingchildren.com

Remember to visit www.pwsbooks.com after you complete this assignment and share your favorite photo! It's a community of enthusiastic photographers and a great place to view what other readers have created. You can also post comments, read encouraging suggestions, and get feedback.

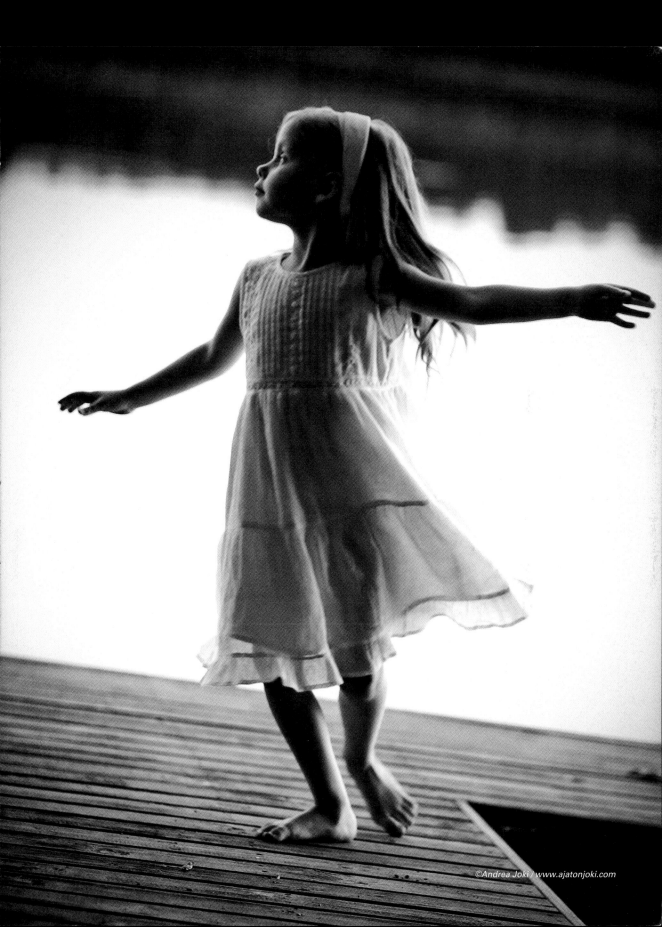

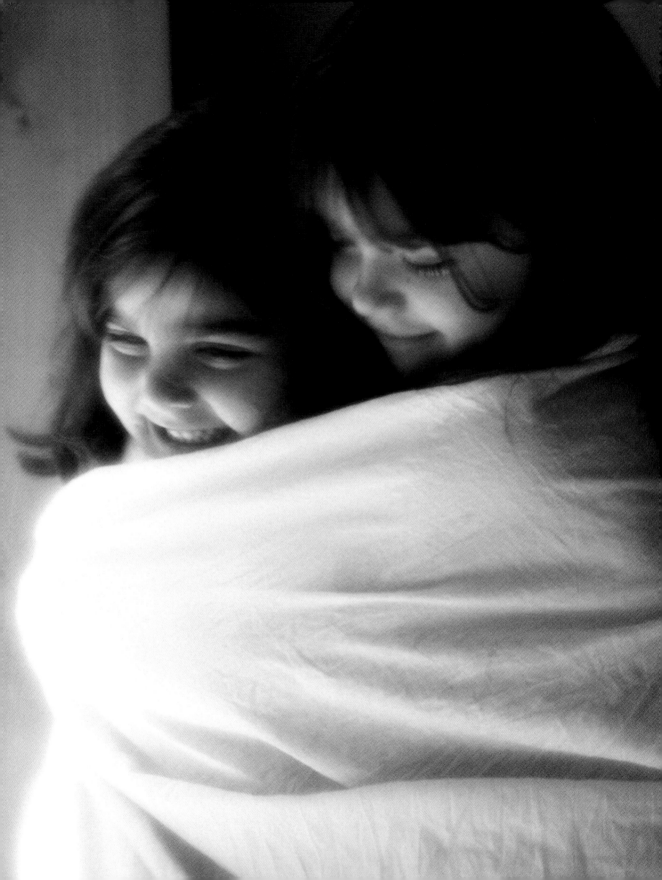

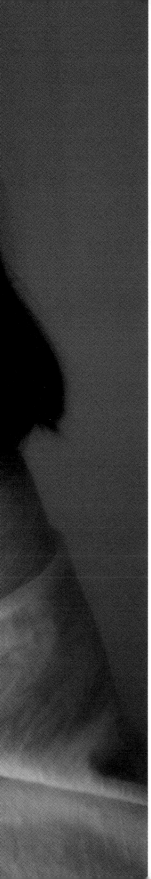

GLOSSARY

ambient light   Refers to the available light in a given setting, whether by natural light or any other light sources in a room/setting. Ambient light does not refer to flash.

angle of view   The area of a scene that a lens can capture, determined by the focal length of the lens. Lenses with a shorter focal length have a wider angle of view than lenses with a longer focal length.

aperture   The size of the lens opening through which light passes. Aperture is referred to by f-stop numbers. See also *f-stop*.

Aperture Priority (Av)   A setting on an automatic camera that enables you to choose the opening in the lens while the camera sets the shutter speed accordingly for the best picture.

back light   Refers to when a subject is primarily lit from behind.

bounce flash   Pointing the flash away from the subject toward a wall, ceiling, or other hard surface, causing it to bounce off that surface before hitting the subject, thus softening the light illuminating the subject. Bouncing the light often eliminates shadows and provides a smoother light for portraits.

catch light   The sparkly reflection captured in the eye of the subject. This catch light gives spark and life to the eyes.

color cast   The color of light in a given photograph. Different light sources have different color temperatures. For example, household lights have a very orange cast, and fluorescent bulbs have a greenish cast.

contrast   The difference between light and dark in a photo. A low-contrast image has a limited range of contrast in that there is no big difference between light and dark tones. A contrasty or high-contrast image has a big difference between light and dark tones.

depth of field   The area in a photo that is in focus. In portraits, especially, a pleasing photo can be taken with a narrow depth of field, in which the person or people are in focus and everything else in the background is out of focus. See also *f-stop*.

diffuser   Refers to anything that diffuses light in some way. It could be a sheet or curtain or a commercial diffuser made specifically for photographers.

digital noise   Comparable to grain in film. When an image is captured at a very high ISO (usually 800 or higher) noise is introduced into the image that makes it appear grainy and less sharp.

direct light   Light falling directly on the subject from its source. Direct light is light that has not been diffused or reflected off of something else.

environmental portraiture   Portraits taken in the subject's environment — a yard, home, garden, workplace, and so on. See also *photojournalistic style*.

exposure   Created when a certain amount of light (controlled by the aperture) hits the camera sensor for a certain amount of time (controlled by shutter speed). Technically speaking, an exposure is a photographic image.

fill flash   Using a flash unit (on-camera or otherwise) to illuminate the subject in order to eliminate shadows. Using a flash for outdoor portraits often brightens up the subject in conditions where the camera meters light from a broader scene. See also *fill light*.

fill light   Any light that is not the primary illumination of a subject. See also *main light*.

filter   Glass or other material that covers a lens to change the color or intensity of an image, soften an image, take away glare, or do any number of things to improve your photos. A filter also can be a post-production software tool that is used to create a variety of effects.

f-stop   A measure of the size of the opening of the lens aperture. As the f-number increases in size (that is, f/8.0, f/9.0, f/22) the size of the aperture opening decreases. As the f-number decreases (f/5.6, f/4.0, f/2.0) the size of the aperture increases. The f-stop determines the depth of field, or the area that is in and out of focus in the frame. See also *aperture* and *depth of field*.

golden hour   The hour before sunset is prized by photographers because the sun is at a low angle in the sky and the light is soft and golden as a result of passing through the earth's atmosphere at a low angle. See also *sweet light*.

Golden Rectangle   An area (based on the Golden Ratio of 1:1.618) of an image considered to be most pleasing to the human eye. The Rule of Thirds is based on the Golden Rectangle divided into thirds to help guide the composition of a photograph. See also *Rule of Thirds*.

hard light   Light quality that casts a harsh shadow and is often unflattering to most subjects. See also *direct light*.

high key   An image that has predominantly light tones and low contrast. The subject stands out because the skin tones appear darker than the clothing and background. The opposite of low-key photography. See also *low key*.

indirect light   Light that has been diffused through or reflected off of something else. Indirect light is not falling directly from the light source. See also *soft light*.

ISO setting   Determines the sensitivity to light in your camera. You can set the ISO to make the camera more or less sensitive to light. The higher the ISO, the better the picture you get in darker conditions. However, you also get more grain or noise in your final image. See also *noise*.

JPEG   An image format that compresses the image data from the camera to achieve a smaller file size. See also *lossy*.

leading lines   Lines in the environment, such as roads, paths, edges, fences, and shadows, that draw the eye to the subject in a photograph or through the photograph in a specific direction.

lossless   A file compression type that discards no image data. TIFF is a lossless file format.

low key   An image that has predominantly dark tones, with the subject usually standing out in light tones. The opposite of high-key photography. See also *high key*.

main light   Light that provides the primary illumination of the subject being photographed. See also *fill light*.

megapixels   Equivalent to 1 million pixels. The higher the pixel count, the bigger the potential print size. For example, 2-megapixel cameras can produce quality 4 × 6 prints, and 8-megapixel cameras can produce great prints up to 10 × 14. See also *pixel*.

noise   A grainy appearance in a photo that is usually the result of low-light conditions and long exposures, particularly when you've set your camera to a higher ISO rating than normal.

photojournalistic style   A style that seeks to capture more candid moments rather than traditional posed portraits. See also *environmental portraiture*.

pixel   Shortened from Picture Elements, this is the unit that makes up a digital image. See also *megapixel*.

point and shoot   A camera that does not have interchangeable lenses and typically is easier to use and more compact than a digital SLR camera. See also *SLR*.

red eye   An effect from flash photography caused by light bouncing from the retina of the eye. It is most noticeable in dimly lit situations (when the irises are wide open) and when the electronic flash is close to the lens and, therefore, prone to reflect the light directly back. It creates a red glow in human eyes.

reflector   A device that can reflect light onto your subject. Reflectors can reflect flash/strobe lights or natural light.

Rembrandt lighting   A lighting pattern that uses a single light source placed at a 45-degree angle to the subject, resulting in an image with a three-dimensional appearance.

rim light   The silhouette and halo effect around the hair of a subject achieved by placing a light in back of the subject.

Rule of Thirds   States that you can divide the frame of your image into three sections vertically and three sections horizontally. The best spots to place your subject are where the lines intersect. This rule keeps you from placing everything in the center of the photograph, which is less compositionally pleasing. See also *Golden Rectangle*.

sepia   Photographs with a brownish tone — a great alternative to color or black and white. Sepia photographs look antique. The tone can be achieved either by a filter on the lens or in digital post-production.

shutter speed   The amount of time that the lens shutter is open to let light in through to the sensor; usually measured in fractions, such as 1/30, 1/60, 1/125, and 1/500 second. The combination of the shutter speed and the f-stop determine the exposure.

SLR   Single lens reflex. A camera that enables you to view the scene from the same lens that takes the photograph. In most point-and-shoot cameras with fixed lenses, you view the scene from a different lens than the one that takes the photo.

soft light   Light quality that creates gentle shadows and is more flattering to most subjects. See also *indirect light*.

specular highlight   The reflection of the light source (sky, sun, or flash) on the subject. Different examples include the catch light you see as a white dot in the eye in a photograph; the too-bright spots on foliage that can be a terrible distraction in a portrait; and the soft line of light that you often see on a nose when light comes in from the side.

sweet light   The light seen at dawn and dusk, when the sun is at a great angle. The effect it produces is soft and gentle and bathes the subject with modeling and often atmosphere light. See also *golden hour*.

TIFF   A type of file storage format that has no compression, and therefore, no loss of image detail. TIFF files can be very large image files. See also *lossless*.

white balance   The colorcast to any given image that may need to be corrected using software or settings in the camera.

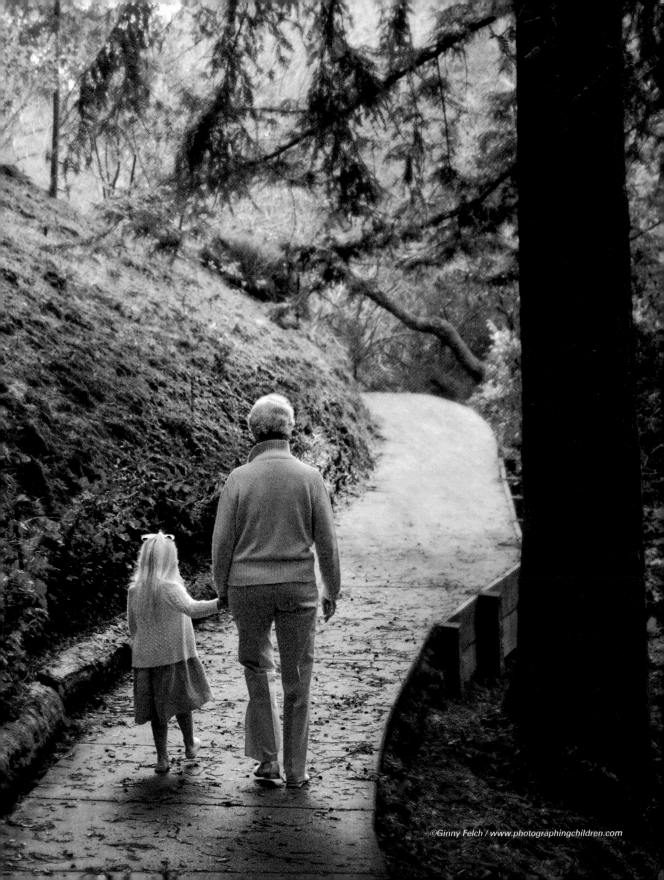

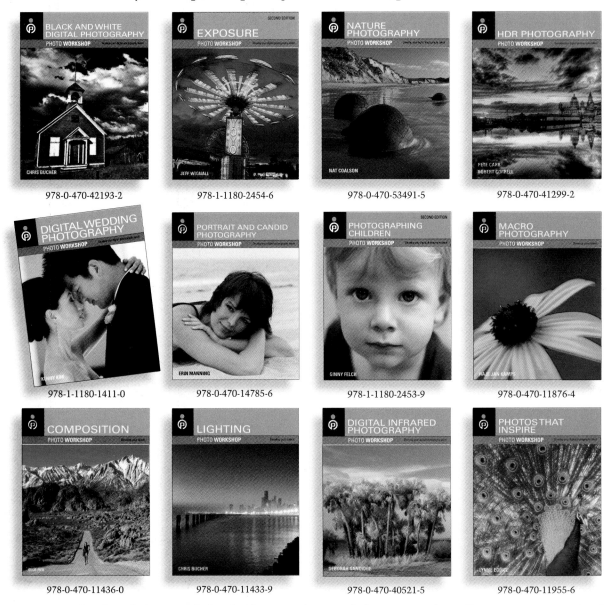